THE INDEPENDENCE
OF THE JUDICIARY

The Independence
of the Judiciary

The View from the
Lord Chancellor's Office

ROBERT STEVENS

CLARENDON PRESS · OXFORD
1993

Oxford University Press, Walton Street, Oxford OX2 6DP

Oxford New York Toronto
Delhi Bombay Calcutta Madras Karachi
Kuala Lumpur Singapore Hong Kong Tokyo
Nairobi Dar es Salaam Cape Town
Melbourne Auckland Madrid
and associated companies in
Berlin Ibadan

Oxford is a trade mark of Oxford University Press

Published in the United States
by Oxford University Press Inc., New York

British Library Cataloguing in Publication Data
Data available

Library of Congress Cataloging in Publication Data
Stevens, Robert Bocking.
The independence of the judiciary: the view from the Lord
Chancellor's Office / Robert Stevens.
p. cm.
Includes bibliographical references and index.
1. Judges—Great Britain. 2. Law and politics. 3. Great Britain.
Lord Chancellor's Dept. I. Title.
KD7285.S74 1993
347.41'014—dc20
[344.10714] 93-15327
ISBN 0-19-825815-1

1 3 5 7 9 10 8 6 4 2

Set by Hope Services (Abingdon) Ltd.
Printed in Great Britain on acid-free paper by
Bookcraft Ltd., Midsomer Norton, Bath

For

Kathie and Robin

Preface

I AM grateful to the many who made this book possible. The research was undertaken over the last decade. Thus I should particularly like to thank those who encouraged me to go on with my research even while engaged in the dubious enterprise of academic administration. John Whitehead and John Jones were successive (and supportive) chairs of the Haverford Board, while I was President of that college. David Gardner, President of the University of California, provided similar support when I was Chancellor of the University of California, Santa Cruz, as well as sabbatical support at the end of my term. I am also grateful to the members of Covington and Burling (and in particular to Jonathan Blake and Charles Lister) for allowing me a few months' grace between my time at the University of California and my joining the London Office of that firm, to complete this book. Finally, I have to thank Sir William Goodhart, QC, and the members of the Executive Committee of Justice (the English branch of the International Commission of Jurists) for appointing me, in 1991, as chair of the Committee on the Judiciary, a role that was important in helping to clarify my thoughts. I should also like to thank the members of that committee for joining in this educational process.

I should like too to thank the library staffs at both Haverford College and the University of California, Santa Cruz, for support. I should also like to thank, at both institutions, my assistants (Shelly Weiss and Judi Tessier), without whose firm guidance nothing would have been accomplished, and my secretaries (Rosanne English and Mara van der Plas), who took pity on me for my ignorance of the technological advances, not only of the twentieth century, but also of the nineteenth. At Covington and Burling, Elizabeth Partridge and Gillian Davies organized the final draft. Paula Juntunen made the Table of Office Holders.

The actual writing of the book was done mainly in New Brunswick and Oxford. At the University of New Brunswick in Fredericton, I should like to thank Dean Wade MacLauchlin and his colleagues (as well as the library staff) for the warmth of their welcome. Most of all, I should like to thank Donald Harris, Director of the Centre for Socio-Legal Studies and his colleagues, who, during two visits to Oxford, took me in and supported me with the minimum of fuss and the maximum of intellectual encouragement. I should also like to thank the members of Keble and Wolfson Colleges for their support, as well as my colleagues at University College, London, where I am currently Visiting Professor of Law.

The penultimate draft of the book was read by a number of persons: Peter Bartrip, Andrew Crawshaw, Jill Cottrell, John Gasson, Cyril Glasser, Robert Heuston, J. Anthony Holland, Anthony Lester, David Pannick, Alan Paterson, Brian Simpson, Katherine Booth Stevens, and William Twining. Their comments were immensely helpful and I am grateful to each of them. They would all, however, I suspect, wish me to emphasize that they might well have drawn very different conclusions and, I am sure, avoided many of my errors.

I must also add something about genesis and acknowledgements. Much of the research for this book was in fact undertaken when I had the naïve whim that I might write a second edition of *Lawyers and the Courts*.[1] I came to realize that I am not capable of second editions. I became increasingly interested, however, in the work of the Lord Chancellor's Office and especially its relationship to the Judiciary. I also became intrigued by the ongoing fascination of the judges with their status, a fascination so often assimilated to judicial independence. I also became interested in the English view of judicial independence and the transformation it may have to undergo if England in fact engages in constitutional reform.

It was these interests that led me to the papers from the Lord Chancellor's Office in the Public Record Office. They are important to this thesis because the Lord Chancellor's Office sees one of its primary roles as being the protection of the independence of the judiciary; and at least until 1971 its main functions revolved heavily around this role. It is unfortunate that the thirty-year-rule prevents us looking at any papers after 1971.

Most of the book is thus concerned with the period up to 1971, and while historians naturally shy away from periods, the "reigns" of the Permanent Secretaries break the book naturally into three parts. The period of Lord Muir Mackenzie lasts from the founding of the Office until 1915 and is discussed in Chapter 1. The Golden Age of the Office—the period of Lord Schuster from 1915 to 1944—is covered in Chapters 2, 3, and 4. The work of the Permanent Secretaries between 1944 and 1968, Napier and Coldstream, is covered in Chapters 5, 6, 7, and 8. While each of these last four chapters looks at some issues from the last thirty years without the benefit of departmental papers, the period from 1971 to 1992 is basically covered in the Epilogue.

While the Lord Chancellor's Office papers drive the bulk of the book, I have not been shy in relying on *Lawyers and the Courts* or its companion volume *In Search of Justice*;[2] and I have been equally generous to myself in relying on *Law and Politics*[3] and *The Restrictive Practices Court*.[4] Parts of this book have appeared in

---

[1] B. Abel-Smith and R. B. Stevens, *Lawyers and the Courts: A Sociological Study of the English Legal System, 1750–1965* (London, 1967; Cambridge, Mass., 1968).

[2] B. Abel-Smith and R. B. Stevens, *In Search of Justice: Society and the Legal System* (London and New York, 1968).

[3] R. B. Stevens, *Law and Politics: The House of Lords as a Judicial Body, 1800–1976* (Chapel Hill, NC, and London, 1983).

[4] R. B. Stevens and B. S. Yamey, *The Restrictive Practices Court: A Study of the Judicial Process and Economic Policy* (London, 1965).

the *Journal of Legal History*,[5] the *Oxford Journal of Legal Studies*,[6] *Current Legal Problems*,[7] *The University of New Brunswick Law Journal*,[8] and the festschrift for Patrick Atiyah.[9] I am grateful to the editors of each of these publications for permission to re-use material in this book.

I also made use of a research talk I gave at the Socio-Legal Centre in Oxford in the spring of 1986 on the appointment of judges; a keynote address I gave to the Western Branch of the British Studies Association in April 1989: 'The Labour Government and the Judiciary, 1945–51'; my inaugural lecture as professor of history at the University of California, Santa Cruz, in January 1990: 'Socialists, Conservatives, and the Separation of Powers'; a faculty seminar on the Lord Chancellor's Office and the Judicial Committee of the Privy Council at University College, London, in June 1990; the 'End of Empire and the Separation of Powers' at a fellows' research talk at Wolfson College, Oxford, in November 1991; and finally, a paper at the Institute of Advanced Legal Studies, London, on Judges and Judging, in April 1992.

I should thank the Public Record Office for permission to cite from the papers of the Lord Chancellor's Office and Department and also to HMSO for permission to quote from Command Papers. The Bodleian Library at Oxford allowed me access to the Asquith and Hanworth Papers, and His Grace the Archbishop of Canterbury allowed me access to the Selborne papers in the Fulham Palace Library.

Clearly a significant part of the book is based on lectures or essays which were intended to be self-contained. A considerable part of the material has been rearranged; a good deal is new. Yet I have deliberately attempted to retain some aspects of that self-containment and some of the informality which infused those parts of the book originally given as lectures. Finally, let me say, while I do not accept the canon of deconstruction that history is but a branch of literature, I do subscribe to the view that even legal history should be readable.

R.S.

1 May 1992

[5] R. B. Stevens, 'Judicial Salaries: Financial Independence in the Age of Equality', 13 *Journal of Legal History* (Aug. 1992), 155–77.

[6] Id., 'The Independence of the Judiciary', 8 *Oxford Journal of Legal Studies* (1988), 222, based on the Blackstone Lecture, Pembroke College, Oxford, June 1987.

[7] Id., 'The View from the Lord Chancellor's Office', *1987 Current Legal Problems* (1988), 181–205, based on a public lecture delivered at University College, London, May 1986.

[8] Id., 'Vignettes from the End of Empire', *University of New Brunswick Law Journal*, 40 (1991), 145–57.

[9] Id., 'The Role of the Judiciary: Lessons from the End of Empire', in *Essays for Patrick Atiyah*, ed. P. Cane and J. Stapleton (Oxford, 1991), 151–78.

List of Contents

List of Abbreviations

CC	Cabinet Committee
CM	Cabinet Minutes
CP	Cabinet Papers
CRO	Commonwealth Relations Office
DO	Dominions Office
FO	Foreign Office
HC	House of Commons
HL	House of Lords
IR	Inland Revenue
LCO	Lord Chancellor's Office
MR	Master of the Rolls
PIN	Ministry of Pensions and National Insurance

Prologue

In the so-called Independent Prosecutor Case, Mr Justice Scalia in the Supreme Court of the United States, in his dissent, gave the American concept of the separation of powers a new lease of life.[1] Montesquieu would have been pleased. It was his *Esprit des lois* that is regarded as having given credibility to the concept of such separation. In so doing Montesquieu misunderstood the English Constitution and helped shape the American.

In fact the concept began before Montesquieu and was to be given an Anglo-American flavour outside his works. John Locke in his *Second Treatise on Government* (1696) used the idea of separation of powers to justify the Glorious Revolution which had brought in William 'our great restorer'.[2] For him, however, the powers to be separated were 'the legislative, executive and federative',[3] and the judiciary did not figure prominently. Moreover, with the clear predominance of Parliament after the Act of Settlement (1700) and the Hanoverian Succession a decade later, the judges were not central in constitutional issues. While, by the time of the *Esprit des lois* (1739), Montesquieu was talking of the power of judging being a balance in the separation of powers, in the English context he looked to the jury to provide such power of judging. In 1743, Bolingbroke saw the judicial as represented by the House of Lords—the final court of appeal.[4] It was left to Blackstone in his *Commentaries* to spell out the concept of the judicial as a co-equal branch of government—and, while it is possible to read Blackstone either narrowly or broadly, it was he who insisted that there had to be judicial independence to protect the judges' law-making role, particularly in the Lords.[5]

It was no doubt from Blackstone that the separation of powers passed into American law. While the British have always remained sceptical of such grand theories,[6] the concept was highly influential in the development of American Constitutionalism. Thus, in the Independent Prosecutor Case, Mr Justice Scalia

---

[1] *Morrison v. Olsen*, 487 US 654, 697 (1988).

[2] Preface to Two Treatises of Government, *The Works of John Locke* (9th edn. London, 1794), v. 209.

[3] Ibid. 424.

[4] M. J. C. Vile, *Constitutionalism and the Separation of Powers* (Oxford, 1967), 43.

[5] Sir William Blackstone, *Commentaries on the Laws of England*, i. *Of the Rights of Persons* (4 vols., Oxford, 1765), saw the case of the separation of powers as being 'each branch being armed with a negative power, sufficient to repel any innovation which it shall think inexpedient or dangerous'.

[6] For an interesting application of the doctrine in an appeal from Ceylon, see *Liyanaje v R* [1967] I AC 259 (PC), where the Privy Council struck down a law where the Ceylonese Parliament had created an *ad hoc* crime, on the ground that the legislature had infringed judicial powers.

made a strict separation of powers argument that would not only have put out of business the independent prosecutor, but under which the regulatory agencies would have disappeared, blown away by the winds of original intent. Scalia cited with approval Article XXX of the 1780 Massachusetts Constitution:

In the government of this Commonwealth, the legislative department shall never exercise the executive and judicial powers, or either of them; the executive shall never exercise the legislative and judicial powers, or either of them; the judicial shall never exercise the legislative and executive powers, or either of them; to the end that it may be a government of laws, and not of men.[7]

Nothing underlines the atheoretical nature of the British Constitution more than the casualness with which it approaches the separation of powers.[8] Political theorists, both before and after W. S. Gilbert, reported the Lord Chancellor as the embodiment not only of all that was 'good and excellent' but also of the legislative, executive, and judicial functions. The Lord Chancellor is not only the senior judge, presiding when available in the final court of appeal for the United Kingdom (the House of Lords) and the vestiges of Commonwealth (the Judicial Committee of the Privy Council), he is also Speaker of the House of Lords presiding in legislative sessions. Equally importantly, he is a member of the Cabinet, and at least from 1880 onwards the Lord Chancellor has run an executive department—the Lord Chancellor's Office, responsible for the judiciary, the courts, law reform, legal aid, and related activities.

This book looks at the status and role of the judges from the viewpoint of that executive office, or, as it has been known since the 1970s, the Lord Chancellor's Department. The Lord Chancellor's Office is a lawyer-ridden department. Until 1990, its Permanent Secretary had to be a barrister, and most of its senior officials are barristers. While with the passage of the Courts Act of 1971 it became a relatively large department, its policy-making role lies in the hands of a relatively few lawyers who were exempt from the basic Civil Service regulations until recently; and, unlike every other government department, until 1990 it was subject to no Select Committee in the House of Commons. While these peculiarities have ameliorated over time, in many ways the Office—now Department—remains one of the most intriguing in Government. Moreover, today it is a significant department, with an annual budget of some £1.4 billion.

Neither the concept of the separation of powers, nor that of the specific role of the Lord Chancellor, has been subject to the most rigorous of analyses.[9] Perhaps the most pungent support for the current role of the Lord Chancellor was provided by Lord Schuster, the most powerful of the Permanent Secretaries

---

[7] *Morrison* v. *Olsen*, 108 US 654, 697 (1988).

[8] The Scott–Donoughmore Committee noted: 'In the British Constitution there is no such thing as the absolute separation of legislative, executive and judicial powers; in practice it is inevitable they should overlap.' See Ch. 2 below.

[9] But see Vile, *Constitutionalism and the Separation of Powers*; and G. Marshall, *Constitutional Theory* (Oxford, 1971), pt. 5.

of the Lord Chancellor's Office. He defended the then existing arrangements in a memorandum written in 1943:

The advantages which accrue to the Cabinet from the presence of a colleague who is not only of high judicial reputation but who can represent to them the view of the judiciary; to the legislature from the presence in it of one who is both a Judge and a Minister; and to the judiciary from the fact that its President is in close touch with current political affairs, are enormous. In a Democracy, whose legislature may be advancing, or at least moving rapidly, and where the judiciary remains static, there is always present a serious risk of collision between the two elements. Where the Constitution is written and the static condition of the Judiciary is absolute, as in the United States, the danger of such a collision is very great. Even in England, with an unwritten Constitution and an unwritten common law, unless there is some link or buffer (whichever term may be preferred) between the two elements the situation would be perilous.[10]

While this book examines that Office or Department, its central focus is the examination of the nature of the judiciary and the mystique of the independence of the judiciary. While there is widespread consensus on the obvious importance of the independence of the judiciary, the literature on it is meagre, and the concept itself has never been fully unpacked. Unpacking is a process worth engaging in.[11]

English political theorists have generally shied away from serious analysis of the judicial function. The same might fairly be said of institutional historians. Much is made of the attempts of Coke, at the beginning of the seventeenth century, to break with the notion of the judges as 'lions under the throne', but after the judges' role in the Glorious Revolution of 1688, the matter was left dangling with the Act of Settlement of 1700. By giving High Court judges security of tenure—subject only to dismissal by both Houses of Parliament, an attenuated form of impeachment—it is frequently asserted that judicial independence was assured. Yet compared with the United States, judicial independence was more of a social status than a legal position. The judges, after 1700, were lions under the mace. Their role was to enforce the will of Parliament. This constitutional function might involve assisting in the drafting of Bills and, as Lord Camden showed, ensuring that Parliament followed its own procedures or at least passed specific legislation if it wished to cut back on fundamental freedoms. There were, however, no fundamental or constitutional laws to follow or to enforce.

The English judges in the eighteenth century were, nevertheless, significant men in society. They sat in Westminster Hall, and they were in London far more frequently than members of the House of Lords or Commons. The judges advised the House of Lords in its judicial activities. They were an integral part of the legislative, judicial, and executive functions of the Privy Council. They reviewed private Bills for Parliament. The Bar was a way by which those of

---

[10] Memorandum, 31 Jan. 1943. LCO 2/3630.

[11] For a recent example see J. Bell, 'The Judge as Bureaucrat', in *Oxford Essays in Jurisprudence*, 3rd ser., ed. J. Eekelaar and J. Bell (Oxford, 1987), 33, 51–2.

modest means might move into the centres of power and amass a fortune on the way. The judges were pillars of the Whig (and to a lesser extent) the Tory Establishment. Chief Justices like Mansfield and Lord Chancellors like Eldon were household names in the politics of the period. Lord Chancellors—as speakers of the House of Lords—were important figures in the Cabinet. Ellenborough, as Chief Justice, sat in the Cabinet in the first decade of the nineteenth century.

The judiciary was small. There were twelve judges sitting in three common law courts. The Lord Chancellor was effectively the Chancery Court. Two or three times a year the law term broke to enable the common law judges to go on circuit to deliver the gaols, to hear *nisi prius* (civil) cases, and to represent the King in a quasi-administrative capacity. The fees which the judges earned from litigants and the sale of offices made them rich men, comparable with many of the wealthiest landowners in the country. Their status was reflected both by the calls they received to the opening of Parliament and the peerages many of them earned at the time when the peerage was appreciably smaller and more powerful than it is today.

That the judicial role was unclear is scarcely surprising. In the Whig hegemony political roles were not clearly defined. Judicial status was assured by the political stability abroad in the land during the age of enlightenment. Judicial independence and judicial status were virtually interchangeable. This status was threatened when, early in the nineteenth century, Bentham challenged the settled concepts intellectually, and Brougham challenged them politically. The reforms of 1825, setting judicial salaries at £5,500 a year, left the judges wealthy men by any standards, yet the curtailing of payment by fees and the ending of the selling of offices meant that the opportunity to compare with the wealthiest men in the land was severely curbed. The cut in salary to £5,000 in 1832, the year of the beginning of modern democracy, was a further blow to the status of judges as grandees.[12] By the time of the final reforms of the courts in the 1860s and 1870s the idea was afoot that the judges might be more public servants than public figures. The interaction between that theme, their status, and their independence provides the background for this book.

If we look at the standard works of constitutional law, the only thing that is agreed is that judicial independence means that High Court judges may not be dismissed without an address by both Houses of Parliament. What this itself means is less than clear.[13] Probably the most extensive, as well as the most recent, analysis of what is meant by judicial independence is contained in the 1991 edition of *Smith and Bailey on the Modern English Legal System*.[14] The basic principle is expressed in these terms:

---

[12] Abel-Smith and Stevens, *Lawyers and the Courts*, pt. 1.
[13] R. M. Jackson, *Jackson's Machinery of Justice*, 8th edn., ed. J. R. Spencer (Cambridge, 1989), 369.
[14] Ed. S. H. Bailey and M. J. Gunn (London, 1991).

Much importance is attached to the independence of the judiciary. By that is meant independence from improper pressure by the executive, by litigants and by particular pressure groups. Reasons given in support of judicial independence are (1) that independence is a condition of impartiality and therefore of fair trials and (2) that it makes for a separation of powers which enables the courts to check the activities of the other branches of government.[15]

In analysing the concept the editors suggest there are six aspects of judicial independence. The first is salary: 'Judges are paid large salaries.' The second concerns the legislative role. Judges cannot be MP's and should not engage in 'political controversies'. With respect to the latter, however, the authors concede that in addition to the complex role of the Lord Chancellor, it is not always easy to explain the behaviour in legislative debates of the Lords of Appeal who also hold life peerages. The same distancing becomes difficult when attempting to define the boundaries of the judiciary and the executive—the third proferred element in judicial independence. Judges do in effect perform executive functions when chairing Commissions and Committees. They cannot avoid taking policy stands when they chair committees on riots, security, Northern Ireland, or industrial disputes.

The three other aspects of judicial independence—as defined by Smith and Bailey—include the duty of the judges not to make public statements (relaxed by Lord Mackay, the present Lord Chancellor) and not to have public statements made about them. The idea that criticizing a judge might be contempt of court was invented by the Court of Appeal in 1900 to protect Mr Justice Darling,[16] but that protection has been on the decline in the last decades. Judicial independence is also said to cover the traditional parliamentary principle of not 'reflecting' on the judges either generally or specifically in either House of Parliament.[17] While the obligation not to discuss matters *sub judice* has survived intact, criticism of the judges seems to have become more acceptable among MP's in recent decades.

The final aspects of judicial independence are thought by the authors of Smith and Bailey to be judicial immunity from suit and the obligation of judges to disqualify themselves for bias. Neither seems controversial yet neither seems to clarify significantly the concept of judicial independence. Perhaps the most acceptable way of characterizing the role of judicial independence in England is to say that, while the independence of the judiciary is casual at best, the English have a strong commitment to the independence of individual judges. In the light of that, this book is an attempt to re-think the issue of judicial independence through an analysis of recent legal history, especially as that history was experienced by the Lord Chancellor's Office.

[15] Ibid. 225.   [16] *R* v. *Gray* [1990] 2 QB 36.

[17] Erskine May, *Parliamentary Practice*, 21st edn., ed. C. J. Boulton (London, 1989), 378–9. See *Ward* v *James* [1965] 2 WLR 455 (CA), where the Court of Appeal seemed to take away the right to jury trial and to put it at the discretion of the judges; Labour MPs attacked the decision. *The Times*, 4 Feb. 1965. Quintin Hogg QC (Lord Hailsham) attacked the MPs for attacking the judges. *The Times*, 6 Feb. 1965.

I

The Lord Chancellor's Office and the Age of Muir Mackenzie

This book, then, looks at the judges, their status, and their independence through the eyes of the Lord Chancellor's Office. It is an analysis which is best attempted historically. Today, the Lord Chancellor appoints the judges (including members of tribunals and the magistrates) and the QCs. The Department is responsible for the Appeal Courts, the High Court, and the Circuit Courts and has recently taken over the responsibility for the Magistrates' Courts; it is the ultimate administrator of the Legal Aid Scheme and thus, as we know from the 1986 litigation,[1] is highly significant in determining the level of payment of the profession. It commissions reports[2] and staffs most of the major commissions and committees that touch on the law;[3] it is responsible for the Law Commission, the Council on Tribunals, the Land Registry, the Public Trustee, and various other bodies; it takes the lead in law reform; it comes close to being, depending on how one defines the term, a Ministry of Justice for England and Wales. It is, however, more than that, for, in a very English way, it continues to present incumbents to Crown livings within the Established Church, as well as being responsible for the formal side of the Queen's Speech at the opening of Parliament, and the Lord Chancellor's political and judicial work.[4]

This book relies heavily on the papers of the Lord Chancellor's Office and Department. The papers partly do no more than confirm what we already knew or suspected about changes in the English legal system. Among other things they remind us that some constitutional skirmishes, like the issue of a Ministry of

---

[1] See e.g. *The Times*, 10, 11, 19, 21, 22, 28 Mar. 1986.

[2] What is perhaps less well known is that the Office also commissions its own reports, some of which are not published: e.g. Committee on Charitable Trusts (1956), LCO 29/94; Committee on Common Market Laws (1961), LCO 29/108. Recently, it has commissioned some significant empirical work.

[3] For some of these files see Compensation for Taking Land 1917–1919, LCO 3/; Beeching Committee, LCO 7/; Committee on Defamation 1971, LCO 13/; Extension of Legal Aid to Tribunals, LCO/14; (Franks) Committee on Administrative Tribunals (1957), LCO 15/; (Winn) Committee on Personal Injuries (1968), LCO 16/; (Lakey) Committee on Age of Majority (1965), LCO 17/; (Benson) Royal Commission on Legal Services (1979), LCO 19/; (Pearson) Royal Commission on Compensation (1978), LCO/20; War Time Adjustment Acts, LCO 26/; (Payne) Committee on Enforcement of Debts (1969), LCO 31/; (Lawrence) Committee to Enquire into Poor Persons Rules (1925), LCO 32/.

[4] See e.g. Returns from Crown Livings, LCO 5/; Crown Office, LCO 6/; Lord Chancellor's Visitors, LCO 9/, 10/, 11/; Sovereign's Speeches, LCO 21/; (Wilson) Committee on Public Records (1982), LCO 27/.

Justice, are resurrected each few decades. They remind us of the simplicities that exist in so many of our discussions of basic concepts like the separation of powers. In particular, they remind us that the notion of judicial independence is at best a vague one within the British Constitution. Judicial independence in England is less a question of one branch of government under the separation of powers; it is a question of how far, and with what political guidance, the civil servants should be choosing members of the judiciary, or what role the judges themselves should play in deciding appointments and terms of service, and in running the courts.

What is intriguing is not merely who set up some committee, but how and with whom the Office talked in deciding its composition, who staffed the committee, who drafted the report, and who negotiated away the rough edges. If legislation was needed for implementation, the Department's or the profession's lobbying could be important; if the report might be implemented administratively, the views of senior members of the Department may have been crucial. If the thirty-year rule keeps us from looking in this way at the immediate past, the messages from an earlier period are important for those considering current legal problems.

One of the difficulties in assessing the role of the Lord Chancellor's Department is that the Department can claim not only the political anonymity of the Civil Service, but the political asexuality of the legal profession, since the Department was, until the 1972 reorganization, staffed exclusively by lawyers rather than regular civil servants. It was indeed a remarkable example of professional self-regulation. An organization that is responsible, in so far as there is managerial responsibility, for running the legal system had until the 1970s no regular civil servants, by which I mean persons who formerly fell in the category dignified by the title 'the Administrative Grade'. Even today the influence of lawyers is strong, despite the fact that in 1990 the Permanent Secretary was no longer required to be a barrister, although preference was given to those serving in the department.

The idea that the Ministry of Defence (or the old War Office) would be solely run by regular officers or the Ministry of Health solely by health professionals would be regarded as risible. If it is the civil servants in the Chancellor's Office who have refused to increase the earnings of the Criminal Bar, it is not solely some Machiavellian act of the regular Civil Service. Whatever the overriding political considerations, in the mechanics of decision-making, lawyers have been heavily involved. Moreover, these civil servants have been strangely sheltered from public examination. Until 1990, the Lord Chancellor's Department was subject to no parliamentary committees and until 1992 there was no minister in the House of Commons to answer parliamentary questions.[5]

---

[5] *De facto*, the Attorney-General answered such questions.

(a) The Founding of the Lord Chancellor's Office

The actual founding of the Office goes back to the two old war-horse Chancellors of the late 1860s, the 1870s, and the 1880s—Selborne for the Liberals and Cairns for the Conservatives—who had, between them, dominated the dramatic restructuring of the English legal system in that period. The logic of the reform of the courts in the 1870s was that there should be a Ministry of Justice, and the Utilitarians almost persuaded the Judicature Commission (1867) to institute such a Ministry within the Home Office. Various select committees suggested that the courts be staffed by professional civil servants and that there be a Ministry of Justice similar to other great departments of state. The judges and the profession, however, were much happier with the Lord Chancellor exercising these new powers. The new-fangled Northcote–Trevelyan vision of life did not sit well with the judicial self-image. The judges' sense of élitism was not a utilitarian or meritocratic one. Since the Lord Chancellor was in any event to be president of the restructured Supreme Court (High Court and Court of Appeal), the judges and the Bar convinced politicians he should be—as far as anyone was used—the person responsible for administration.[6] The Home Office was, however, left with responsibilities not only for the police and prisons but for the running of Quarter Sessions (and the appointment of recorders and chairmen) as well as the management of Magistrates' Courts.[7]

In 1880, when Selborne returned to the Woolsack, he brought in Sir Kenneth Muir Mackenzie as Clerk of the Crown in Chancery, and as such Muir Mackenzie was also referred to as Principal Secretary. The appointment, however, was unlike the Permanent Secretaries in the reformed Civil Service; the appointment had been made by Selborne, and it was not absolutely clear that Mackenzie would stay when Selborne disappeared. Already in 1882, however, Muir Mackenzie was suggesting that the two offices might be merged;[8] and Selborne was pushing the idea of a permanent staff for the Lord Chancellor. The crucial move came in an 1882 letter from Cairns to Selborne, in which the former—although out of office—announced, 'I have come to the conclusion that the new Judicature System has thrown around the Chancellor such a network of departmental business . . . that . . . it will not be possible to prevent serious inconvenience to the public business on a change in the Great Seal . . . without a really efficient Permanent Secretary.'[9] The following year, 1883, Selborne sought Cairns's support in approaching the Treasury for a permanent establishment, 'in fact, a permanent secretary of the Ministry of Justice.'[10]

---

[6] P. Polden, *Guide to the Records of the Lord Chancellor's Department* (London, 1988), 15.
[7] It retained the first until 1971 and the second until 1991.
[8] Letter, Muir Mackenzie to Selborne, 24 Sept. 1882, LCO 2/262.
[9] Letter, Cairns to Selborne, 29 Mar. 1882, ibid.
[10] Letter, Selborne to Cairns, 16 Aug. 1883, ibid. Letter, Cairns to Selborne, 28 Aug. 1883, ibid. Selborne was suggesting £1,200, a figure he knew Muir Mackenzie would accept. He was in fact

The Treasury put up little resistance and by 1884 agreed that the work in the Office since 1874 had changed dramatically. The memorandum to the Treasury saw the work as of two types: first, the confidential and political variety for which the Lord Chancellor should have a political Private Secretary, and second, that 'belonging to a permanent Ministry of Justice' which 'will be best performed by a permanent staff . . . on whose experience each successive Lord Chancellor may rely'. This role was to be fulfilled by the new Permanent Secretary, who was to be a barrister of seven years' standing, exempt from the Civil Service entry regulations. The Treasury also assumed that this person would serve, among other things, as secretary to the Council of Judges (that is, the parliament of the judges of the Supreme Court of Judicature called for in the 1873 legislation) and, by vetting all Bills presented to Parliament, would act as parliamentary draftsman—two revenue-saving dreams that were not to be fully fulfilled.[11] The basic scheme, however, went through, and on 28 May 1884, Mackenzie became the Permanent Secretary to the Lord Chancellor and Viscount Wolmer the 'political' Private Secretary.

The significance of the financial concessions made by the Treasury in establishing the Lord Chancellor's Office has undoubtedly affected the course of law reform. The permanent civil servants were exempt from the meritocratic fervour of the Northcote–Trevelyan reforms of the Civil Service. Compared with other departments there has been a predominance of senior appointments and, at least until the 1970s, the Office managed to beat off attempts to change that situation.[12] One of the results has been that the Department has seen its role not as one primarily of managing the areas for which it was responsible but rather as that of a lobbyist for quasi-independent activities, like the judges or the courts. Until recent times, this was the context for the Department's view of judicial independence.

The fact that the Office operated largely outside the regular Civil Service also gave great power to the Permanent Secretary. He (and they have all been males thus far) is likely to have spent his whole career in the Department. Historically the incumbents have stayed as Permanent Secretary far longer than persons in similar positions in other departments, since retirement in the Department was not until 72 or, with permission, 75 (although, in 1990, legislation provided that future Permanent Secretaries had to retire at 62). The deputy, since the first one was created in 1915,[13] has invariably succeeded as Permanent Secretary; and the files make it clear that, historically, it has often been the outgoing Permanent

---

prepared to pay £1,500, but not until one of the existing clerks resigned. Letter, Selborne to Cairns, 24 Mar. 1884, ibid.

[11] Treasury to Selborne, 3 May 1884, ibid.

[12] During the 1960s the Treasury, responsible for Civil Service staffing, grumbled regularly about this. LCO 4/23.

[13] Since 1972 there have been two Deputy Secretaries (Grade 2).

Secretaries, rather than the Head of the Civil Service, who *de facto* chose the new Permanent Secretary.[14]

The Department's history falls into three clear parts. For the first thirty years (1884–1915), the Office was Muir Mackenzie. The next fifty-seven years (1915–72) were the years when the Office exercised its mystical powers. While it was still more a private office than a genuine Department, its power—and its control of reform—was awesome. This period in the Office's history was dominated by Lord Schuster (Schuster was made a peer at the end of his term as Permanent Secretary) and Sir George Coldstream. Schuster took over in 1915 and retired in 1944, to be replaced by Sir Albert Napier, Permanent Secretary 1944–54,[15] followed by Sir George Coldstream (1954–68).[16]

Since the book is based largely on the papers of the Lord Chancellor's Office, and they are subject to the thirty-year rule, there is less comment in depth on the four most recent Permanent Secretaries: Sir Denis Dobson (1968–77),[17] Sir Wilfred Bourne (1977–82)[18] Sir Derek Oulton (1982-89),[19] and Sir Thomas Legg (1989-date).[20] The work of the Office has evolved more into that of a Department, although it lacks, in some areas, effective managerial powers. The staff now includes more persons at the policy-making level who are either not lawyers or whose legal qualifications are perhaps not their most significant attributes as administrators. Specific individuals, however, continue to be important in shaping the thinking of the whole Department; and most of them are lawyers.

(b) The Muir Mackenzie Era

Muir Mackenzie[21] was only 35 when he became Clerk of the Crown in Chancery; he was to retire forty years later, in 1915. He then served (being by then Lord Muir Mackenzie) as a Lord-in-Waiting and ultimately a Minister during the two minority Labour administrations of 1924 and 1929. (He was, incid-

[14] In 1953, Napier effectively told Bridges (Head of the Civil Service) that Coldstream would be replacing him. Formally the Prime Minister has to approve the choice of Permanent Secretary to the Lord Chancellor. The Queen still has to approve the joint appointment as Clerk of the Crown in Chancery, LCO 4/23.

[15] Born 1881; educated at Eton and New College, Oxford; barrister, 1909; Private Secretary to Lord Chancellor, 1915–19; Deputy Serjeant-at-Arms, House of Lords, 1916–19; Deputy Secretary, Lord Chancellor's Office, 1919–44; Permanent Secretary, 1944–59.

[16] Born 1907; educated at Rugby and Oriel College, Oxford; Parliamentary Counsel's Office, 1934–9; Lord Chancellor's Office, 1939; Deputy Secretary, 1944–54; Permanent Secretary, 1954–69.

[17] Born 1908; educated at Charterhouse and Trinity College, Cambridge; solicitor, 1933; barrister, 1951; Deputy Secretary, 1954–68.

[18] Born 1927; educated at St Edward's, Oxford, and King's College, Cambridge; Ph.D.; private practice, Kenya, 1952–60; Lord Chancellor's Office, 1961; Deputy Secretary, 1968–77.

[19] Born 1922; educated at Eton and New College, Oxford; Bar 1949–56; Lord Chancellor's Office, 1956; Deputy Secretary, 1972–82.

[20] Born 1935; educated at Frensham Heights School and St John's College, Cambridge; Lord Chancellor's Office, 1962; Deputy Secretary, 1982–5.

[21] Lord Muir Mackenzie, born 1845, educated at Charterhouse and Balliol College, Oxford; barrister, 1873 (pupil of Lords Bowen and Davey); Lord Chancellor's Office, 1880.

entally, the oldest person to hold government office in this century.) Muir Mackenzie created the office of Permanent Secretary to the Lord Chancellor; and he was the Lord Chancellor's Office. It is unclear from the Lord Chancellor's papers who ensured that this would be the style of the Lord Chancellor's Office: lean in numbers, responsible rather than managerial, a highly effective force in a limited number of areas.

It is quite clear, however, that after the Judicature Acts and certainly after Muir Mackenzie's arrival, all communications to the Lord Chancellor passed through his Permanent Secretary. Any other member of the Cabinet who had views on the legal system, or, more importantly, wished to express views about the Judiciary, wrote to Muir Mackenzie. Thus the Home Secretary who, prior to the Judicature Acts, had felt free to deal directly with the judges, thereafter dealt through Muir Mackenzie. While Muir Mackenzie insisted he was but 'the Lord Chancellor's postman',[22] a reading of the files of that period shows a man increasingly the *éminence grise* in dealing with the High Court judges and, more obviously, a power in dealing with other judges and the profession.[23]

Muir Mackenzie, for instance, was heavily involved in working out a reformed Judicial Committee of the Privy Council as the implications of Dominion status became clear, although the Selborne vision of an Imperial Court of Appeal was dead.[24] Muir Mackenzie was in office when the Criminal Appeal Act of 1907—setting up the Court of Criminal Appeal, first suggested by the Council of Judges in 1892—was passed.[25] It was he who acted as spokesman for the judges as the County Courts Bill of 1903 was going through its various stages.[26] In his later years, however, Muir Mackenzie did not use the powers of the Permanent Secretaryship to their full effect, having apparently lost his early energy for reform. His successor Sir Claud Schuster later wrote confidentially:

Muir Mackenzie . . . was a man of subtle brain and keen wit. He hated waste or disorder, and he was industrious to an almost incredible extent. He was also extremely ingenious. He learned his business under Lord Selborne, and had imbibed many of Lord Selborne's views . . . to it (the Permanent Secretaryship) he devoted his very considerable mental and physical powers. But he was a man naturally secretive, unwilling to trust to his subordinates either his plans or their execution, and though an advanced Radical in politics, he was in many matters exceedingly conservative. He, for example, detested the use either of shorthand or of typewriting. So far as he allowed any record to be kept of what took place in the office or of what letters issued from it, he noted these matters in a very

---

[22] R. F. V. Heuston, *Lives of the Lord Chancellors, 1885–1940* (Oxford, 1964), 502.

[23] Muir Mackenzie was also a man of humour. See e.g. his advice to the Lord Chancellor as to the dangers of the Prince of Wales (later Edward VII) eating the food designated for the judges at the Lord Chancellors' breakfast. Ibid.

[24] Stevens, *Law and Politics*, 72–6.   [25] LCO 2/232.

[26] See generally LCO 2/153. Muir Mackenzie's soliciting of judicial views appears in LCO 2/154 and 155. After the first Bill in 1903, Halsbury introduced a further Bill, which was not passed, calling for selective jurisdictional increases, LCO 2/157, 158, 160. The County Court judges seemed mainly interested in a increase of salary to £2,000 p.a. (LCO 2/159, 209, 210), a goal not achieved until the 1930s (LCO 12/40). For the County Court legislation of 1907–11, see LCO 2/206, 207, 208, 209.

summary fashion in his own handwriting. He wrote his letters himself and kept no copies, and he directed the envelopes and stuck them up. He kept no record of the understandings or pledges to which he became a party. By reason of his unwillingness or inability to delegate, he took care to be served only by those who were unlikely to oppose his will. Furthermore, during the long reign of Lord Halsbury he gradually lost heart in the reforms which he had either planned himself or the idea of which he had inherited from Lord Selborne. Hence during the last years of his office, though he remained skillful and laborious, he ceased to make any attempt to accomplish reforms which he knew to be necessary . . . [27]

The work of the office was done by Muir Mackenzie as Permanent Secretary and by Adolphus Liddell, his Private Secretary, seconded from the Parliament Office, who was allowed to decide nothing.[28] The Assistant Serjeant-at-Arms of the House of Lords acted as Muir Mackenzie's secretary. In addition, there were two clerks and an odd job man. That was the Office.

In some ways it is not easy to reconcile the two visions of Muir Mackenzie—the spare administrator and the *éminence grise*. Despite the secretiveness, and the paucity of staffing, Muir Mackenzie established the reputation of the Office as guardian of the legal profession and 'administrator' of the judiciary. These were not easy times. Perhaps the best example of the way he operated was his dealings in the first few years in implementing the Judicature Acts. Those Acts established the Court of Appeal, retained the judicial functions of the House of Lords, merged the common law divisions, purported to merge the substantive systems of common law and equity, and established a High Court. The actual implementation was highly complex; while we tend to think about the legislation, it was the Statutory Instruments and the informal decisions that actually shaped the way the English legal system would develop. Obviously the most important actors were the two branches of the profession and the judges themselves, but the Cabinets—particularly Liberal Cabinets—had strong views; and Muir Mackenzie was no mere cipher.

Two things must, however, be borne in mind. First, Muir Mackenzie was operating in an atmosphere which underlines Dangerfield's arguments in the *Strange Death of Liberal England*. The Irish issue did change the face of English politics, and strangled the liberal reform movement. While Cairns, who had been Disraeli's Lord Chancellor until 1880, was certainly a reformer, he was not a liberal reformer in the way that Selborne was; and Halsbury, Cairns's successor as Conservative Lord Chancellor, was more interested in protecting the preroga-

---

[27] Memorandum by Lord Schuster, 31 Jan. 1943, pp. 4–5. LCO 2/3630. Schuster later wrote: 'You will bear in mind that Muir Mackenzie was completely unscrupulous in interpreting a statute and disregarding its provisions if they did not suit him.' Schuster to Coldstream, 12 July 1955, LCO 2/5233.

[28] 'Liddell was the most charming of men. He had passed many years in the office, but had never been allowed to decide anything and was not of a temper to oppose, or even to criticize, such of Muir Mackenzie's designs as were made known to him.' Schuster, Memorandum, 31 Jan. 1943, p. 5. See also A. G. C. Liddell, *Notes from the Life of an Ordinary Mortal* (London, 1911).

tives of the judiciary and the profession. Similarly, the Liberal Home Secretaries were far more convinced of the need for reform than were their Tory opposite numbers; and the frequency of Conservative Cabinets, at least until 1905, as a result of the Irish question and the Liberal split over Home Rule, meant that decisions were made primarily by Conservative politicians who generally had less concern for the litigant than for the professionals. Halsbury did not regard reforms as a benefit.

Since the decline of liberal England is significant in understanding how the spate of reform that began with Brougham petered out in the 1880s and 1890s, a weakening that Muir Mackenzie obviously felt, one should remember that Selborne, categorically, and Cairns, significantly, spent their time chivvying and bullying judges and the profession into accepting reforms and putting their own houses in order. The judges feared commissions. Imagine, then, what a Selborne or Cairns would have done if they had received a printed memorandum from the Lord Chief Justice calling for a Royal Commission on the Judicature, to examine, among other things, the cost of appeals, the backlog of cases in Chancery, the expense of litigation as a whole, the weakness of the appeal system in criminal cases, and the collapse of commercial work. Yet this is precisely what Halsbury received from the Lord Chief Justice, Coleridge, in 1891.[29] Halsbury, to the horror of Muir Mackenzie, wrote back to say the time was not ripe and the Council of Judges should address the issues.[30] The Council was not to prove a fruitful source of law reform. An opportunity to complete the work of the Judicature Commission of the 1860s and 1870s was lost. The bipolarization of politics resulting from the Irish issue made it possible for later Lord Chancellors—and especially Halsbury—to stifle reform.

The second thing that becomes clear about the decisions shaping the English legal system in the 1880s was that many of them were taken for the convenience of the profession and, even more so, for the convenience of the judges. While Lord Chancellors might occasionally take strong decisions, the Office was neither staffed nor structured to institute reform. In its most extreme form, the Office was seen as primarily responding to the concerns of the more senior judges and protecting the amorphous concept of judicial independence.

It was the Conservative Home Secretary, Assherton Cross, who in 1876 attempted to rationalize the circuit system by grouping county towns for criminal business and having the judges on circuit only visit them in rotation; more importantly, he increased from three to four the number of assizes each year in order to provide regular criminal proceedings around the country and more general civil assizes. The judges fought the changes vigorously. While there was

---

[29] Coleridge was also interested in the codification of English law. As Attorney-General, in 1872, he had argued for this, as well as for merging the two branches of the profession. He had also favoured a Ministry of Justice: E. H. Coleridge, *Life and Correspondence of John Duke, Lord Coleridge, Lord Chief Justice of England* (2 vols., London, 1904), ii. 89–92.

[30] Letter, Halsbury to Coleridge, 2 Jan. 1892, LCO 2/242.

much talk about the needs of litigants, at bottom it was a battle about the nature of the English judiciary and the status of the judges. The judge as embodiment of the law did not easily give way to the judge as public servant. Within ten years of the Cross proposals, the judges had their way—at least on the issue of assizes. The Lord Chancellor's Office papers both record these changes and illustrate Muir Mackenzie's role.

The Liberals were anxious to go further than the Conservatives, and have permanent courts in the major cities of the country. The Liberal Home Secretary, Sir William Vernon Harcourt, put it this way in 1884:

To break up the whole judicial staff of London four times a year utterly disorganizes the administration of the law in the metropolis and produces vast delay, cost and inconvenience to everyone. Much [sic] fewer judges would do the London work a great deal better if it was done continuously and without interruption.

He went on:

You might dispose with circuits altogether and their paraphernalia of grand juries, sheriffs, javelin men and the rest of them. Civil business of the district would be continuously and satisfactorily disposed of as regards proceedings of the first instance by younger and more vigorous men fresh from their practice at the Bar. The older and less locomotive sages of the law would remain in London. Instead of the outcry against the general gaol delivery with which you are now pestered, there would be a monthly trial of assize prisoners to which the accused are as much entitled in the provinces as in London. This simple division of labour would save time, money and injustice but I know that the judges and leading lawyers fight 'in their courses' against it.[31]

To get some sense of the opposition, one should perhaps look at Lord Justice Fry, a Quaker and one of the more liberal judges. 'I think any attempt to require the residence in Lancashire of the judges of the High Court whether by means of an obligation cast on the junior judges for the time being or by a rota of all the number, would have a disastrous effect on judicial office. If I judge others by myself I believe it would form a grave obstacle to the acceptance of a judgeship and so seriously affect the character of the Bench.' It was not until the Courts Act of 1971 that the Liberal goal was, at least partially, achieved.

The story was, of course, complex. From 1878 onwards the Council of Judges was strongly against the Winter Assize as the fourth assize was called. Baron Huddleston noted in a letter to the Lord Chancellor that 'it was almost unreasonable to call upon the judges many of whom are of advanced years . . . to be exposed at Assize towns to the unusual inclemency of the weather at that period of the year.' On the other hand, the Council of Judges resolved collectively that:

we say nothing about the inconvenience to the judges. They must discharge such duties as the general good of the country imposes upon them and they will always discharge them in a cheerful and ungrudging spirit but the office of the judge is becoming less and less

[31] LCO 1/2.

desirable and it would be a result to the country really disastrous if that office ceased to be an object of desire to the best of the profession. It is not only the profession that would suffer by its best men declining judgeships, the whole country would suffer grievously, far more grievously than it suffers because in a small minority of cases prisoners are kept too long in gaol.[32]

The Conservative Home Secretary Cross wrote to the Conservative Chancellor Cairns agreeing that sometimes the system was inconvenient but that it would be 'retrograde' to go back on the fourth assize. When the Liberals returned in 1880 it was suggested one way of adding judicial time would be to cut the long vacations by ten days, a suggestion opposed by the Council of Judges by a vote of twenty to four.[33]

Even after the government made various concessions, including a generous circuit allowance, Mr Justice Manisty went to the Newcastle Assizes and lectured the populace on the awfulness of the new system. Selborne's reaction, drafted by Muir Mackenzie, was chilly:

After the general concurrence of the Judges in the most recent Assize arrangements and after all that had taken place with respect to the allowance of circuit expenses, on the faith of these arrangements by the Treasury, I must own I was not prepared for a denunciation of them in an address by the Judge to a Grand Jury at the Commencement of an Assize in an important town upon the first occasion of their being put into practice, least of all from a Judge whose disapproval of them I had received no notice.[34]

After the Chancery and Court of Appeal judges were excused from going on circuit, the only other group thereafter who were supposed to go on circuit were the judges of the Probate and Divorce Division. Selborne was displeased when, in 1882, they had bluntly refused to go. As he wrote to the Master of the Rolls, 'the disposition recently shown in the Probate Division to refuse circuit duty will, I fear, increase those difficulties and perhaps make it necessary to think of remedies for them of a different kind which have hitherto not found favour with the judges or the Bar but for which (unless I deceive myself) a demand is growing both in the House of Commons and in the country.'[35]

So at least the Queen's Bench judges went on circuit and the Divorce Judges were put under pressure to go, but the judges still wanted the fourth assize killed and they did not want any grouping of circuit towns. Having failed under the Liberal administration to get rid of the fourth assize and the grouping of assize towns, the judges tried again when Lord Halsbury returned to the Woolsack in 1885, keeping Muir Mackenzie as his Permanent Secretary. The judges voted at their first meeting in 1886 formally to get rid of the fourth assize and to end grouping for criminal cases. What they were prepared to do, they said, was to

---

[32] LCO 1/4.
[33] Report of the Committee of Judges to the Council of Judges, Apr. 1878, ibid.
[34] 16 July 1884, LCO 1/7.   [35] 15 Apr. 1889, LCO 1/11.   [36] LCO 1/8 and 9.

have grouping for civil cases; moreover, they were prepared to have all litigation in the Home Counties heard in London.[36]

Halsbury had a good deal more sympathy for the personal preferences of the judges than had Selborne. Selborne thought the judges were pampered. Halsbury accepted the report of the committee established by the Council of Judges and drafted an Order in Council to give effect to it. While some old-time judges like Mr Justice Day were anxious to return to the system when circuit riding and London sittings did not overlap, and while some of the younger judges like Mr Justice Cave would have been happy to see more grouping and more work given to the County Courts, the basic judicial position seemed reasonable to Halsbury, who tried to implement it. Halsbury, however, had less experience with the judiciary than had Selborne; and he did not have the scepticism, nor the sense of the judges as public servants, held by Muir Mackenzie.

No sooner had Halsbury published a draft Order in Council attempting to implement the advice of the judges than Mr Justice Grantham, famous later as the last of the judges to be threatened with impeachment, announced it as 'unconstitutional, ill-considered and most injurious to the interests of all those concerned'. Perhaps the most bizarre outburst, however, came from the Chief Justice, Lord Coleridge, the advocate of the reform.[37] The new arrangement for civil work was 'revolutionary' and it would 'virtually destroy the circuit system', he said. Halsbury was unable to understand Coleridge's letter but agreed to do nothing because of his opposition. Meanwhile Muir Mackenzie's minutes on the letters from the judges became more acerbic. Of the Chief Justice he said, 'He seems to have forgotten that the principle of the scheme was settled by a unanimous vote of all the judges present at the first Council and the scheme confirmed by a large majority afterwards.'[38] The English solution of having neither the judges nor the Lord Chancellor's Office clearly responsible for the supervision of the courts left an uncomfortable vacuum. In particular, it enabled judges to avoid their responsibilities as public servants.

The matter was tabled, and a new committee of judges was set up, this time with Coleridge as a member. The judges had their way on the fourth assize. They had their way on the grouping of the criminal assizes, and the Lord Chief Justice Coleridge had his way—supported by lobbies from County towns: there would be civil assizes in the Home Counties. In other words, with the support of Halsbury, all the changes since 1877 were abandoned within a decade.[39] (All

---

[37] He had, after all, been Liberal Solicitor-General, 1868–71, and Attorney-General, 1871–3. When he was appointed Chief Justice of Common Pleas in 1873 he wrote to his constituents: 'my political principles are as strong as ever, and my political sympathies as keen as ever; though henceforth I can allow them, as a judge, neither influence nor expression.' Coleridge, *Life of Lord Coleridge*, ii. 231.

[38] LCO 1/9.

[39] Although, not unnaturally, the assizes continued to cause trouble. There was a suggestion in 1892 that the number of assize towns be dramatically reduced; and again in 1896. Abel-Smith and Stevens, *Lawyers and the Courts*, 89. The judges tinkered with the circuit and assize system throughout the Edwardian period: LCO 2/242.

that remained were Selborne's generous circuit expenses, destined to become an important bargaining chip in the 1940s.) If this capitulation made Muir Mackenzie's role as factotum of the judiciary more tolerable, it certainly did not help what he saw as the Office's responsibility for reform.

The whole episode emphasizes the peculiar direction that the English sense of separation of powers, and particularly the notion of judicial independence, had taken. At a time when the judges might have been expected to be drawn into the operation of central government with a significant role, that did not happen. Equally, at a time when, in their capacity as triers of fact, it might have been expected that they would assume the utilitarian pose of the period, they strove to retain old forms and procedures, and became increasingly concerned with their status.

(c) The Imperial Dimension

The Muir Mackenzie years spanned vital years in the modern history of the Judicial Committee of the Privy Council. The idea of Dominion status—the forerunner of the Commonwealth—was born in 1867 with the British North America Act; and the period between then and the First World War was the Golden Age of the Judicial Committee. While the Lord Chancellors were in the public eye, it was Muir Mackenzie who was, in many ways, at the centre of the inevitable political pressures which grew as the new Dominions developed their own political cultures.[40]

As the independent Dominions grew in number—Australia was added in 1900, New Zealand in 1907, South Africa in 1909—they became more articulate and made greater use of and demands on the Privy Council.[41] Once Cairns had destroyed the idea that after the Canadian Supreme Court had been established in 1875, there should be no further appeals to London,[42] the various Imperial Conferences, beginning in 1887, put pressure on the British government to ensure an adequate judiciary in the Privy Council. The first major public criticism of the Judicial Committee had been heard in Canada in the 1880s.[43] When

[40] See generally, J. Eddy and D. Schreuder, eds., *The Rise of Colonial Nationalism: Australia, New Zealand, Canada and South Africa First Assert their Nationalism, 1880–1914* (London, 1988).

[41] In 1900 the Privy Council received 16 appeals from Canada, 27 from Australia, 11 from South Africa, and 6 from New Zealand: *Civil Judicial Statistics, 1900*, 53. In 1910 the figures were Canada, 38; Australia, 16; South Africa, 8; New Zealand, 5: *Civil Judicial Statistics, 1910*, 24.

[42] C. G. Pierson, *Canada and the Privy Council* (London, 1960), 16–21.

[43] One of the first problems was the relationship between the Judicial Committee of the Privy Council and Canadian criminal appeals. In the Connors case, in 1885, an attempted appeal by a convicted murderer, the Attorney-General and Solicitor-General (Webster and Gorst) advised the English Cabinet that, while the 1867 act allowed Canada to abolish appeals in criminal cases, until the Canadian Parliament legislated, the right to appeal survived. Unfortunately, acting on the advice of the Canadian ministers, the Governor-General (the Marquess of Lansdowne) had refused Connors a stay of execution. LCO 1/2.

It was also at this point that the Judicial Committee, after an initial decision in *Russell v The Queen*, 7 App. Cas. 829 (PC 1882), favouring the broad federal powers intended by the 1867 Act, decided

Chamberlain, at the 1897 Imperial Conference, broached the idea of economic union, if not of federation, the role of the courts took on added significance. In this atmosphere the first arrangements were made in 1895 to have 'Dominion' judges as opposed to ex-colonial judges sit with the law lords in the Privy Council,[44] and before long, more dramatic gestures were being considered.

By 1900 the Dominions and colonies were expressing considerable dissatisfaction about the somewhat random arrangements for staffing the Judicial Committee:[45] the four Lords of Appeal and six judges of the Court of Appeal, various other English privy counsellors who had held 'high judicial office', two appointees under the 1833 Act,[46] together with an Indian judge and certain Dominion judges under the 1895 Act.

Although by this time the urge to merge the House of Lords and the Privy Council—pushed by Selborne in the 1860s and 1870s—had largely evaporated, by 1900 a plan was developed to add four more Lords of Appeal to satisfy the demands of the self-governing colonies. Behind the scenes, Joseph Chamberlain, Lord Halsbury, and Sir Courtenay Ilbert (former Law Member of the Governor's Council in India and by then Parliamentary Draftsman) worked out a compromise. Ilbert drafted a bill to add four more law lords, appointed for seven-year terms,[47] and it was assumed that overseas judges appointed under the 1895 Act would become the new Lords of Appeal. With horror, Ilbert specu-

Hodge v. The Queen, 9 App. Cas. 117 (PC 1883), which appeared to espouse Mowatt's theory of the co-ordinate relationship of the federal and provincial governments. D. C. Creighton, *Canada's First Century, 1867–1967* (Toronto, 1970), 49.

Meanwhile, the Australian judges were complaining because the Judicial Committee did not allow dissents, and at a meeting of the Australian State court judges in 1888, they voted 'that their lordships be requested to obtain the necessary powers to enable them to deliver judgements individually if they see fit'. Among those consulted by the Lord Chancellor, to whom the petition was referred, was Selborne. He wrote on 28 Nov. 1888: 'I am extremely sorry to hear of a Colonial movement against the accustomed mode of delivering Privy Council judgements; which I have always thought wise; and I think that a departure from it, much as you say certain Colonial Judges now desire, might tend to great discontents in India and in the Colonies in many cases in which there is now a satisfactory degree of acquiescence.' Lord Bramwell (2 Dec. 1888) was less charitable: 'I suppose the Australian judges think that sometimes their dignity would be saved by a minority opinion.' None of the English and Scottish judges consulted was prepared to endorse the Australian view. LCO 2/33. Between 1929 and 1966 (when dissents were allowed) no Australian judge sat in the Privy Council on the ground that they would not sit in a court in which they could not dissent (unpublished paper by Alan Paterson).

[44] The 1833 Act had provided for the appointment of two former colonial judges as members of the Council and two former Indian judges to be paid £400 per year. The 1871 Act allowed four paid members to be chosen from among the judges of the English Superior Courts or from among the Chief Justices in Bengal, Madras, or Bombay. The 1887 Act reduced to one the former Indian salaried judge under the 1833 Act (and fixed his salary at £800). The 1895 Act allowed up to five Canadian, Australian, and South African judges to be appointed as members of the Judicial Committee.

[45] Nor were they entirely pleased with the behaviour in it. Lord Halsbury was reported as 'hopping' between the House of Lords and the Privy Council, hearing cases concurrently.

[46] At that time, Hobhouse and James.

[47] 'Its object was probably to secure the existence of colonial Lords of Appeal who should be not too much out of touch with the course of law and justice in the colonies which they were to represent.' LCO 2/179.

lated that '[T]here would at least be a risk that a strong self-governing colony would claim a substantial voice in the appointment of a Lord of Appeal.'[48]

In July 1901, the Conference on the Final Court of Appeal met, chaired by David Mills, Minister of Justice in Canada. From the outset, the inherent absurdity of achieving agreement among such a heterogeneous group of emerging nations was plain. Mr Justice Hughes of the Supreme Court of Victoria insisted on pushing the merger of the Privy Council and the House of Lords,[49] a suggestion that Chamberlain thought 'quite futile'.[50] An unseemly debate ensued about who would pay for any new judges,[51] and tangential debates went on about allowing dissents in the reconstituted Privy Council. New Zealand argued in favour. Sir James Prendergast, the former Chief Justice, argued,

An English judge first makes his reputation in the House of Lords; he continues to make his reputation, and that reaches us. If our appeals are to be disposed of by gentlemen who first made their reputation in India or in the Roman-Dutch colonies, and then have their mouths closed in the Privy Council, then we do not know by whom our cases are being disposed of.

Halsbury did not agree.

Lord Selborne took the very strongest view against it, and I am bound to say I think he was a good deal actuated by the difficulty of satisfying public opinion in India rather than in this country. The sort of notion was that the dissentient judges' opinion might be made the subject of great discussion in India, and would be rather likely to promote litigation. Some of the qualifications and disagreements that you occasionally find in the judgments in the House of Lords he thought might be very safely left to expert opinion in England to form a judgment upon, but he did not wish that, particularly by comparatively half-educated Hindoo lawyers.[52]

It soon became clear that while there was dissatisfaction in the colonies and especially in the Dominions, any new imperial court was liable to cause even more dissension than the Privy Council. The Canadian Privy Council had already resolved that 'with the information they at present possess the creation of the four Colonial Law Lords suggested would not inspire any additional confidence in the Judicial Committee'; and the New Zealand representative announced at the conference: 'In my opinion a Member or Members appointed from the Dominion of Canada or the Commonwealth of Australia or from

---

[48] Ibid.

[49] There was some evidence that he had been put up to this by Edmund Barton, the Prime Minister of Australia. Letter from Barton to Hughes, *Correspondence Relating to the Proposed Establishment of a Final Court of Colonial Appeal* (HMSO, 1901), 24.

[50] 'To attempt a change of that kind, with all the difficulties attending it, when we are under the impression that a majority of the Colonies would object to the change, would be, of course, quite futile.' *Conference Report* (1901), 24.

[51] Chamberlain noted, 'I thought that possibly they might think it was a little infra dig, that a Judge appointed specially as the representative of a Colony should be paid for by the Mother-country.' Ibid. 25.

[52] Ibid. 26.

South Africa would afford no better guarantee nor bring any further satisfaction to the Colony of New Zealand than is afforded by the presence of Great Britain or others under the existing laws at the hearing of appeals from New Zealand.'[53] The Colonial Office, not surprisingly, reported that the views expressed at the Conference were 'too diverse' for any action to be taken. While reform of the Judicial Committee remained a perpetual agenda item at Imperial Conferences, its fate was uniform. Whatever the failings of the Privy Council, the powerful Dominions were not prepared to risk the alternatives.

At the 1907 Imperial Conference, for instance, Canada once more defended the Judicial Committee. Prime Minister Laurier said, 'So far as Canada has any concern, we have an appeal to the Judicial Committee of the Privy Council; and it has, as a general rule, given very great satisfaction.'[54] At the 1911 Conference, there was further talk of an 'Imperial Court of Appeal'.[55] Once again, however, although the project was by then being pushed by Australia and New Zealand, Canada opposed it. The British government made firm commitments to improve arrangements for hearing appeals in the Privy Council by creating two additional Lords of Appeal: 'That they should add to the highest court of appeal, both for the United Kingdom, and the Dominions and Colonies, by selecting two English judges of the finest quality; that the quorum should be fixed at, say, five, and that the court should sit successively in the House of Lords for United Kingdom appeals and in the Privy Council for appeal from the Dominions and Colonies.'[56] After some delay a bill was introduced to allow an increase in the number of 'colonial' judicial members of the Council, under the 1895 Act, from five to seven[57] and to increase the number of Lords of Appeal from four to six. Yet even these additions were not sufficient to assuage growing doubts in the Dominions. In Canada political rumblings were being heard that the right to appeal to London was an extravagance, coupled with irritation at any suggestion that the Dominion was not free to end appeals. The Lord Chancellor's Office was uncomfortable.[58]

[53] *Conference Report* (1901), 26.

[54] *Colonial Conference Papers*, Cd. 3524 (1907), 210.

[55] Haldane followed the Lord Chancellor's remarks with the observation that '[i]t is understood that this final Court of Appeal for the whole Empire is not merely to be of the strength of the existing one. We have agreed to strengthen it, and propose to add to it, as the Lord Chancellor said, two hand-picked lawyers.' *Proceedings of the Imperial Conference*, Cd. 5745 (1911), 244.

[56] Ibid. 222–3.

[57] New Zealand felt it had not been fairly represented under the 1895 legislation. It was anxious to have Sir Joshua Williams appointed. He was, on 14 May 1914. Sir A. Fitzroy, *Memoirs* (2 vols., London, 1925), ii. 549.

[58] The *Montreal Star*, Memo (7 Mar. 1913) upset Sir Kenneth Muir Mackenzie by arguing that while 'the right of appeal to an impartial tribunal has been of the greatest value to us in delicate constitutional questions—especially those in which race and religion are involved', it was inappropriate in cases where corporations were involved. (It may not be irrelevant that Loreburn's decisions upholding federal power under s. 91 had been largely corporation cases.) The *Star* also dismissed the argument that it was not open to Canada to abolish appeals. '[T]his sort of talk, leaving the impression that Canadian law for Canadians is made by somebody outside of Canada, is more mischievous when forced upon a democratic community such as ours.' LCO 2/287.

The appeals, however, still flooded in. In 1913 the House of Lords sat for 115 days hearing sixty-four appeals and the Privy Council for 124 days to hear ninety-two cases. Far from having the same panel sitting alternately in Lords and Privy Council as he had hoped,[59] Haldane was faced with such a backlog of cases that he reconciled himself to having the Privy Council sit in two panels or divisions.[60] The law officers gave their opinions that this might not be done without legislation;[61] an act legitimating the arrangement was pushed through in 1915.[62] By 1916, the Lords of Appeal were often staffing three appellate panels. In the Lords, the panel was supplemented by other peers qualified to sit, while in the Privy Council these two groups manned panels helped by those appointed under the 1833, 1884, 1895, and 1913 Acts.[63] The arrangement was perhaps not the ideal setting for distinguished jurisprudential contributions.[64]

(d) The Changing Concept of the Judiciary

Muir Mackenzie's period as Permanent Secretary coincided with important changes in the social, political, and economic role of the judges. Despite all the law reforms of the nineteenth century, the judges in the 1870s were still seen as the Great Officers of the State, above mere politicians and certainly above the bourgeois meritocrats in the Civil Service. By the time of the First World War,

---

[59] The Clerk of the Privy Council, after noting that Australia and New Zealand were more reasonable at the 1911 Imperial Conference than they had been in 1907 in their demands for merging the Privy Council and the House of Lords, recorded that Loreburn agreed to 'the introduction of a more flexible system in the distribution of the judicial power available, to create what will be in effect one Supreme Court sitting in two divisions. No doubt his concessions in form had been brought about by the influence of Haldane and Asquith (both being present), who have on different occasions subscribed to the principle.' Fitzroy, *Memoirs*, ii. 448–9.

The Imperial Conference of 1917 once more took up the issue of judicial appeals. Fitzroy summarized the situation in the following terms: 'On Hughes' (Australia) resolution on the subject of a Supreme Court of Appeal . . . everyone subscribed to the theory of such a court, but with no concrete expression of the idea before them, they declined to commit themselves to its urgency. The only fruitful result of the discussion was the testimony elicited from the representatives of Canada, New Zealand, South Africa and India to the extremely satisfactory way in which the Judicial Committee did its work . . . The two obstacles to the realization of Mr Hughes' dream of one Supreme Tribunal for all Appellants resident within the Empire, however attractive in appearance are (1) a matter of finance—will the Dominions contribute to its cost on an adequate scale?—and (2) a matter of repute—will a court largely recruited from Dominion Judges enjoy the confidence of British litigants either at home or beyond the seas?' Ibid. 679.

[60] With the outbreak of World War I, the Privy Council had the additional burden of hearing 'prize' cases from the English courts. By 1915, there were twenty-eight prize cases waiting to be heard. LCO 2/92.

[61] Sir Rufus Isaacs (Attorney-General) and Sir John Simon (Solicitor-General). LCO 2/287. Two years later (5 Dec. 1915) Loreburn wrote to Buckmaster saying that he could see no reason, in law or practice, why the Judicial Committee should not sit in two divisions. LCO 2/292.

[62] Judicial Committee Act of 1915. LCO 2/292. The Committee began sitting in two divisions on 14 Feb. 1916. The second division began by hearing prize cases.

[63] See L. Blom-Cooper and G. Drewry, *Final Appeal* (Oxford, 1972), ch. 6.

[64] W. I. Jennings, 'The Statute of Westminster and Appeals to the Privy Council', 52 *Law Quarterly Review* (1936), 173.

that perception was changing. Judges were seen, increasingly, to be public servants, albeit public servants with an exalted status—the representatives of the
Queen on circuit and the embodiment of status in the Royal Courts of Justice.

In part, these perceptions reflected changes in the political perception of the
judges by the public at large. In 1880, when Muir Mackenzie had taken the reins
at the Lord Chancellor's Office, it was assumed that the appeal courts, and particularly the House of Lords, had some responsibility for law-making. The political pressures which, in the 1870s, insisted that the final appeal court must remain
with the hereditary upper house and not become part of an Imperial Court of
Appeal, managed to cloak the judicial activities with some of the aura of the legislative body. Nor was it a legislative body that saw itself as particularly circum-
scribed—it was not until the Parliament Act of 1911 that the legislative powers
of the House of Lords were curbed.

While the 1873 Judicature Act, which set up the Supreme Court, consisting of
a Court of Appeal and a High Court, gave a boost to the idea of the courts as a
public service and the judges as public servants, it was all a long way from the
utilitarian dream. Judges were chosen from the Bar, and many leading members
of the Bar were members of the House of Commons. Lord Halsbury, the Lord
Chancellor from 1885 to 1886, from 1886 to 1892, and from 1895 to 1905, did
not hesitate to appoint to the bench members of the Bar more for their politics
than their standing at the Bar.[65] The situation began to change with the return
of the Liberals in 1905 and the appointment of Lord Loreburn as Lord
Chancellor. At least in the Supreme Court, politics became far less important in
the appointment of judges, a position underlined by the resolve of Lord
Haldane, who became Lord Chancellor in 1912, not to appoint to the High
Court or Court of Appeal as a form of political reward. Even the Liberals and
certainly Birkenhead, Lord Chancellor in the Lloyd George Coalition of 1919–
22, continued to appoint those with political connections as law lords—judges in
the final court of appeal, the House of Lords.

With the changes, which brought professional judges to the High Court and
Court of Appeal, there was, however, increasingly a more formalistic approach
to the common law and to statutes. The courts seemed to be looking more frequently to Parliament to change the law and for the courts to interpret the law as
if it were a self-contained objective system of rules. The Employers' Liability Act
of 1880, the Employers' Liability Act of 1893, and the Workman's
Compensation Act of 1897, all seemed to push in these directions. There were
political reasons for accepting the limited role of judges implicit in Dicey's
concept of the Rule of Law. The series of politically insensitive decisions about
the labour unions at the turn of the century[66]—another contribution of
Halsbury's—undoubtedly left the judges interested in reaching the objective high
ground. Tax statutes began to be interpreted formalistically;[67] and in *Local*

---

[65] Heuston, *Lives of the Lord Chancellors, 1885–1940*, 36 f.
[66] Stevens, *Law and Politics*, 92–8.   [67] Ibid. 170–6.

Government Board v *Arlidge*[68] the courts appeared to be giving up responsibility even for procedural due process in administrative law cases.

The Liberals—and it was the Liberal law lords who decided *Arlidge*—seemed consciously to be removing the regular courts from decision-making in the new welfare state. When Lloyd-George introduced Old Age Pensions in 1908, disputes were to be settled by local Pensions Committees. Disputes about benefits under the National Insurance Act 1911 were settled by local Courts of Referees. Where judges began to get more work was in chairing commissions and committees—primarily in the area of 'lawyers' law'. Lord Hereford chaired the Royal Commission on Accidents to Railway Servants, in 1899–1900,[69] Lord Dunedin the Royal Commission on Registration of Title in 1906–10,[70] and Lord James the Royal Commission on the Selection of Justices of the Peace in 1909–10.[71] Whille the Parnell Commission in 1888 was a judicial inquiry, it was not until after the Tribunals of Enquiry Act, 1921, that it became common for judges to chair public inquiries outside 'legal' areas.

Nevertheless, as the political element in judicial appointments declined, and as the judges were removed or removed themselves from decision-making in politically sensitive areas, and as they increasingly came to treat their role as a more objective mechanistic process, they came to be in greater demand as chairs of outside fact-finding bodies and increasingly as chairs of groups designed to produce policies which, in their own way, might be highly controversial. In some ways the new status of the apolitical judges was underlined by the demise of the public freedom to criticize the judges. What had been described by the Privy Council as 'obsolete' in 1899[72]—namely, the criticizing of judges being contempt of court—was found to be the law of the land in 1900 in an effort to prevent press criticism of the extrovert Mr Justice Darling.[73] The complex historical environment of the English judiciary was being adapted to the twentieth century.

---

[68] 1915 AC 120 (1914).   [69] Cd. 41.   [70] Cd. 5316.   [71] Cd. 5250.
[72] *McLeod* v. *St. Aubyn* [1899] AC 549 (PC).   [73] *R.* v. *Gray* [1900] 2 QB 36 (CA).

The Schuster Era: High Policy

While Muir Mackenzie was far more than the 'postman' he pretended to be, there is little doubt that his was something of a passive role—especially in his later years. In these years, he humoured the judges; he soothed the Bar; he even began to pamper solicitors. His original hope of moving to complete the reforms of the Judicature Acts of the 1870s had, however, evaporated. Perhaps, in any event, the staffing of the office made a proactive style unlikely. This existing style was not to the liking of Lord Haldane, a Liberal reformer, when he took office as Lord Chancellor in 1912. Muir Mackenzie was replaced in 1915 by the man who became the most powerful of the Permanent Secretaries—Sir Claud (later Lord) Schuster.

Schuster's family had come to England from Frankfurt in the early nineteenth century and became successful Manchester merchants.[1] Educated at Winchester and New College, Oxford, Schuster began practice on the Northern Circuit, only to give up when his father 'suffered financial reverses'. Schuster then joined the Civil Service, working first in the Ministry of Education under Sir Robert Morant and then with Lloyd George on the National Insurance Bill. In 1915, Haldane, anxious formally to establish a Ministry of Justice,[2] appointed Schuster as his Permanent Secretary; and Schuster rapidly established himself as the dominant force in the Office and a power in the wider professional and political arena. The size of the Office increased somewhat, but perhaps the most significant aspect was that, within a few years, Schuster was seen as the *alter ego* of the Lord Chancellor and a moving force in Whitehall.

Schuster's style was decisive and directive. It was not a style which was popular with all the judges. Schuster, nevertheless, undoubtedly achieved a great deal. The Law of Property Acts of 1922 and 1925,[3] his work on the County Courts, his reform of procedure and evidence, the beginning of comprehensive criminal legal aid, the slightly more relaxed approach to judicial manpower—which led to the gradual increase in the numbers of High Court judges—and his support of the Law Revision Committee established in 1934 were all significant. His successor, Napier, was undoubtedly right in describing Schuster as a 'quick reader, fluent on paper and lucid in stating a case . . . always alert, his reaction to the news immediate, his course of action soundly planned and quickly put in train'.

---

[1] Schuster was anxious to rebut any suggestions that he was of Jewish origin.

[2] See e.g. a memorandum, apparently written in Sept. 1917, LCO 2/601.

[3] A. Offer, 'The Origins of the Law of Property Acts, 1910–25', 40 *Modern Law Review* (1977), 405.

It was also true that he 'gave pungent expression to his dislikes'.[4] It was not true, as Napier also suggested, that all the judges, excepting Hewart, liked Schuster.[5]

(a) The Machinery of Government and the Long Weekend

In the relationship between the executive and the judiciary—and especially between the Supreme Court and the Lord Chancellor's Office—little served to cause more friction than the suggestion in the Committee on the Machinery of Government (1918)[6] that there should be a Ministry of Justice in England. It is difficult at this distance to see what all the fuss was about. Many of the reformers in the 1870s assumed they had created a Ministry of Justice in establishing the Lord Chancellor's Office. The Committee itself was, in some ways, a canard. At its most cynical, the Committee may be viewed as a way of keeping Lord Haldane employed. He had been removed from the War Office, mainly because of the totally unfair suggestion that, because he had studied at Göttingen, he was pro-German.[7] Reading the recommendations of the Committee in the 1990s, they seem both moderate and a natural historical evolution from the nineteenth century. Yet, as the judicial establishment chose to read the recommendations of the Committee, they were seen as an affront to the Rule of Law as epitomized in the writings of Dicey. Had the English judicial establishment taken an intellectual approach to the separation of powers, the recommendations would have tested a series of important hypotheses. As it was, paranoia, strongly influenced by the Report, set the theme for relations between the judiciary and the Civil Service in the 1920s and 1930s.

What Haldane suggested in the chapter on 'Justice' in the Report of the Committee on the Machinery of Government was an Imperial Court of Appeal—a glorified Judicial Committee of the Privy Council. To this would go appeals from Commonwealth and Empire, as well as from England, Scotland, and Ireland,[8] a scheme regurgitating the plan originally devised by Selborne and Cairns in the 1860s and 1870s. Haldane did not, however, look for an end to the co-mingling of the judicial, executive, and legislative functions in the Lord Chancellor, as is sometimes suggested.[9]

His ideas were no doubt influenced by the period he had already served in that

---

[4] See e.g. his testy reaction when the Treasury failed to live up to its promise that the Chancellor's Office should have one 'free floating' Knighthood in every Honours List: Memo, Schuster to Lord Simon, 18 Mar. 1942, LCO 4/7.

[5] A. Napier, 'Schuster', *Dictionary of National Biography, 1951–1960* (London, 1971), 867.

[6] *Report of the Machinery of Government Committee*, Cd. 9230 (1918).

[7] S. E. Koss, *Lord Haldane: Scapegoat for Liberalism* (New York, 1969).

[8] *Report of the Machinery of Government Committee*, 64, 72.

[9] See memorandum by Lord Schuster, dated 31 Jan. 1943. LCO 2/3630. This extensive memorandum is relied on at different points in this book. The following year, after Schuster's retirement, Henry Hollond of Trinity College, Cambridge, wrote to Schuster, congratulating him on the peerage that he had received and urging him to write an extensive memorandum on the role of the Permanent Secretary to the Lord Chancellor. Hollond to Schuster, 31 Aug. 1946. LCO 2/3028.

office (1912–15). Haldane thought the Chancellor should remain in the Cabinet as 'a legal and constitutional adviser of the highest standing'. He would be the President of the Imperial Court of Appeal, but would be 'freed from the duty of daily or even frequent judicial sitting'.[10] Since the Upper House of the legislature, at least according to recommendations of the Report, was to be drastically restructured, the Lord Chancellor would cease to be the Speaker of that House. At the same time, the Lord Chancellor—rather than the Treasury—would be the conduit between departments introducing legislation and the Parliamentary Counsel's Office which, under the British system, drafts nearly all legislation.

These were not the changes which disturbed the judicial establishment, however; there were three other recommendations. First, the Lord Chancellor would become the focal point of judicial appointments. Not only would he continue to appoint High Court judges, County Court judges, some of the Masters and the Justices of the Peace, he would take over from the Prime Minister appointments of the Law Lords and Lords Justice; from the Home Secretary appointment of Recorders and Stipendiary Magistrates; and from the senior judges the appointment of certain Masters. Second, in making judicial appointments, the Chancellor would be advised by a Committee.[11] Third, all other aspects of the running of the legal system would be in the hands of a Minister of Justice, who would take over most of the functions of the Home Secretary.

It was in this context that the judges faced the issue of their own status. The Bar Council caught the atmosphere of the moment as it reviewed the possibility of a Ministry of Justice: 'This aroused a fear that . . . an Inspector should be appointed whose business it would be to observe, and report on, the conduct by the judges of the cases before them—a proposal against which we consider it would be impossible to protest too strongly.'[12] While the Report of the Committee on the Machinery of Government was largely ignored in the nation at large, the status of the judiciary, as allegedly reflected in the Report, became almost an obsession with the legal profession. As real power ebbed away and there appeared to be less deference to the judicial role, the judges sought reassurance through the medium of ritual and salary. It was to be a theme heavily emphasized in the 1920s and 1930s.

As the nation addressed the implications of the peace, the upper classes—into whose ranks their salaries still thrust the High Court judges[13]—began to feel that Edwardian England would never return. They were right. While the great

---

[10] *Report of the Machinery of Government Committee*, 73.

[11] Composed of the Prime Minister, the Minister of Justice, any ex-Lord Chancellors, and the Lord Chief Justice.

[12] General Council of the Bar, *Report of the Special Committee on a Ministry of Justice*. 17 Dec. 1918. LCO 2/3630.

[13] The judges generally came from upper middle-class rather than upper-class families. Of the appointments to the senior judiciary between 1921 and 1950, 15.4% of the judges were from the landed upper classes, 14.3% from the professional classes, 43.3% from the upper middle classes, 8.8% from the lower middle class, and 11% from the working class. Cited, J. A. G. Griffith, *The Politics of the Judiciary* (4th edn. London, 1991), 31.

Liberal reforms of the period after 1905 were developed from a position of strength and confidence, by 1919 there was an ominous—and accurate—sense that England was on an economic decline. Reforms in the legal system accelerated, and change was coming not only from Parliament but, so it seemed, from the civil servants in the Lord Chancellor's Office. In the Machinery of Justice section of the Report Section, it was provided that the new Minister of Justice would have 'experts charged with the duty of watching over the necessities of law reform and of studying the development of the subject at home and abroad'.[14]

Trying to understand the frame of mind of the judges during these years is not easy. The judges felt they had been loyal soldiers during the First World War. They had given decisions sympathetic to the administration;[15] and they had performed a wide range of public duties. With the war over, however, there seemed less role for the judges. Administrative law, even at a procedural level, had been largely abandoned. While there were occasional outbursts in public law—as in *Roberts* v. *Hopwood*[16]—reasserting *ultra vires* over local authorities, the senior judiciary was increasingly uninvolved with great matters of state. The Civil Service had grown larger; and the Permanent Secretary loomed larger and his influence was reflected in a salary closing in on that of the High Court judges.[17] Meanwhile, the judges of the Supreme Court were excluded from the War Bonus and denied the pay increase that Birkenhead had sought.

An increasingly testy mood was afoot. Schuster recorded it faithfully in the Lord Chancellor's Office files. He noted that it was true that in the last quarter of the nineteenth century a number of important powers had been taken from the courts. With a dig at Hewart, Schuster also noted that 'particularly during the War and largely under the influence of the then Attorney-General, who has since become Lord Chief Justice, Parliament was persuaded to withdraw from the Courts, and grant to the executive, powers which might in ordinary times have been thought more suitable for exercise by the former. But the deep and more underlying truth seems to be that Judges, however subconsciously, desire to retain or obtain for the judiciary problems more fit for executive decision.' Schuster felt that this psychological state of mind on the part of the judiciary was unfortunate: 'In recent years . . . it has been difficult for the State to obtain justice from the Judges of the High Court. It is not too much to say that in recent years, the weight of prejudice against the State in the minds of many members of the Court of Appeal and Judges of the High Court has been such as seriously to affect the Administration of Justice.'[18]

For Schuster, 'it may safely be asserted that no system of administration could be

---

[14] *Report of the Machinery of Government Committee*, 74. That part of the Report was clearly Haldane's own work. F. Maurice, *Haldane*, ii (London, 1939), 62–4; Heuston, *Lives of the Lord Chancellors, 1885–1940*, 228.

[15] e.g. *R v Halliday* [1917] AC 260.

[16] [1925] AC 578.

[17] In 1910, Permanent Secretaries had earned £2,500. By 1920, it was £3,500.

[18] Schuster, memorandum, 25 Mar. 1929. LCO 2/1133.

worse than administration by judicial officers. Any system which commits administration to the Courts is likely to bring the courts into disrepute, since Judges have too little experience or skill to deal with such questions, and is likely in the long run to bring the Courts and the executive Government into violent collision.'[19] Meanwhile, C. K. Allen, of Oxford, became a publicist for the other side:

it is exactly from the executive officers' efficiency and zeal that we must save ourselves—and him. His business is to get things done. He knows best what is to be done and the most convenient means of doing it: he is the expert, with special means of knowledge at his command: and when principles of law are put in his way, he is apt to be impatient of them as mere pedantic obstructions . . . Say what you will of the administrator's merits—and they are eminent—he is not the best person to be either legislator or judge, except under the close control of those who are trained to look beyond the practical means of attaining an immediate object to the principles which may be involved in its attainment. Under that control he may be a valuable, indeed an indispensable, part of the general administration of law.[20]

The debates during the inter-war years went on in this atmosphere. In 1922, there was a committee to look into the assize system.[21] In 1923, the Committee on Criminal Procedure recommended a restructuring of the relationship between Petty Sessions, Quarter Sessions, and Assizes.[22] Complaints about the operation of both civil and criminal courts, however, continued. In the early 1930s, the Hanworth Committee on the Business of the Courts again tackled these issues, as well as the assizes, and it recommended shortening the Long Vacation for the High Court, together with changes in appeals.[23] The Administration of Justice (Appeals) Act, 1934, abolished the automatic right of appeal to the House of Lords and cut out the Divisional Court as a normal part of the appeal process from the County Courts. In that same year the Peel Commission on the Dispatch of Business at Common Law was appointed, and by the time it had finished its work, there were recommendations about assizes, evidence, mandatory retirement of High Court judges at 72 with proportional pensions, and increases in jurisdiction for both Quarter Sessions and County Courts.[24] Some of these recommendations were implemented by the Administration of Justice (Miscellaneous Provisions) Act, 1938, although not those relating to the judges.

---

[19]   Schuster, memorandum, 25 Mar. 1929. LCO 2/1133.
[20]   C. K. Allen, 'Some Aspects of Administrative Law', (1929) *Journal of the Society of the Public Teachers of Law*, 10. Allen's theme was continued, resulting, ultimately, in C. K. Allen, *Law and Orders* (London, 1945).
[21]   See *Report of the Committee to Consider what Rearrangements of the Circuits can be Effected so as to Promote Economy and the Greater Dispatch of the Business of the High Court*, Cmd. 1831 (1923). By the Administration of Justice Act, 1925, the Lord Chancellor was allowed some latitude in reorganizing the circuit system. Abel-Smith and Stevens, *Lawyers and the Courts*, 101.
[22]   *Report of the Committee on Alterations in Criminal Procedure (Indictable Offences) 1921*, Cmd. 1813 (1923). Abel-Smith and Stevens, *Lawyers and the Courts*, 103–4.
[23]   Abel-Smith and Stevens, *Lawyers and the Courts*, 104–5.
[24]   Ibid. 106 f.

While these structural changes were being suggested or implemented, there was a new spate of reform of substantive law. For some judges even this appeared threatening. The dramatic reforms of English land law by the Law of Property Acts, 1925, drafted by Benjamin Cherry, sprang chiefly from the political support of Lord Birkenhead. The Divorce Reform Act of 1937 was the work primarily of A. P. Herbert, MP. By the 1930s, however, there was a Law Revision Committee, staffed by the Lord Chancellor's Office, which tidied up the law in such diverse areas as the award of interest in civil proceedings[25] and contribution between tortfeasors. Over the decades, the regular judges also found themselves increasingly excluded from the new trends in government. Intellectually the judges sought refuge in the claim that they were guardians of value-free principles which were objectively derived and impartially applied.[26] Inwardly, both socially and politically, they seethed.

(b) A Little Matter of Constitutionalism

While economic, social, and political conditions were unsettled during the 1920s, Britain suffered less immediate trauma than the United States as a result of the collapse of the Stock Market in 1929. The major crisis in fact came in 1931 with the ending of the Gold Standard, the collapse of the second Labour Government, and the formation of a National Government under the Labour leader, Ramsay MacDonald. The economic effects of the First World War finally became clear. The reaction by the judges to the cutting of their salaries under the National Recovery Act of that year can only be understood in terms of the general mood of the country and specifically in the light of the role of the Chief Justice, Lord Hewart, and especially his interaction with Sir Claud Schuster.

Hewart came from a relatively humble background (his father was a Lancashire shopkeeper), practised on the Northern Circuit, and began political life, after he entered Parliament in 1912, on the Radical Wing of the Liberal Party. He was in favour of votes for women and Home Rule.[27] As a supporter of Lloyd George, he moved steadily to the right, prosecuting Irish terrorists vigorously. He was offered both the Irish Secretaryship and the Home Secretaryship, but stayed on as Attorney-General which, at least at that time, was assumed to hold the right of reverter to the Lord Chief Justiceship—the post Hewart had always wanted. When Lloyd George needed the incumbent Chief Justice, Reading (Rufus Isaacs), to become Viceroy of India, various schemes were

---

[25] Law Reform (Miscellaneous Provisions) Act, 1934.

[26] T. E. Scrutton, 'Work of the Commercial Courts', 1 *Cambridge Law Journal* (1921), 8, admitted the danger of class bias.

[27] R. Jackson, *The Chief: Biography of G. Hewart, Lord Chief Justice of England, 1922–40* (London, 1959). Only on the legal system was he conservative. When discussing the Royal Commission on the Law's Delays, he noted: 'I venture to express, with suitable diffidence, the hope that no inconsiderate hands will be laid upon the circuit system, and especially upon the Northern Circuit, to which honourable members in all parts of the House are bound by ties of filial duty and affection.' Ibid. 65–6.

hatched, all of them unseemly, to enable Hewart to stay as Attorney-General but be assured ultimately of the Chief's job.

The scheme which prevailed, and which was allegedly blessed by the King, called for an elderly judge to be appointed Lord Chief Justice and to give in return an undated letter of resignation. The tiresome Lord Darling lobbied for the part, but it actually went to A. T. Lawrence, who was created Lord Trevethin. The proceedings not unnaturally offended the judges, some of whom refused to attend Lord Reading's farewell. Even Lord Birkenhead, no stranger to intrigue or the unethical, called the plan illegal: 'it would make the Lord Chief Justice a transient figure subject to reversal at the will of the Government of the day and the creation of political exigency.' It certainly did. As the Lloyd George administration collapsed in 1922, Trevethin read of his resignation in *The Times.*[28]

Hewart turned out to be a poor judge. Having taken the Chief Justiceship he came to realize what Coleridge had discovered in the 1890s,[29] that the Judicature Acts of the 1870s had taken most of the administrative powers away from the Lord Chief Justice and lodged them with the Lord Chancellor. While a Lord Chief Justice might still allocate work to the individual judges of the King's Bench Division, he had lost control over the officers of the courts and the administration of the court system. In court Hewart was bad-tempered and took sides early.[30] It was almost inevitable that he would become deeply hostile to Schuster, the Permanent Secretary to the Lord Chancellor, to whom he referred as 'Shyster'.[31]

When Hewart was denied extra King's Bench judges in 1927, he described it as 'petty larceny' and invoked Magna Carta to the delight of the *Daily Telegraph.*[32] His obsession with the growing power of the Civil Service and Parliament at the expense of the judiciary took full flight in his book, *The New Despotism*, published in 1929. In it, Hewart fumed against delegated legislation and all aspects of administrative law, which 'has the effect of placing a large and increasing field of departmental authority and activity beyond the reach of the ordinary law'.[33] Allowing civil servants to decide quasi-judicial matters was 'grotesque'. 'One would have thought it perfectly obvious that no one deployed in an administrative capacity ought to be entrusted with judicial duties in matters connected with its administration . . . his position makes it probable that he would be subject to political influences.'[34]

This situation, he argued, made it even more vital that judges be independent.

---

[28] R. Jackson, *The Chief: Biography of G. Hewart, Lord Chief Justice of England, 1922–40*, 126–44.

[29] '. . . if I could have seen, as perhaps I ought, how the Judicature Acts would have worked, I would have resigned sooner than be a party to it . . . the enthroning of the Chancellor upon the neck of all of us . . . I find the great traditional influences of the Chief Justice and the deference to him lessened materially, in every way, year by year . . .'. Coleridge, *Life and Correspondence of Lord Coleridge* ii. 359.

[30] Jackson, *The Chief*, 157, 160–1.   [31] Ibid. 258.   [32] Ibid. 214.

[33] Lord Hewart, *The New Despotism* (London, 1929), 11.   [34] Ibid. 46.

At this point, Hewart took up his analysis of the Ministry of Justice, which he saw as 'an effort to hand over the appointment of judges to the Permanent Secretary of the Lord Chancellor's Office'.[35] This, coupled with 'a concerted endeavour to subtract from the Law Courts important decisions, and to get those decisions made, behind the backs of the parties interested, by a Department or a Departmental Committee',[36] meant that England was creeping towards a Continental concept of administrative law, 'which is fundamentally opposed to the English conception of the "Rule of Law"'.[37] While some of the points made by Lord Hewart were legitimate concerns, his style was not designed to make friends. Whitehall was furious about the book, no civil servants being more angry than those in the Lord Chancellor's Office.[38]

There were more temperate voices who shared some of Hewart's concerns. In 1929, Sir John Marriott, the MP for Oxford University, asked parliamentary questions, which had considerable impact in Whitehall, about the increase in the amount of delegated legislation.[39] *The Times*, in a leader, expressed concern for the number of bills where the jurisdiction of the courts was excluded as well as calling for a commission to examine the role of delegated legislation.[40] Shuster, who felt that 'the time has come for a serious and deliberate consideration of the problem', wanted to ensure that the two different streams were kept separate. He distinguished between the two positions: Marriott's concern was that delegated legislation was taking away the powers of Parliament, while the 'complaint made by those, of whom the Lord Chief Justice is an example, is that by recent legislation matters which should have been decided by the Courts of Justice as between parties, have been withdrawn from the Courts and sent for decision by Government Departments'.[41]

It was in this context that the ground was laid for the Committee on Ministers' Powers. Even before *The New Despotism* came out,[42] Schuster was busy drafting the terms of reference, and, with the new Labour Chancellor, Lord Sankey, he pressed for an early decision. Writing to the Acting Prime Minister, Sankey noted that ever since he had come into the office he had had in mind 'a committee to consider the question of the powers exercised by Public Departments, both in the realm of substantive legislation and in the field of legal and quasi-legal decision'.[43] Thus was born a committee to be chaired by Lord Donoughmore, who was responsible for House of Lords' committees and who eventually ceded chairmanship of the Committee to Lord Justice Scott. At least one future Lord Chancellor, Lord Simonds, then a QC, was on the Committee,

---

[35] Ibid. 108.   [36] Ibid. 135.   [37] Ibid. 37.   [38] Jackson, *The Chief*, 214.
[39] For the impact, see LCO 2/1133.   [40] 5 Mar. 1929.
[41] Memorandum, 25 Mar. 1929. LCO 2/1133.
[42] Writing for Sankey, Schuster noted that it was 'highly expedient that the Government should be beforehand in this matter and should have indicated the desire to investigate it before such a publication stirs up further public excitement on the question'. Sankey to Chancellor of the Exchequer (Acting Prime Minister). 11 Oct. 1929, ibid.
[43] Ibid.

but the core of the Committee was undoubtedly the three senior civil servants: Sir Warren Fisher, Sir John Anderson, and Sir Claud Schuster.[44] It was a triumvirate that many felt ran Whitehall in the 1930s. It was a committee before which Hewart refused to appear: 'They've got my book, why should I appear—especially with Schuster on the Committee'.[45]

The Committee reported in 1932, and its Report was the high point of the Diceyan view of the Rule of Law. The Report assumed the objectivity of rules of law and that statutes could be interpreted literally and impartially. It attempted to define and distinguish cleanly judicial and administrative acts. It sought to buttress notions of the separation of powers.[46] Schuster was said to be the author of the Report, and in some ways it might be thought odd that he would have endorsed such an approach which caused Professor Harold Laski, another member of the Committee, to file a dissent which he described in a letter to Mr Justice Holmes as a 'fight against regarding a judge as an automatic slot-machine into whom you put the statute and from whom you get a construction in which there is no articulate major [premiss]'.[47] After citing Dicey's definition of the Rule of Law, the Committee declaimed that 'on the maintenance of the principles evolved by that process the liberty of the subject and the protection of his rights depend'.[48] Yet by drawing a clear line between a judicial decision 'which disposes of the whole matter by a finding upon the facts in dispute and an application of the law of the land to the facts so found, including where required a ruling upon any disputed question of law' (appropriate for the judiciary) and a quasi-judicial situation where such process was replaced by 'administrative action' which might involve 'considerations of public policy' and 'discretion'[49] (suitable for decision by the Civil Service), Schuster achieved his goal. The judges were kept within their narrow field; the Civil Service was left with broad decision-making powers.

Ironically, in the year in which the Committee on Ministers' Powers was appointed, 1929, Hewart himself appeared to violate the separation of powers when he accepted appointment as a member of a Liberal Party committee. When a political storm broke, Hewart wrote to *The Times* to express astonishment: '. . . in addition to being Lord Chief Justice of England, I am also a peer of the United Kingdom, and in that capacity am summoned by writ . . . to be present in the House of Lords "to treat and to give counsel" upon the affairs of State . . . These are not principles to be enjoyed. They are responsibilities to be discharged.'[50] One of the difficulties of working out High Policy was that there

---

[44] For a criticism of Schuster's behaviour on the Committee see H. H. Slesser, *Judgment Reserved* (London, 1941).

[45] Jackson, *The Chief*, 215.

[46] *Report of the Committee on Ministers' Powers*, Cmd. 4060 (1932), 73–5, 81–2.

[47] Laski to Holmes, 8 Mar. 1932. *Holmes–Laski Letters*, ed. M. de W. Howe (2 vols., London, 1953), ii. 1368.

[48] *Report of the Committee on Ministers' Powers*, 73–82.   [49] Ibid. 74–81.

[50] Jackson, *The Chief*, 217.

was little rationality in the concept of separation of powers. Judicial independence was at best idiosyncratic.

(c) The Hewart Explosion

There were a number of players in the next outburst. Hewart had proved himself an undistinguished judge.[51] He had run foul of the Court of Appeal, and especially of Lord Justice Scrutton, a brilliant commercial judge who had become bitter and vindictive;[52] while the latter also took out many of his feelings on Mr Justice McCardie.

McCardie was in his own way a most interesting human being. His biographer claimed for him 'unnatural brilliance'.[53] He certainly had a meteoric rise from his practice at the Birmingham bar, from which he was appointed a High Court judge in 1916, without ever having taken silk. He was outspoken on many issues. His views on the 'Amristar Massacre' upset the Lord Chancellor's Office, and his views on women caused his more conservative brethren discomfort. While he never married, he was reputed to have a mistress in the country, while a titled lady in London claimed to be pregnant by him.[54] He certainly was in favour of abortion and thought the divorce laws, as they existed, awful and absurd.[55]

His friction with Lord Justice Scrutton, author of the seminal work on charterparties, however, may have come from his rhetorical question, posed from the Bench: 'What is of more concern to most women: the construction of a charter party or their own self expression through the clothes they wear.'[56] He opined that 'clothes well chosen and well worn, whether they be the gown of a marchioness or the one and only frock of a typist, can reflect the mind and temperament of the wearer'. In return, Scrutton observed that 'If there is to be a discussion of the relationship of husbands and wives, I think it would come better from judges who have more than third hand knowledge of husbands and wives. I am [a] little surprised that a gentleman who has never been married should, as he has done in another case, proceed to explain the proper under clothing that ladies should wear.'[57] These various squabbles had bubbled to a head in 1932, with Lord Hanworth, the Master of the Rolls, attempting to mediate between McCardie and Scrutton.[58]

---

[51] 'A dreadfully bad judge', C. P. Harvey, *The Advocate's Devil* (London, 1958), 32; I. Adamson, *A Man of Quality* (London, 1964), 160–3. Cf. Professor Hanbury's views that Hewart was 'a model of justice and rectitude . . . of the nature of law he had the loftiest views'. He was courteous 'to learned counsel' and noted for his 'gentleness on the bench'. *The New Despotism* was 'learned and well-reasoned'. Hanbury, 'Lord Hewart', *Dictionary of National Biography, 1941–1950* (London, 1959), 382.

[52] See *Hardie* v. *Chilton* [1928] 1 KB 663, where Hewart was rude about Scrutton, and *Hobbs* v. *Tinking* (unreported), where Scrutton attacked Hewart. See Hanworth papers, *passim*.

[53] G. Pollock, *Mr Justice McCardie* (London, 1934), 1.

[54] D. Pannick, *The Judges* (Oxford, 1987), 12.   [55] Pollock, *Mr Justice McCardie*, ch. 9.

[56] Ibid. 120.   [57] Pannick, *The Judges*, 22.

[58] Hewart said McCardie was 'obsessed with sex and dark thoughts of death'. Jackson, *The Chief*,

While Hewart was to take few public positions over the judges' salaries (he still hoped to return to politics), his dislike for Lord Chancellor Sankey (like Hewart, the son of a draper) and his Permanent Secretary, Sir Claud Schuster, was once more making the running. The issues finally surfaced in connection with a series of events in 1934. First, when the Commission on the Dispatch of Business at Common Law was established under Lord Peel,[59] Hewart took its appointment personally. He thought it was an effort by Schuster to humiliate him. Hewart complained to Sankey, 'We are always being enquired into . . . It does no good, and only makes people think there are arrears, which is not true. Things are much better than they used to be.'[60] Sankey tried to bring Hewart and Schuster together, but Hewart rejected the overture.[61]

237. McCardie ultimately committed suicide, shooting himself while at Lewes Assizes. Ibid. 239. After McCardie had announced his interest in social science in *Place* v. *Searle*, Scrutton on appeal said: 'The Learned Judge tells us that he is a student of Sociology; I don't know what the word means, it sounds nasty—in my view the less a judge knows about it the better.' Slesser, *Judgment Reserved*, 251. *Place* v. *Searle*, 48 TLR 428 (1932), was a case where a greengrocer's assistant sued Dr Searle for 'enticing away' his wife. McCardie entered judgment for the defendant.

McCardie tried to get the Master of the Rolls to protect him from Scrutton: 'I have today read the offensive remarks upon me yesterday by Lord Justice Scrutton in the case of *Place* v *Searle*. In my view they are gravely and deliberately discourteous. He appears to have been as insulting as he could toward me . . . The time has come when his influence and malice should cease. Several appeals from me are pending . . . I must ask you to be good enough to arrange that these appeals shall not be heard by a Court of which Lord Justice Scrutton is a member . . . He is, in my view, unfit to be a member of a judicial tribunal.' McCardie to Hanworth, 7 May 1932, Hanworth Papers, Box C 949.

This led the Master of the Rolls to write to McCardie, regretting the manner in which he had recently been trying cases. (Hanworth to McCardie, 10 May 1932, ibid.) McCardie replied: 'I anticipated that your loyalty to your colleague would lead you to defend, so far as possible, Lord Justice Scrutton.' McCardie denied that he had been rude in court, while he resented Scrutton's 'impertinent and deliberate references to me as a bachelor'. (McCardie to Hanworth, 23 May 1932, ibid.) In a second letter that day, McCardie demanded that Scrutton be 'denounced'. (Ibid.)

McCardie became more outspoken. The following day, Hanworth wrote, acknowledging the request about Scrutton, and saying, 'the matter has assumed rather a serious aspect since your public statement in court this morning', and asking McCardie to come to see him. (Hanworth to McCardie, 24 May 1932, ibid.) What McCardie had done was to say in open court that he regretted 'that it had become necessary to administer this political rebuke to Lord Justice Scrutton'. The rebuke consisted of McCardie saying 'Before I start this case I wish to say a few words. I shall take my usual note of the evidence which will be given, and it may be that an appeal will take place. If there be an appeal, I shall not supply any copy of my notes until I am satisfied that Lord Justice Scrutton will not be a member of any court which tries the appeal.' Pollock, *Justice McCardie*, 213. The day after this, McCardie acknowledged that the Master of the Rolls would issue a formal statement the next day. (McCardie to Hanworth, 25 May 1932, Hanworth Papers.) The following day, McCardie reported that he had made a public statement 'in response to your courteous and dignified observations'. (McCardie to Hanworth, 26 May 1932, ibid.) The Dowager Duchess of Montrose congratulated the Master of the Rolls on 'the very dignified speech you made in the Court of Appeal, pointing out to Mr Justice McCardie that he should maintain the well-known tradition of judges'. (Dowager Duchess of Montrose to Hanworth, 29 May 1932, ibid.)

The lull was temporary. By July, the Lord Chancellor was lamenting about McCardie: 'I was afraid our colleague's return to sanity was only temporary. His extra-judicial pronouncements increase my morning mail.' (Sankey to Hanworth, 23 July 1932, ibid.)

[59] It reported in 1936. Cmd. 5065.   [60] Jackson, *The Chief*, 259.

[61] Ibid. 260. There was some improvement in relations for a short while, but a deterioration set in after Schuster failed to show Hewart the list of new silks before they were announced.

In the summer, Scrutton died, and this made another crisis possible. Lord Hanworth, the Master of the Rolls, decided he would preside in common law cases in the Court of Appeal[62]—until then the responsibility of Lord Justice Slesser, who had been less than comfortable with the role[63]—and a Vice-President of the Court of Appeal would be appointed to preside in Chancery appeals. Slesser, soon to be the senior Lord Justice, felt 'passed over' when this provision was put in the Administration of Justice Bill, 1934. Slesser, a Fabian, had been Solicitor-General in the Labour Government of 1924 and eventually an MP for Leeds.[64] Hanworth, the Master of the Rolls, had been Conservative MP for Warwick and Leamington, and Attorney-General in the Lloyd George Coalition.[65] Lloyd George's old Attorney-General and former Liberal MP, Chief Justice Hewart, rushed to Slesser's defence. Slesser warned the Master of the Rolls that Hewart ('I regard his views as conclusive') 'advised me to refuse to sit if the occasion arise, otherwise than in my rightful place; this advice I propose to act upon'.[66]

The third element in the crisis arose out of an event in October, when Schuster wrote to Hewart to tell him that the Cabinet had decided to authorize two new King's Bench judges in the pending legislation, but the actual filling of the slots would require a resolution of Parliament. The letter was marked 'secret', and, apparently, Hewart threw it in the fire unread. Thus when Hewart saw the draft of the Supreme Court of Judicature Bill 1934 on 7 December, he hastily called a meeting of judges and set sail for the House of Lords.[67]

On 11 December 1934, Sankey proposed a Second Reading of the Bill with what might be thought two uncontroversial sections: the addition of an eighteenth and nineteenth King's Bench Judge and provision for a Lord Justice to preside in one of the divisions of the Court of Appeal.[68] These Lord Hewart attacked,[69] running together his various causes:

On November 23 of this year there was sent to me, not by the Lord Chancellor but by a secretary, a letter. I have had experience of five Lord Chancellors now. The others used either to write to me or at any rate to sign the letter, but now it is always from a secretary, and the answer in future will be from a clerk. On November 23, I got a letter from a secretary saying that it had been decided that a certain inquiry should be conducted by a Royal Commission, the terms of reference of which and the members of which were shown on the two accompanying slips; and there followed the terms of reference, of a most exhaustive character. . . . I wonder who drafted the terms of reference . . . Unless my judgment is wholly at fault, I think I know this hand . . . let me say that I was not

---

[62] On the advice of Sankey. Sankey to Hanworth, 27 Aug. 1934, Hanworth Papers, Box C 949.

[63] 'Uneasy' was his own word. Slesser, *Judgment Reserved*, 257.

[64] He was a very English socialist. He spoke no modern language except English, although fluent in Latin and Greek. His only trip abroad was two days in Hamburg.

[65] Hanworth Papers, Box C 432.   [66] Slesser, *Judgment Reserved*, 261.

[67] Jackson, *The Chief*, 262.

[68] *Parliamentary Debates* (5th ser.), HL vol. 95, cols. 219–24 (11 Dec. 1934).

[69] Ibid., cols. 224–37.

consulted for one moment as to the terms of reference or as to the personnel of the Commission. And may I remind you that I am not speaking for myself. I happen to be the Lord Chief Justice of England, and I have to think of my office, and of my successors forever. Not one word was said to me either upon the terms of reference or upon the members of the Commission . . .

That Royal Commission having been appointed behind my back, this Bill is drafted. Now you would have thought, would you not, that as a mere matter of ordinary courtesy the Lord Chief Justice of England would have been given an opportunity of seeing at any rate a draft or a proof of the Bill, or would have been told what the Bill was going to contain. Not a bit of it! This is Tuesday. I came out of my Court last Friday afternoon, and my invaluable clerk, who had happened—merely happened—to look through the papers delivered to me, not as Lord Chief Justice, but as a member of this House, said: 'Here is a document which I think you ought to read,' and it was this Bill . . . And it was in that purely accidental fashion, at that eleventh hour, that I was made aware of the existence of this Bill . . . I immediately summoned for yesterday (Monday) a meeting of the Judges of the King's Bench Division.

He then attacked not the adding of two new judges, but the need to have a Parliamentary Resolution before appointing them—first because it put too much power in the hands of the Parliamentary Whips and second, because, while the Resolution was awaiting a vote, the practices of leading candidates could be destroyed as solicitors refused to brief those expected shortly to leave for the bench. Then Hewart, a strong opponent of a mandatory retirement age for judges, questioned observations on the judges:

Sometimes they take cold in the winter. They are away for a few days. When they are, if they happen to occupy a certain position, you are certain to find paragraphs, inspired from quarters I well know, because I have taken the trouble to ascertain, that they are going to retire. I have been pursued by that kind of thing for three years. I regard them now not with contempt, which is an active feeling, but with indifference, which calls for no exertion; but I have been very much annoyed by them.

Hewart then moved on to the Vice-Presidency of the Court of Appeal. He related the story about his advice to Slesser.[70] Clause 2 meant that 'the Lord Chancellor or one of his secretaries, or one of his secretaries, by the stroke of a pen or a telephone message to me or somebody can say: The person to preside in the second Court of Appeal is So-and-so . . . When is it going to stop? . . . I wonder if the Members of your Lordship's House think it desirable that, if this Bill is passed in the present form, when the General Election takes place there should be flaming posters on the wall "Rigging the judicial Bench in order to affront a former Labour Minister"?'

Hewart concluded with a reprise about one of his favourite *bêtes noires*, the Ministry of Justice:

[70] *Parliamentary Debates* (5th ser.), HL vol. 95, col. 234. 'My right honourable friend Lord Justice Slesser holds some opinions with which I may say I profoundly disagree, but he is the next senior Lord Justice.'

. . . when I became Attorney General at the beginning of 1919, when the late Lord Birkenhead first became Lord Chancellor, a little scheme was put before him whereby the Lord Chancellor was to cease to exist, all judicial patronage was to be taken from the Home Secretary, and all powers were to be invested in a new person to be called, after the Continental fashion, a Minister of Justice. And that scheme had strong backing from some entity the origin of which I do not know, the legal foundation for which I do not know, the personnel of which I do not know, called the Lord Chancellor's Department. The Lord Chancellor was to go, the Home Secretary as a person appointing judicial officers was to go, and we were to have a Minister of Justice. Why? It is perfectly obvious why. Because if that were done, it would no longer be necessary to have in this country a lawyer as political head of the Judiciary. You might have a layman, a successful merchant, a successful tradesman. And what would follow that? What would follow would be this— that Minister could be ignorant of the personnel of the Bar; he would not have leaders of the Bar habitually appearing before him in the final Court of Appeal in the House. When a vacancy occurred he would have to turn to somebody and say: 'Whom shall I appoint?' And who would that somebody be? The permanent officials of the Lord Chancellor's Department.

The outburst was so strong that the debate was adjourned but not before Lord Hanworth had tried to put part of the record straight:

I think I should best consult the dignity of this House and the dignity of the Judiciary and my own by not replying to the general observations which have fallen from the Lord Chief Justice but . . . let me repel at the earliest possible moment the suggestion that I had anything to do with the genesis of Clause 2. I never had anything of any sort or kind to do with it. It is not an interpolation in the Bill by me; it is not a late interpolation in the Bill. The reason I spoke with Lord Justice Slesser was that the Lord Chancellor had told me that the clause was in the Bill . . .[71]

When the debate continued three days later, Lord Ponsonby for the Opposition referred to the Bill as containing 'highly disputable, highly controversial and rather offensive provisions'.[72] Lord Hanworth restated his innocence with respect to clause 2.[73] Lord Hailsham, Secretary of State for War and a former Lord Chancellor dealt with the attack on civil servants:

It has been a long established and well-recognized tradition of this country that a civil servant is debarred from any right to defend himself or to take any part in public controversy. The speech which . . . the Lord Chief Justice made contained . . . a scathing and a substantial attack upon the head of the Lord Chancellor's Department . . . I should be failing in my duty to Sir Claud Schuster, knowing that he is debarred so long as he remains in his office from making any reply, if I were not to take up the cudgels on his behalf, and if I were not to tell your Lordships, as I propose to do, not only that he is incapable of such conduct as is imputed to him, but also that I can lay before your Lordships facts which I think will satisfy you that the impression which the Lord Chief Justice . . . held, is one which is based on false premises.

---

[71] Ibid., col. 238.   [72] Ibid., col. 375 (14 Dec. 1934).   [73] Ibid., col. 378.

In particular, Hailsham attacked the silliness about the Ministry of Justice: '. . . the impression conveyed by (Hewart's) language is that there was a plot launched by the Lord Chancellor's Department, that is to say, by Sir Claud Schuster and those who were working under him, to substitute for the Lord Chancellor a Minister of Justice in order that they might have a say as to who should be appointed to the judicial offices of this country'.[74] Hailsham had no difficulty showing that the idea of a Ministry of Justice went back to Brougham, and had been resurrected by Haldane. Hailsham alleged that Schuster had opposed the concept. Hailsham also put both clauses 1 and 2 of the current bill in a rational context and exposed Hewart's various factual errors, concluding: 'I profoundly regret that this debate should ever have taken place. I cannot think it will redound either to the dignity of the Bench or to the public estimation of the administration of justice.'[75]

Lord Sankey then spoke, saying of Hewart's speech that it 'took me entirely by surprise. It amazed me.'[76] With respect to Schuster, he described his respect for Schuster and the respect in which he had been held by six other Lord Chancellors, concluding: 'I greatly deprecate, however, attacks on permanent officials. Their lips are sealed. They cannot defend themselves. The people answerable for their acts are their ministerial superiors. It is contrary to all Parliamentary practice, and . . . to the whole spirit of the Constitution that attacks should be directed against them personally.'[77] He patiently explained the communications and discussions there had been with Hewart on the increase in the numbers of judges and on the Peel Commission, and that discussions on clause 2 had gone on with Hanworth, as the effective head of the Court of Appeal, rather than with the Lord Chief Justice, the Head of the King's Bench Division. By the time he came to the Ministry of Justice point, Sankey lost his temper, calling it 'moonshine' several times. It was all rather a let-down; and Hewart ultimately managed something of an apology.[78] It was the end of a tawdry affair that had not helped the standing of the judiciary and had clouded still further their constitutional status.

The decade continued, with Hewart continuing his somewhat erratic course. In 1936, he was plotting with Lloyd George to return to politics to renew the Liberal Party.[79] In that same year he announced at the Lord Mayor's Dinner that 'His Majesty's Judges are satisfied with the almost universal admiration in which they are held.'[80] The following year, he supported A. P. Herbert's Bill on Divorce, and saw no reason why County Courts and Quarter Sessions could not hear divorce cases.[81] He came to regret having written *The New Despotism*,[82] realizing that for the Welfare State to succeed, civil servants needed discretion.

[74] *Parliamentary Debates* (5th ser.), HL vol. 95, cols. 381–2.
[75] Ibid., col. 401.   [76] Ibid., col. 402.   [77] Ibid., col. 405.   [78] Ibid., cols. 415–19.
[79] Jackson, *The Chief*, 300.   [80] Ibid., 245.
[81] Lord Hewart, *Not Without Prejudice* (London, 1937), 121, 130.
[82] Jackson, *The Chief*, 216.

Ironically, his undistinguished term, somewhat like that of his predecessor, came to an end when he received a telephone call from 10 Downing Street asking for his resignation. Hewart had helped import the sleazy qualities of 'the Long Weekend'[83] into both constitutional debate and the role of the judiciary.[84]

[83] For many in Britain the years between the First and Second World Wars were 'The Long Week-end'. See the popular social history of the period: R. Graves and A. Hodge, *The Long Week-end* (London, 1940).

[84] Typical of his behaviour was that when he felt he had not been appropriately consulted about the appointment to the High Court of Cyril Asquith (son of the former Prime Minister) by Lord Chancellor Maugham in 1938, he assigned Asquith to the Old Bailey to hear criminal cases, an area about which Asquith knew little, in the hope of discrediting him. Cited, Pannick, *The Judges*, 23.

3

Schuster and the Judges

Schuster's interaction with the judges on detailed issues is particularly revealing of the Schuster style. Was it true that the Lord Chancellor reigned, but the Permanent Secretary ruled—as critics claimed? Certainly these years were in marked contrast to the later Muir Mackenzie years, even though Muir Mackenzie was reputedly active in judicial appointments. The independence of the judges as a concept was tested both by the political and civil service involvement in choosing them and by the judicial assumption that independence included financial independence.

(a) Choosing the Judges

From 1905 onwards, and certainly after 1912, choosing High Court and Court of Appeal judges because of their political connections was effectively over.[1] While political experience was still thought relevant by some Lord Chancellors, party political affiliations ceased to be important during the chancellorships of Lords Loreburn and Haldane (1905–15), at least in the Supreme Court. Schuster, who became Permanent Secretary in 1915, was therefore operating in a different environment from Muir Mackenzie. Moreover, while the Prime Minister still appointed Law Lords, and Lloyd George and Birkenhead fought over them, by the late 1920s the political element had largely departed from that process, too. In short, Schuster was operating what was essentially a new system. While some Lord Chancellors were active in the process, it fell heavily to the Permanent Secretary to take soundings with Bench and Bar, to make recommendations to the Lord Chancellor (or provide a slate), and to humour senior judges who were uncomfortable with the decisions. It was a long way from a Northcote–Trevelyan process, but it was an important step towards a system of meritocracy based on success at the Bar. It also put a powerful weapon in the hands of the Civil Service.

When Schuster was faced with a vacancy for the High Court his briefing paper to the Lord Chancellor, Finlay, seemed to leave the latter little discretion.

---

[1] Alan Paterson has drawn a useful distinction between political 'motive' appointments on the part of the appointer and 'traits' among the appointees. This latter is further subdivided into 'party political' and 'political experience'. A. A. Paterson, 'Judges: A Political Elite?', 1 *British Journal of Law and Society* (Winter 1974), 118–35. For a series of reasons, mainly relating to expectations of the Lord Advocate and the Dean of the Faculty, 'party political' and 'political experience' have both remained more important in Scotland than in England. See A. A. Paterson, 'Scottish Lords of Appeal, 1876–1888', *Juridical Review*, 1988, 241–3, for the background to this.

In 1917, for instance, he offered the Chancellor a list of senior silks, but added, 'All these were in their time *papabili*, but they are now so old that the appointment of any one of them would be an infraction of the recommendations of innumerable Royal Commissions . . .'. Of a list of QC MPs, he noted:

Salter seems the most considerable both in the eyes of the party and professionally. It seems to me . . . that if you wish to make an appointment from the House of Commons it is difficult to look beyond him . . . Of those who are not M.P.s you will have no difficulty passing over Marshall Hall, Powell, Langton, Ashton, Gregory, Compton, Schiller and Charles[2] and it is not necessary for me to give the reasons . . . There remain Gore-Brown, Talbot, Greer, Disturnal and Hawke.

Of these, Hawke was too young; Gore-Brown 'too much of a Chancery man'; Disturnal was 'very undistinguished'; Greer at least 'could be safely trusted with the Commercial List'; Talbot's appointment 'would be in every way distinguished'. Finally, he noted that Roche was the one regarded as best by the Bar but he probably could not be induced to take a judgeship.[3]

Schuster, however, put out feelers and later reported that 'if an offer were made now to (Roche) his decision would be different . . .'.[4] Thus Lord Finlay prevailed where Buckmaster, Haldane's immediate successor, had failed and Roche accepted. The next appointment went to one of the other favourites, Greer, and shortly thereafter Talbot was promoted. In the Chancery Division, Schuster told Finlay: 'I think our list should be very short indeed.' It consisted of only P. O. Lawrence and Mark Romer. The next appointment to the Chancery Division was P. O. Lawrence. Mark Romer ('He has always seemed to me to have the most distinguished mind of any leading practitioner of the Chancery side') had to wait a few years but was almost at once promoted to the Court of Appeal.[5] In baseball terminology, Schuster was batting five for five.[6]

Finlay was elderly, some would say senile,[7] and there were undoubtedly Lord Chancellors with whom Schuster had to be less direct than in the incident just described. Birkenhead no doubt had his own list, and, as already noted, he clashed with the Prime Minister over appointments of Law Lords.[8] Despite his recommendations in the *Report of the Committee on the Machinery of Government* for greater openness in judicial appointments, Haldane in fact remained rather secretive during his second chancellorship. Sankey consulted Hanworth and others extensively;[9] but apparently not always the Lord Chief Justice and the

---

[2] Later Langton, Compton, and Charles were in fact appointed.
[3] LCO 2/601.   [4] Memorandum, 20 Sept. 1917, LCO 2/601.
[5] Memorandum, 18 Jan. 1918, ibid.
[6] Even in his first year in office, Schuster was capable of killing appointments. When the Irish Solicitor-General, Campbell, was lobbying for an English judgeship, Schuster warned Buckmaster that the mood of the Bar was such that such an appointment would be regarded as 'outrageous'. Heuston, *Lives of the Lord Chancellors, 1885–1940*, 272.
[7] Heuston, ibid. 339.
[8] P. Polden, *Guide to the Records of the Lord Chancellor's Department* (London, 1988), 32.
[9] See Hanworth papers, *passim*.

President of the Probate, Divorce, and Admiralty Division. Hailsham was a strong Chancellor. Yet in all their chancellorships, Schuster's voice was very much present. It was almost certainly during this period that the system of records in which comments were (and are) kept at voluminous length began. Not all the concerns of Chief Justice Hewart were unjustified. In judicial appointments, the Civil Service (albeit in the form of the Lord Chancellor's Office) had, since the decline of political appointments, become much more important.

For instance, Viscount Simon was a vigorous intellect, but Schuster was capable of limiting his discretion. When Mr Justice Langton's seat was to be filled in the Probate, Divorce, and Admiralty Division in 1942, Schuster advised Simon that he might wish to talk with Merriman—the President—although the implication was that it would not be of much value. Then Simon was told of the 'possible' silks on the Admiralty side, with heavy emphasis on their public school, university, and war service. Some were discussed peripherally: 'There is also Lewis Noad, but you may perhaps not think it necessary to trouble yourself with any prolonged consideration of his name.' Others on the Admiralty side were then discussed at greater length:

Of these men, Trapnell, though, as I have already stated, he purports to practise in the court, has never really had any footing in it; if I had had to comment on Carpmael a short time ago, I should have said that he was not regarded professionally as the equal of his competitors, and it appears to be accepted that he is a poor advocate and not very good tempered. Recently, however, I have heard that he is a better lawyer than an advocate and that his faults of temper are largely due to diffidence. Seller's [*sic*] activities really lie elsewhere; Willmer, though by common repute the ablest of all, is still very young, and incidentally is serving actively in the Army. The choice, if it be made from among those practising in this court, therefore, appears to lie between Hayward and Pilcher. I do not think it appropriate to comment on their respective merits which you have recently had ample opportunity of judging. Pilcher is a personal friend of my own.

If you turn to the Divorce Side, the silks are: Middleton, Glazebrook, Barnard and Bush James, all of whom took silk in 1939.

I do not trouble you with any details about these men as I do not think that in any circumstances you would be disposed to recommend any one of them for a Judgeship.[10]

Pilcher was appointed. In such an amateur process, the views of the Permanent Secretary were inevitably seen by Bench and Bar as close to decisive.

The power can be seen at work in other ways. With respect to commissions, Schuster played a crucial role. This role in the Committee on Ministers' Powers has already been noted. Even when committees or commissions were created by other Departments, if they remotely affected 'the law', Schuster's hand was to be seen. For instance, in 1939 the Prime Minister (Chamberlain) had appointed a Royal Commission on Workman's Compensation (which was also to cover common law rights) under the chairmanship of Sir Hector Hetherington, the

[10] LCO 2/3829.

Principal of Glasgow University. The War affected the Commission and when, over the objection of the Civil Service, Beveridge was appointed in 1943 to look at the future of National Insurance, it was assumed that a separate committee would be established to look at Employers' Liability outside Social Insurance—the so-called alternative remedies. The War-Time Committee on Reconstruction Priorities agreed in June 1943 that 'for political, historical and other reasons some special and extra provision must be made for victims of industrial disease outside the social security system'. The power of the TUC, as well as the legal establishment, made it inevitable. The Committee on Reconstruction Priorities emphasized that a chair 'whose name would carry weight' would be needed and William Jowitt, the Minister without Portfolio, suggested Lord Rushcliffe or Lord Atkin.[11]

The Home Office, in charge of the Committee, talked of the need to have 'a prominent member of the legal profession'. In fact the Permanent Secretary, Sir Robert Bannatyne, talked of a chair who would be 'a legal expert of high judicial standing'. Simon responded in a way that Jowitt would not have understood: 'it is very undesirable that a judge, who is now discharging his judicial functions, should take the principal part in advising on this sort of question. The question is essentially one of politics and of administration.'[12] Although the Lord Chancellor thought Peake, the Parliamentary Under-Secretary at the Home Office, would be good, he was not favoured by Schuster. The Permanent Secretary preferred Rushcliffe ('would do admirably') or Soulbury ('O.K.').[13] In fact, Morrison, the Home Secretary, offered the job to Hetherington.[14]

It was at this point that Hetherington was made Chair of the Committee of Vice-Chancellors and Principals and withdrew as Chair of the Committee on Alternative Remedies.[15] By December 1943 there was a scurrying around for a new chair. The two names that the Home Office floated were Sir Arnold McNair, the Vice-Chancellor of the University of Liverpool, and A. L. Goodhart,

---

[11] RC (43) 12th Meeting, PIN 12/94. For background to these areas and analysis of the paper, see P. W. J. Bartrip, *Workmen's Compensation in Twentieth Century Britain* (Aldershot, 1987), esp. 224 ff. See also P. W. J. Bartrip, 'Beveridge, Workmen's Compensation and the Alternative Remedy', 14: 4 *Journal of Social Policy* (1985), 491–511.

[12] Thus Lord Greene (Master of the Rolls) was neither available nor suitable. Peake (Parliamentary Under-Secretary at the Home Office) would be good. Napier (next Permanent Secretary to the Lord Chancellor) should be on the Committee. Lord Simon to Schuster, 29 Mar. 1943, PIN 12/85.

[13] Memorandum to file, 6 Apr. 1943, ibid. There is evidence that the Lord Chancellor's Office favoured Rushcliffe as a chair of committees because he could be 'controlled'.

[14] Morrison to Hetherington, 18 June 1943, ibid. The balancing of the committee was fascinating. There were to be two TUC members, two employers' representatives, one English QC, one Scottish QC, one County Court judge, three legal experts. Bannatyne to Schuster, 5 Aug. 1943, ibid. Simon was quite happy to have Hetherington. As English QCs, he suggested Beney, Sellers, or Lynskey. Memorandum, 11 June 1943. The Board of Trade wanted a representative of the insurance industry. E. H. S. Marker (Board of Trade) to Bannatyne, 16 July 1943. The Home Office thwarted that idea. Ibid.

[15] Hetherington to Morrison, 6 Dec. 1943, ibid.

the Professor of Jurisprudence at Oxford.[16] Sir Owen Davison at the Home Office favoured McNair. Jowitt did 'not think you could do better than'[17] McNair, while Simon thought him an 'excellent choice'.[18] Both, however, appeared to give their blessing to Goodhart as the back-up candidate; the Home Office actively checked out the latter's background, especially his acceptability to the unions.[19]

Despite his apparent approval—indeed enthusiasm—about these candidates, Simon at this point, in a letter drafted by Schuster, appeared, after McNair turned the job down, to take a diametrically opposed tack:

As [McNair] has refused there is no harm in my saying that I really do not think a man with no experience of litigation, with an academic qualification which is largely in the realm of International Law, would have been a very good choice, though, of course, he is an excellent Chairman, thorough and painstaking to a degree and a very nice fellow. I make this comment because I have a message on the telephone that one of the names you were thinking of was Goodhart, the Professor at Oxford. Here again, the trouble is that he knows nothing about workmen's compensation which is a statute and not common law, and though he is a very good lawyer, primarily American, I really do not think he is the kind of choice you should make. Why do you not consider A. T. Denning, K.C.— one of the best brains at the Bar I think and certainly a very quick and active mind? . . . An even better name, perhaps, would be G. J. Lynskey, K.C., of Manchester.[20]

While the Lord Chancellor's Office files on what caused the change of heart are silent—they have been heavily 'gutted' for the last few years of the Schuster secretaryship—the files from the Ministry of Pensions and National Insurance make it clear that the change of heart was prompted by Schuster. In a memorandum to Herbert Morrison, the Minister, the civil servants reported that although he had told them to write a letter to Professor Goodhart appointing him as chair, 'Bannatyne and I have since seen Sir Claud Schuster, and Sir Claud, while expressing admiration for the ability and character of Professor Goodhart, says that his talk and manner are so strongly Jewish that he feels sure he could not be counted on to control such a Committee as we have in mind'.[21]

Morrison, Simon, and Jowitt then got together and agreed on Sir Walter Monckton.[22] On 24 January, only a week after the Schuster bombshell, a letter

---

[16] Memorandum from C.A.D. 14 Dec. 1943, ibid. It said of Goodhart: 'Well known as a lawyer and he has I think already undertaken a certain amount of public work . . . would take immense trouble to do the job thoroughly . . . very good at getting on with people . . . there is against him the fact that he is not a British Subject—he is an American citizen who lives here—he has an English wife.'

[17] Jowitt to Morrison, 16 Dec. 1943, ibid.   [18] Simon to Morrison, 16 Dec. 1943, ibid.

[19] Memorandum, 3 Jan. 1944. 'The important question is—has Professor Goodhart any political attitudes which will be regarded as important by T.U.C.' On 7 Jan. 1944, C.A.D. reported to Bannatyne that there was no evidence he was *persona non grata* to the TUC. On 7 Jan. 1944, C.A.D. reported that the TUC knew nothing about Goodhart. Ibid.

[20] Simon to Bannatyne, Jan. 1944, ibid.

[21] Memorandum from C.A.D., 17 Jan. 1944, ibid.

[22] Simon to Morrison, 19 Jan. 1944; Jowitt to Morrison, 20 Jan. 1944, ibid.

went from Herbert Morrison to Monckton, assuring him that 'The Lord Chancellor and I agree there is nobody who could do this important job better than yourself.' Within a week he had accepted,[23] and although later in the year the Foreign Office wanted Moncton to head the Legal Division of the Control Commission for Germany, he was allowed to finish the Committee on Alternative Remedies first.[24] Lord Simon had realized by April that the Beveridge Committee's suggestion that employers' liability at common law should be restricted would have a profound effect—not least on Bar and Bench. He told the War Cabinet Reconstruction Committee that the suggestion was 'impracticable' and that the Committee on Alternative Remedies should be activated before the White Paper on Beveridge was published.[25] The work of the Committee then moved ahead and, to the relief of the unions—including lawyers' groups—the alternative remedy was saved.[26]

(b) County Court Salaries: The Doctrine of Unripeness

The views of the Permanent Secretary were also vital—sometimes determinative—in matters of salary. The County Court judges, for instance, had been recommended for an increase in salary from £1,500 to £2,000 by a House of Commons Select Committee in 1878, as well as for a two-thirds pension after twenty years of service. The lobbying for such improvements had been going on at least since 1905.[27] During the First World War and after, however, the County Court judges were paid a war bonus, the amount of which varied

---

[23] His final acceptance was 1 Feb. 1944, ibid.   [24] Ibid.   [25] PIN 12/94.

[26] It was Lord Jowitt as Lord Chancellor who introduced the Law Reform (Personal Injuries) Bill, 1947, even more favourable to the unions and the legal profession than the Monckton compromise. Bartrip, 'Beveridge, Workmen's Compensation and the Alternative Remedy', 507.

[27] See Special Meeting of the Society of the Judges of the County Courts, 5 Jan. 1905, LCO 2/159. The battle on this occasion became enmeshed in the dispute over the selective increase in the jurisdiction of County Courts. Judge Selfe took the view that if salary increases were given to judges on circuits where the work was heaviest, 'I think the government would have no difficulty with the Bill. It would be idle to pretend that the judges would be satisfied, as they think they are entitled to an increase all round. I need not say that I should be very glad if this were granted and I only submit my suggestion on the assumption that, as you have told me more than once, the Treasury will not agree to a general increase.' Selfe to Muir Mackenzie, 26 Jan. 1905, ibid.

The following year, Muir Mackenzie replied to Judge Roberts, advancing the usual arguments: 'It is impossible for his Lordship to close his eyes to the fact that a County Court judgeship with its present salary and work is regarded as an entirely desirable office by a very large number of most competent men at the bar.' Muir Mackenzie to Roberts, 26 Feb. 1905. Roberts replied, somewhat testily, that the fact that there were competent men prepared to do the job was not the point. The point was that their work had increased in both quantity and quality—i.e. it was becoming more serious and complex. 'As matters now stand, the difference in work, jurisdiction and responsibility between the Judges of the High Court and those of the County Courts is not so great as to justify the great disparity at present existing between the position and emoluments of the two classes of judges.' Roberts to Muir Mackenzie. 15 Mar. 1906, ibid.

In a letter to Muir Mackenzie, five years later (15 Aug. 1911) the Treasury confirmed its view that in the light of the number of days County Court judges sat in 1910 (157) they were not underpaid or overworked compared with other public servants. A salary increase could only be justified if the number of judges were reduced and sittings significantly increased. Ibid.

between £200 and £750 p.a., depending on the cost of living. During that same period, the County Courts were put on a more professional basis. In 1915 the registrars and clerks, who were still paid by fees and who had little incentive for integrity, were put on a salaried basis. In 1926 the Vote and Pay Offices of the County Court were taken from the Treasury and given to the Lord Chancellor's Office. In 1919, a mandatory retiring age of 72 (which might be extended to 75) was imposed on the County Court judges, but they were given pension rights (rather than *ex gratia* payments)[28] on a sliding scale up to two-thirds of their salary. They were even given a uniform—a mauve and black robe. (Previously each judge had made up his own court regalia.)

Yet robes, pensions, and even the war bonus did not compensate for an absence in real increases in salaries, and the County Court judges set out in 'the land fit for heroes' to achieve what they felt they had been promised in 1878— namely a salary of £2,000 p.a. The campaign began in 1921 when the County Court judges heard the rumour that High Court salaries were to be increased and, as they put it, they did not want, two years down the road, to be told that they should have applied when the High Court salaries were raised.[29] The Lord Chancellor's Permanent Secretary did not find that argument convincing.[30]

The County Court judges renewed their pleas in 1924. This time they emphasized 'that in respect of difficulty and importance the work of the judges is now twice as great as in 1865', the year their salaries had been fixed. This change, they argued, had been caused by the smaller number of judges, the extension of the County Court jurisdiction, the arrival of the motor car, and the enormous production of statutes by Parliament—especially the Rent Restriction Acts ('no judges of any class or period have ever had to perform duties more burdensome or harassing'). It was on these grounds they felt their pay rise was justified and not 'upon such grounds as the increased cost of living or taxation, which of course apply to all persons occupying a similar position . . .'.[31]

The County Court judges, however, had to be satisfied with honeyed words. On behalf of the Lord Chancellor, Schuster wrote:

---

[28] Lord Schuster reported that one County Court judge was given an *ex gratia* pension after one day on the bench. Schuster, memorandum, 31 Jan. 1943, LCO 2/3630.

[29] Judge Bray to Sir Claud Schuster, 11 June 1921, LCO 12/40. At this point, with the war bonus, they were earning £2,250.

[30] Schuster to Bray, 13 June 1921: 'For one thing, the High Court judges have up to now received no additional remuneration by reason of the increase in the cost of living, whereas the County Court judges have had a bonus for some little time.' Bray to Schuster, 14 June 1921: 'It is true that the High Court Judges received no bonus, but I suppose that the proposed increases in their salaries will be permanent.' Ibid. In fact, Schuster had already undercut the County Court judges. In December 1920 he had written to Sir Warren Fisher, 'I am not sure whether the additional sums they are now receiving are wholly war bonuses or are partly war bonuses and partly salary revision, but however that may be, no one would claim that they ought to receive more than the sums which they are receiving at present.' Schuster to Fisher, 10 Dec. 1920, LCO 2/467.

[31] Quotes from an 8-page 'Statement of Facts from the Council of County Court Judges to the Lord Chancellor', 29 Mar. 1924, LCO 12/40.

The Lord Chancellor has very much sympathy with the case of the County Court Judges and he appreciates the force of the reasoning in the memo . . . The great success of the County Court system and the confidence which the court enjoys are due to the successful and devoted labours of the judges . . . The Lord Chancellor further realizes that £1,500 p.a. is not, having regard to the financial burden involved and to the cost of living, a satisfactory remuneration for persons occupying the office of the County Court Judges. Both he and his predecessors have from time to time considered the situation with some anxiety and have contemplated proposals for increasing the salary . . . Unfortunately the Lord Chancellor, like his immediate predecessors, finds himself hampered by the general national financial situation; and like them, he has been reluctantly forced to the conclusion that the circumstances of the time are unpropitious to carry through such a proposal. He will not lose sight of the matter . . .'[32]

Lord Haldane, once again the Chancellor, did however see a delegation of judges and, while sympathetic, told them that the time was not ripe, lest it set off a process of leap-frogging in salaries.[33] In fact behind the scenes Schuster tried to be helpful, writing to Sir Warren Fisher at the Treasury urging that County Court salaries be raised to £2,000.[34] At that point, however, the judges misplayed their hand. Judge Parry sent a copy of the memo directly to the Lord Privy Seal. Schuster was furious.[35] Schuster's next memo to Fischer was more devious:

It is true that a County Court Judge's work has been much increased in the last ten years and we could get better men if we had more to offer and perhaps we ought to get better men. It is certainly impossible to do anything to increase the County Court Judges' salary while leaving the King's Bench Masters' salaries untouched. Both sets of officials are drawn from the same class . . . if I had to choose between getting good County Court judges and getting good King's Bench Masters, I should prefer the latter. Our whole judicial system would break down if the quality of King's Bench Masters were lowered. The economy and efficiency of our system in the High Court depends on the devolution from the Judge to the Master of the interlocutory work.[36]

Although clearly regarded as an inferior form of judicial life, the County Courts judges kept up their pressure and, with the collapse of the Labour Government later that year, they petitioned the new Chancellor, Lord Cave. They sent essentially the same memorandum they had sent to his predecessors, and they met with Cave in December 1924. Cave assured the judges that they had a 'strong case' but that the time was 'inopportune'.[37] When the judges took

[32] Schuster to Bray, 1 Apr. 1924, ibid.

[33] 18 June 1924. Schuster wrote to Bray that same day. Ibid.

[34] Schuster to Fisher. The judges would then give up their war bonus which at that time stood at £212. Ibid.

[35] 'He knows quite well that he ought to come to us.' Schuster to A. F. Hemmings. 25 July 1924, ibid.

[36] Schuster to Fisher, 6 Aug. 1924, ibid. The leap-frogging argument was strengthened when, in early August, the Metropolitan Police Magistrates petitioned the Home Secretary asking for an increase in their salaries. Ibid.

[37] Meeting of 10 Dec. 1924, ibid.

the matter up again in October 1925, the wave of industrial unrest was leading inexorably to the General Strike.[38] This time Schuster warned that while he and the Lord Chancellor were anxious to see salaries increased, the time was 'more unpropitious than ever'.[39] With the General Strike on, the judges tried yet again in 1926, this time emphasizing the rapid increase in revenue to the Treasury through increased County Court fees. Schuster was irritated this time because the judges wrote directly to the Lord Chancellor, and, while he was prepared to let High Court judges make the argument about court fees, he was unsympathetic to the argument in the mouths of the County Court judges:

I do not think that the matter is assisted one way or another by the condition of County Court finance. We ought to pay judges a proper salary whether the State bears or does not bear the expense of dispensing justice in the County Court . . . if the State were to decide to turn the County Courts into a revenue collecting Department, that would not afford an additional argument for an increase of the County Court Judges' salaries any more than an increase in returns in income tax would justify an increase of the salaries of tax officials.[40]

In 1927 the judges adopted their version of public relations. Judge Crawford made some public comments about the situation and the *Law Journal* began championing the judges' cause:[41] 'It is unthinkable that these hard-worked servants of the State should "agitate" for redress of a recognized grievance; and inconceivable that they should have recourse to the popular "strike" weapon. Yet a printed statement of the case, restrained, brief, and unanswerable, is in existence . . . when justice involves expenditures, the Government will deliver it only at the point of the pistol.' Early in 1928, Lord Cave was moved to write to the Chancellor of the Exchequer, Winston Churchill, urging a salary of £2,000, otherwise he might have difficulty attracting good candidates.[42] Churchill saw through that:

You tell me that unless the remuneration of these Judges is improved, you anticipate increasing difficulty as time goes on in inducing the most suitable men to accept appointment. If indeed it were the fact that the present rates of remuneration are already insufficient to attract and retain the services of well-qualified candidates, there would have been no choice but to increase them. But I do not think, nor does your letter suggest, that this would be a true picture of the present position.[43]

Lord Cave nevertheless produced a paper for Cabinet,[44] and Lord Hailsham, who became Chancellor later that year was sent the printed memo[45] and was waited upon by the County Court judges.[46] In the letter the judges wrote to Schuster, they claimed that the Lord Chancellor had said he would think about

[38] Judge Bray cheerfully predicted, however, that the trade unions would not oppose the increase: 'I think we are in their good books and have their confidence.' Bray to Schuster, 4 July 1925, ibid.

[39] Schuster to Judge Scully, 15 Oct. 1925. See also Scully to Schuster, 17 Oct. 1925, ibid.

[40] Schuster to Judge Scully, 26 Oct. 1926, ibid.   [41] *Law Journal*, 1 Oct. 1927, ibid.

[42] Cave to Churchill, 6 Feb. 1928, ibid.   [43] Churchill to Cave, 15 Feb. 1928, ibid.

[44] CP 52 (28), ibid.   [45] 25 July 1928, ibid.   [46] 18 July 1928, ibid.

their claims.[47] Schuster denied that was what the Chancellor had said.[48] The *Law Journal* continued to believe that the County Court judges were 'overworked and underpaid.'[49] Two days after the collapse of Wall Street in 1929, the judges paid a visit to the new Lord Chancellor, Lord Sankey. This time Judge Crawford asked for £2,500, because the County Courts were no longer small debt courts, but courts of 'responsibility and importance'. Judge Rowlands added that he thought their work was more important than that of assizes.[50] This latter theme continued to be stressed by the *Law Journal*, even after the financial and political collapse of 1931.[51]

During the 1930s, however, the County Court judges' luck changed. The War Bonus for civil servants (which the County Court judges received) had finally been cancelled in 1934, and in 1936 the Treasury wanted to cancel it for those paid out of the Consolidated Fund.[51] Schuster basically agreed; but by the spring he was suggesting that it should be offset by a salary increase,[52] after he had been lobbied by the County Court judges.[53] The Treasury was more agreeable than usual and suggested an increase to £1,800. Schuster suggested £2,000.[54] There followed the usual leap-frog discussions. When the Treasury asked whether such an increase would mean the stipendiary magistrates' salaries would have to be raised, the Lord Chancellor's Office said it was none of their business. That was not the view of the Home Office, who at that time appointed the stipendiaries. In turn it was agreed that the King's Bench Masters' salaries would have to be increased, and the Attorney-General said he needed to increase the salary of the Official Solicitor and the Director of Public Prosecutions.[55]

Finally a bill was introduced in October 1936, but there were problems with the Financial Resolution. Also some High Court judges were upset. They thought the County Court judges should be better paid than the stipendiaries;[56] and they were concerned, too, that an effort was being made to cut the salaries of High Court judges' clerks and to transfer their appointment away from the judges. Meanwhile the County Court judges urged action and a backdating of their pay claim.[57] The Financial Resolution finally passed the House of Commons in June 1937. Judge Allesbrook, writing from Nottingham to the Lord Chancellor's Office, could not understand why his salary had not gone up. Napier tried explaining the legislative process: 'My dear Allesbrook . . . Powerful as the House of Commons is, it needs more than a Financial Resolution to

[47] Judge Crawford to Schuster, 27 Oct. 1928, ibid.
[48] Schuster to Judge Snagge, 31 Oct. 1928, ibid.   [49] *Law Journal*, 15 Dec. 1928.
[50] Memo of 31 Oct. 1929 Meeting, LCO 12/40.
[51] Treasury to Schuster, 1 Jan. 1936, LCO 12/41.   [52] Schuster to Treasury, 2 Mar. 1936, ibid.
[53] Judges Hargreaves to Schuster, 3 Jan. 1936. They (Maxwell, Hargreaves, Snagge) called on Schuster on 6 Mar., ibid.
[54] Schuster to Sir James Rae (Treasury), 3 Apr. 1936, ibid.   [55] Ibid.
[56] Mr Justice Croom-Johnson to Colville, 9 Feb. 1937, ibid.
[57] Judge Snagge to Attorney-General (Donald Somervell), 26 Apr. 1937, ibid.

amend the section of the County Courts Act which fixes judicial salaries.' He explained that there had to be three Readings of the Bill in the House of Commons and then the Bill went to the Lords. All the stages were, however, completed by July 1937.[58] The world was, indeed, changing. The County Court judges had finally received the salary recommended by the Select Committee fifty-nine years before when the pound had been worth at least twice as much as it was in 1937.

(c) Pay Claims: The High Court and High Drama

The High Court judges had traditionally regarded themselves as in a defensive position where their salaries and generous non-contributory pensions were concerned. When they were put on salary in 1825 it meant a reduction from the remarkable perquisites they had received from fees and the sale of offices. The puisne judges' £5,500 was cut to £5,000 in 1832.[59] Yet they found themselves having to defend even their £5,000 p.a. In 1873 Gladstone had had the audacity to suggest a cut to £4,000 p.a., writing to his Lord Chancellor that 'not only their salaries but also their pensions were extravagantly high'.[60] The judges were furious. When invited to comment on the Judicature Bill, then before Parliament, and designed totally to restructure the legal system, most judges limited their comments to the rumour that their salaries were going to be cut. They were outraged. As Chief Justice Bovill of Common Pleas pointed out, 'since the judges' salaries were fixed everything, especially house rents, servants and horses, have become very much more expensive.'[61] The pressure forced Gladstone to withdraw his suggestion.

At least, however, it is arguable that during the nineteenth century the value of the High Court judges' salaries did not decline. The concept of the cost of living over time is a complex issue. If one means by it the composite cost of a group of consumables, it is arguable that the cost of living actually dropped between 1825 and 1900. What is equally clear is that there was a dramatic increase of 250 per cent in the cost of living between 1900 and 1920. The judges—especially when tax was taken into account—really were suffering a serious diminution in status.[62] In the early 1920s, it looked for a while as if the

[58] Napier to Allesbrook, 30 June 1937, ibid.

[59] The 1825 Act set the salary of the Chief Justice of the King's Bench at £10,000 (with a pension of £8,000), the Chief Justice of Common Pleas at £8,000 (pension £3,750), the Chief Baron of the Exchequer £7,000. Puisne judges in all three common law courts were set at £5,500 (with a pension of £3,500).

The 1832 legislation reduced the puisne judges to £5,000. The Chief Justice of the King's Bench remained at £10,000, but Denman agreed to accept a lower figure. When Campbell was appointed Lord Chief Justice by Lord John Russell in 1850, he agreed to take the lower figure (£8,000) that Denman had received. LCO 2/1667.

[60] Gladstone to Selborne, 27 Jan. 1873. Selborne Papers, Letters, vol. xii.

[61] Letter from Bovill to Selborne, 7 Feb. 1873, ibid.

[62] J. Burnett, *A History of the Cost of Living* (Harmondsworth, 1969), 328.

High Court judges might actually receive an increase. In July 1920, the Council of Judges agreed on a statement:

The impending increases in the Court and other fees payable by suitors seems to afford a fitting opportunity for calling the attention of the Cabinet to the position of the Judges. Their salaries were fixed many years ago when the pound sterling was of a very different value to what it is at the present time, before any tax was payable,[63] and at a time when the present incomes earned at the Bar were unknown. Under present conditions the net amount which remains after deducting the income and super tax is not only very much less than it was a few years ago but its purchasing power has materially decreased. For instance, in 1914, each £1,000 of salary was worth after deductions of just about £950, in 1919, this had fallen to about £690, the purchasing power of which was £200 or thereabouts. While we do not complain of having had to curtail expenditures in many directions we venture to think that it is not desirable that we should be forced into a standard of living which is hardly consistent with the position held for so many years by Her Majesty's Judges.[64]

The judges had hit the right ear. The Lord Chancellor, Birkenhead, always spent more than he earned, thought he should be paid far more,[65] ideally tax-free, and was thus sympathetic to the plea. He persuaded Austen Chamberlain that a large increase in income was in order. Schuster reported that the two had agreed on a £1,500 permanent increase.[66] In consulting the Secretary of State for Scotland and the Chief Secretary of Ireland, Chamberlain said he was proposing a 30 per cent increase for English High Court judges and a 25 per cent increase for appeal judges. It was left to Schuster and Sir Warren Fisher at the Treasury to work out the total scheme, including 'lesser judicial luminaries', for the Cabinet.[67] In fact the memorandum produced for the Cabinet, while it set out the arguments of the judges, was probably not a profound debating document.[68] The Treasury had had the Inland Revenue sample the earnings of leading counsel. It turned out that in 1920–1, these averaged some £6,814. When contrasted with the High Court's £5,000 p.a. and a particularly attractive non-contributory pension (50 per cent of salary after fifteen years), not to mention the prestige and the knighthood, the contrast was hardly persuasive. Indeed, it suggested that the Lord Chancellor was still in a buyer's market as far as recruiting High Court judges was concerned.

[63] In the early part of the 19th cent., the judges were exempt from income tax.

[64] LCO 2/467. Included in letter from Mr Justice Eve to Lord Chancellor, 21 July 1920.

[65] Birkenhead circulated one of the most arrogant Cabinet papers of modern times on his own salary. He found it totally inadequate, as was the pension of £4,000. The memo included the strong implication that, as in the 18th cent., it should be permissible for the Lord Chancellor to amass a personal fortune while in office. LCO 2/480.

[66] Schuster to R. P. M. Gower, Private Secretary to Chancellor of Exchequer, 19 Oct. 1920, LCO 2/467.

[67] Fisher to Schuster, 4 Dec. 1920. The Judicial Salaries Bill print is dated 24 Feb. 1921. Ibid.

[68] Of the memorandum, Lord Justice Atkin wrote: 'It is as attractive a way of presenting the case as could be devised. I sincerely trust it will soon be successful.' Atkin to Schuster, 20 June 1921, LCO 2/467.

The memorandum to Cabinet therefore tried to explain away the Revenue's statistics by noting that they represented a three-year average, and because of 'the delicacy of the questions' the names probably included 'a number who are not within the narrow circle from which a promotion would be made if a vacancy were to occur'. The memorandum thus fell back on hearsay and war stories about leading counsel earning £13,000 or more:

At all times promotion to the Bench has been accompanied equally by some reduction in income, but that reduction has been of such an extent as not to outweigh the benefits involved in a relaxation of the strenuous life of a very busy leader, and the dignity of the position. A man still in the prime of his life with children whose education is still incomplete, or who are not launched upon a remunerative profession, cannot afford to give up an income of some £6,000 or £7,000 a year with a tendency to increase . . . So serious is the situation, that certain judges . . . have been forced to consider the question of returning to the Bar . . . The temptation is very great, and if such an event were to happen the blow at the prestige of the Bench and at our whole judicial system would be calamitous and irretrievable.[69]

Time, however, dragged on. The national financial situation weakened noticeably during 1921. By November, Birkenhead was suggesting more modest increases for the Judges, but with two-thirds salary by way of pension.[70] Birkenhead opined that 'the Judges will consider that the modified proposals are not in themselves sufficient to meet the additional burden cast upon them, but they would, I am sure, be prepared to accept the suggested increase as a settlement.' He was apparently wrong. Thirteen days later he was writing to the new Chancellor of the Exchequer, reminding him that his predecessor had agreed to the original package and while there had been no discussion in Cabinet, there was no evidence that anyone there disagreed. Birkenhead had talked with the Prime Minister (Lloyd George) and 'he concurred with the view that the matter should be put in hand immediately'.[71] Time was, however, running out. During 1922 Lloyd George's Coalition Government broke up and Bonar Law and his Lord Chancellor were less susceptible to wheeling-and-dealing than their predecessors. In any event, economically and socially the country appeared to be coming apart at the seams.

The 1920s were a time when the High Court judges were not so foolhardy as to question their comfortable salaries and pensions, with the cost of living dropping and the Bar, at best, erratic in its prosperity. Not asking for more, however, was one thing; a cut was another. With the collapse of 1931 the High Court judges were required, along with all public servants, to take a cut in their salaries. The National Economy Act and a related Order in Council cut the salaries of all judges—including High Court and County Court judges, whose salaries were

---

[69] Draft of Cabinet Memorandum, 18 Mar. 1921, LCO 2/467.
[70] Memorandum by Lord Chancellor, 3 Nov. 1921, ibid.
[71] Birkenhead to Sir Robert Hume, 21 Nov. 1921, ibid.

charged to the Consolidated Fund rather than being dependent on an annual vote of Parliament.

The reactions from senior judges began in a relatively orderly way.[72] Lord Merrivale, President of the Probate, Divorce, and Admiralty Division, wrote to Stanley Baldwin, 'as a member of the House of Lords addressing the leader of the Conservative Party', suggesting the right 'constitutional process' would have been for 'the Treasury to conclude with the several persons concerned agreements under which these persons shall surrender for the time being an agreed proportion of their stipends'.[73] Baldwin pleaded the fiscal situation had been one of extreme urgency, but he also argued that public faith was as deeply involved in the case of teachers and the unemployed, and any delay by negotiating with the judges would have dragged the judges into the political arena. The Consolidated Fund argument 'would seem to others in the present excitement a distinction without a difference, invented by the Conservative Party for the protection of a particular class. It seemed to me best therefore to rely on the patriotism of the eminent and patriotic body to which you belong and to assume their acquiescence'.[74] The assumption was misplaced.

Sankey, the Lord Chancellor, had lobbied the Cabinet against the cut, not so much on constitutional grounds, but on financial ones. The High Court judges had never received the war bonus, and, on a net income of £2,600,

they certainly cannot keep up on that figure the position which hitherto it has been thought desirable that a High Court judge should maintain . . . their prestige will be lowered. They will be addressed in court by leaders of the Bar who sometimes make in 2 or 3 days as much as a judge makes in a year. There are obvious reasons why it should not be in the power of any Government to decrease the salary of a Judge. His independence must be secured.[75]

The more the judges thought about the National Economy Act, the more outraged they became. The most extreme—perhaps not surprisingly—was Mr Justice McCardie. He wrote regularly to the Lord Chancellor: 'The prestige of the Judges will be substantially lessened by the reduction in their salaries.'[76] It was 'a matter of deep regret for me that the one British institution which has retained the respect of foreign nations should have been enfeebled at a time when a strong judiciary is more needed than ever'.[77]

[72] Sankey reported: 'It is most unfortunate that the Lord Chief Justice has for many weeks been unable to attend to his official duties. Originally he wrote a letter in which he said, as far as I can remember, that the judges would cheerfully comply with the cuts which the Government thought necessary.' Heuston, *Lives of the Lord Chancellors 1885–1940*, 513.

[73] Merrivale to Baldwin, 12 Sept. 1931, LCO 2/1666.

[74] Baldwin to Merrivale, 15 Sept. 1931, ibid.

[75] Memorandum, Lord Chancellor Sankey to Cabinet, 25 Sept. 1931, LCO 2/1666. Nevertheless, Inskip, the Solicitor-General, wrote to Lord Hanworth (Pollock), Master of the Rolls: 'I am distressed at the judges' cuts. It really is too bad and I think Sankey ought to have explained enough to stop them.' Inskip to Pollock, 30 Sept. 1931, Hanworth Papers, Box C 948.

[76] McCardie to Lord Chancellor, 21 Sept. 1931, LCO 2/1666.

[77] McCardie to Lord Chancellor, 30 Sept. 1931, ibid.

Meanwhile, McCardie wrote to all his King's Bench colleagues warning that 'if *a Government of a certain type should obtain a majority in the House of Commons*, it can practically *destroy* the High Court judges by a *mere Order-in-Council*, reducing their salaries to a *minimal* figure. We have been placed in a position *inferior* to an ordinary civil servant.'[78] Meanwhile, Mr Justice Rowlatt was threatening the Chancellor that he and others would retire, since they could earn more in retirement than they would if they stayed on the Bench. The Lord Chancellor's Office was somewhat panicked by the prospect of six simultaneous retirements, for this was a period when it was still believed that more meant worse. As Schuster put it, 'I very greatly doubt whether there are at the Bar six people fit to be appointed and ready to accept office.'[79] Thus Rowlatt was reassured both about the tax implications of staying on and the important contribution he could make. ('You are still in the full vigour of mind and body and capable for many years of making a notable contribution to the administration of justice.')[80] Rowlatt agreed to stay on for a year,[81] and, on his retirement, he was rewarded with a Privy Counsellorship which enabled him to accelerate the end of Canadian appeals to the Privy Council.[82]

By then the judges were bent on producing a memorandum for Cabinet.[83] Mr Justice McCardie drafted his own, including the lines that 'in view of the special duties which fall upon the judges, it would be a salutary thing if the salaries of all judges were paid free of direct taxes . . . It will be found that the salary of the Permanent Secretary of the Lord Chancellor has been almost doubled within the last twelve years.'[84] Hanworth managed to calm McCardie down (the memorandum 'appears to me to be incorrect in several important respects; and, moreover, to be written in a style and tone quite unsuited to the occasion . . . it seems to me most undignified, as well as exceedingly bad tactics, to introduce comparisons with others, such as the Lord Chancellor's secretary').

Meanwhile, the Government and the Civil Service were wrestling with the judicial tantrums. Without Schuster's knowledge the Prime Minister, the Lord Chancellor, and a former Lord Chancellor, Lord Hailsham, met together to draft a letter to the judges.[85] Schuster heard of it from the Treasury and managed to abort the 'madness'.[86] The Civil Service was worried about the impact in Scotland and Ireland. There were problems in Scotland where, as a result of the cuts, the Lord President received a lower salary than the Lord Justice Clerk. Fortunately, in Northern Ireland, just before the cuts were announced, Sir John

---

[78] McCardie to King's Bench judges, 7 Oct. 1931, ibid. The letter was sent on to the Master of the Rolls (Lord Hanworth) by Mr Justice Romer: 'What he says is, no doubt, true. But I think it is a thousand pities that he should say it in public, as he seems inclined to do.' The judges should 'bear it cheerfully'. Romer to Hanworth, 9 Oct. 1931, Hanworth Papers, Box C 948.

[79] Schuster to James Roe (Treasury), 11 Nov. 1931, LCO 2/1666.

[80] Lord Chancellor to Mr Justice Rowlatt, 13 Nov. 1931, ibid.

[81] Rowlatt to Lord Chancellor, 16 Nov. 1931, ibid.   [82] See Ch. 4 below.

[83] Decided at a Council of Judges, 12 Oct. 1931, Hanworth Papers, Box C 948.   [84] Ibid.

[85] Anderson to Schuster, 12 Nov. 1931, LCO 2/1666.

[86] Schuster to Anderson, 13 Nov. 1931, ibid.

Anderson, Permanent Secretary at the Treasury, had warned the Chief Justice of Northern Ireland what was afoot. The Chief Justice of Northern Ireland called a meeting of his colleagues to tell them their salaries were being cut and 'rumour has it that the meeting wound up its proceedings by singing "God Save the King"'.[87] Schuster replied: 'English judges are in a mood where they are far more likely to sing "The Red Flag" than "God Save the King".'[88]

By then—the beginning of December 1931—the judges were ready with their formal memorandum. Its tone was predictable:

we think beyond question that the judges are not in the position occupied by Civil Servants. They are appointed to hold particular offices of dignity and exceptional import-ance. They occupy a vital place in the Constitution of this country. They stand equally between the Crown and the Executive and between the Executive and the Subject. They have to discharge the gravest and most responsible duties. It has for over two centuries been considered essential that their security and independence should be accounted invio-late.

The Act of Settlement made clear provision for this . . .

It was long ago said that there can be no true liberty in a country where the judges are not entirely independent of the Government . . . Article III of the Constitution of the United States . . .

In this matter, our country has set an example to the world, and we believe that the respect felt by the people for an English Judge has been partly due to his unique position, a feeling which will survive with difficulty if his salary can be reduced or if he were an ordinary salaried servant of the Crown.

We must express our deep regret that no opportunity was given to the Judges of offering a voluntary reduction of salaries for an appropriate period; but we recognize that the Government was in a grave difficulty and the time for consideration was very short.

. . . When we consider the long line of exceptionally distinguished and able men who have occupied the position which we now hold, we cannot avoid expressing a fear that if the salary and the prestige of the High Court Judge are to remain as at present, those who will succeed us will probably not, as in the past, be drawn from the leaders of the Bar . . .[89]

The Master of the Rolls, Lord Hanworth, sent along the memorandum to the Prime Minister. Mr Justice Maugham, later briefly Lord Chancellor, was not eas-ily assuaged.[90] His advice to the Lord Chancellor, in order to redress the damage done by treating judges 'as if they were policemen or postmen', was to make the job more financially attractive. It was only because judges were regarded 'as standing on pedestals . . . that barristers would be found to give up £20,000 or more a year to occupy these exceptional positions—a pecuniary sacrifice to which there is no parallel in the world . . . Law indifferently administered by

---

[87] Schuster to Anderson, 12 Mar. 1931, ibid.

[88] Schuster to Anderson, 13 Nov. 1931, ibid.

[89] 4 Dec. 1931, ibid. The *Morning Post* of that date reported, 'Hardship Plea to Cabinet'.

[90] Lord Maugham claimed authorship of the memorandum. Lord Maugham, *At the End of the Day* (London, 1954), 356–7. This seems improbable. The memorandum appears to be the work of Hanworth.

second-rate judges may well (as in the United States)[91] cost the country indirectly many millions a year; for what is inaccurately called the law abiding instinct of our people is largely due to the great respect held for the judges themselves in recent times.' Maugham suggested two things should be done. The judges should be promised their salaries free of income (but not super) tax, and, second, fees received by barristers after they had taken their places on the Bench should be taxed at a low rate. Then, he felt, the judges might be prepared to agree to a voluntary reduction in salary.[92]

Lord Hanworth, in writing to the Lord Chancellor, was more moderate. In his view the Government should admit that the independence of the judiciary had been threatened, that it had been a 'terrible mistake', and that instead they were going to ask the judges to take a voluntary cut.[93] Schuster, however, was becoming increasingly frustrated with his charges. He remonstrated with the Lord Chancellor,[94] adding that it was 'nonsense' to suppose an attack on the judiciary had been involved. 'As long as the judges go on talking about the Act of Settlement, which has nothing whatsoever to do with the question, it is very difficult to deal with people who do not seem able to see that we cannot introduce legislation dealing with them and leaving the Police and unemployed untouched.'[95]

The behaviour of the more extreme judges did not help. Mr Justice Macnaghten, the undistinguished son of a distinguished father, called on the Lord Chancellor, announcing

he had a vision. The judges had to resist the power of the Crown in Stuart days, and had done so successfully. Now they had to resist the power of the Executive . . . on (the reduction of judicial salaries) . . . the legislation of the last fifty or sixty years had made great inroads on the independence of the judges . . . He then went on to rail against the superior civil servants . . . Whereas the power and remuneration of the Civil Servants had been increased in the last twenty years, the power and prestige of the judges had been reduced . . . He said that the judges were now in the power of Civil Servants, and he considered his position was no better than that of an office-boy at the Home Office.[96]

McCardie, too, continued his tirades, dissociating himself from the memorandum by the judges on the ground that it would preclude him from resigning and 'I must be free to resign whenever I wish.'[97] The group of judges appointed to

---

[91] As usual, the USA was invoked on both sides of the argument.

[92] Maugham to Sankey, 7 Dec. 1931, LCO 2/1666.

[93] Hanworth to Sankey, 11 Dec. 1931, ibid.

[94] Memorandum, Schuster to Sankey, 11 Dec. 1931, ibid.

[95] Ibid. He continued: 'Naturally salaries charged on the Consolidated Fund have always been looked upon as sacrosanct since there was a Consolidated Fund. But that is a comparatively short period and during that period . . . it has not hitherto been found necessary for the State to make a composition with its creditors.'

[96] R. F. V. Heuston, *Lives of the Lord Chancellors, 1885–1940* (1964), 517.

[97] McCardie to Hanworth, 24 Jan. 1932, Hanworth Papers, Box C 948. Mr Justice Talbot noted, 'McCardie is rapidly becoming a public nuisance of the first magnitude . . . I quite tremble when I see his name in the papers . . .'. Talbot to Hanworth, 8 Dec. 1931, ibid.

negotiate (Lord Hanworth, Master of the Rolls, Lord Merrivale, President of the Probate, Divorce, and Admiralty Division, Mr Justice Avory, and Mr Justice Maugham) met with the Lord Chancellor and then with the Prime Minister, the Lord Chancellor, and the Chancellor of the Exchequer.[98] The discussions were, to put it mildly, tortuous. Ramsay MacDonald's approach was described as 'very sympathetic throughout'—something, one suspects, which was less true of Sankey and Baldwin. In this atmosphere the Prime Minister offered, and the judges accepted, an arrangement whereby the Government would publicly express doubts about the validity of the Order in Council and the judges would then voluntarily agree to abide by the Order for one year (a 20 per cent cut from October 1931 to October 1932), and the Government would ensure that they would be taxed as if they had made a required payment rather than a voluntary one. This was agreed on 25 January and the judges adopted a more conciliatory stance. Lord Wrenbury, responding to the ongoing work of the (Hanworth) Committee on the Business of the Courts, suggested that the judges should sit from 10 until 4 and on Saturdays. and that such changes would help the salary issue.[99] Hanworth, by quoting Homer, even brought McCardie around.[100] MacDonald thanked Hanworth for solving the crisis,[101] but even as he wrote the arrangement was coming apart.

While Neville Chamberlain, the Chancellor of the Exchequer, was willing to have judges pay taxes at the lower amount (i.e. as if it were a mandated cut), he insisted that the judges could not move the tax years around to suit their convenience ('I cannot suppose the judges ever contemplated seeking a privileged position in matters of taxation').[102] By this time the agreement had become a 10 per cent reduction for two years, but other legal complications had come into play. Encouraged by the judges, two academics had rushed out papers claiming that legally the Economy Act and the Order in Council did not apply to judges.[103] The Lord Chancellor's Office did not discourage a contrary conclusion by E. C. S. Wade of Cambridge, who opined that 'it would be illegal for the Treasury to make any concession to the judges so long as the Order-in-Council as a whole stands and that an Act of Parliament is necessary to restore the judicial salaries, unless the whole Order-in-Council is withdrawn—an improbable event.'[104]

At this point, the Auditor-General, sharing the concerns expressed by Wade, referred the legal issue to the law officers, arguing that he would not give

[98] Hanworth, MR, prepared a memorandum about these various meetings, dated 6 Apr. 1932, LCO 2/1666.

[99] Wrenbury to Hanworth, 25 Jan. 1932, Hanworth Papers, Box C 948.

[100] McCardie to Hanworth, 27 Jan. 1932, ibid. Hanworth to MacDonald, 28 Jan. 1932, ibid.

[101] MacDonald to Hanworth, 3 Feb. 1932, Hanworth Papers, Box C 949.

[102] Neville Chamberlain to Sankey, 5 Feb. 1932, LCO 2/1666.

[103] P. Langdon, *The Times*, 17 Nov. 1931; W. S. Holdsworth, 'The Constitutional Position of the Judges', 48 *Law Quarterly Review* (Jan. 1932), 25–34—but circulated before the publication date to the judges. Maugham to Sankey, 7 Dec. 1931, LCO 2/1666.

[104] Sir Lyndon Macassey to Schuster, 16 Feb. 1932, ibid.

immunity to the judges from the Economy Act and Order-in-Council without some appropriate legal basis beyond an offer by the Prime Minister. The law officers found no such legal foundation. The judges were once again outraged. Mr Justice McCardie had already written to the Lord Chancellor demanding the return of the portion of his salary 'illegally retained',[105] while Mr Justice Rowlatt wrote to Schuster that he 'must accelerate the selection of a retired spot to end my days in'.[106] The problem was then that the Government would have to pass legislation to achieve the judges' goals. As Hanworth put it in a later memorandum,[107] 'This they [the Government] thought could not be done, for in the Constituencies, no clear distinction would be drawn, or could be explained, between the position of the Judges and of the Police, Teachers and Civil Servants, and in view of this the House of Commons would probably refuse to pass the Bill.'[108]

It was all back to the drawing-board. The Auditor-General's decision, coupled with the opinion of the Attorney-General and Solicitor-General, led to the formation of a Cabinet Committee under Stanley Baldwin,[109] which once again met with the representatives of the judges. After negotiations and a series of further meetings, the judges decided not to press the Government to implement the original agreement. Instead, the judges agreed to settle 'for a declaration on the Constitutional position of the judges, to be made by Mr Baldwin in answer to a question to be put to him in the House of Commons'.[110] On 25 February 1932, the declaration was duly made, with Baldwin referring to the 'special position' of the judges.[111] Unfortunately, in a supplementary reply, he seemed to assume the matter was purely a technical one. Once again the judges were outraged. At a meeting of the judges 'opinions were strongly expressed that the mistake made in the terms of the supplementary answer should be rectified in some formal manner, for the judges were anxious to make it plain that they had never acquiesced in the reduction of their salaries, and thought that their exceptional position as judges called for exceptional treatment'.[112] Fortunately, they decided to do nothing further as a body except to send the memorandum of their treatment to Stanley Baldwin, as Leader of the Conservative Party.

That, of course, did not stop individual judges protesting. Macnaghten wrote

---

[105] MacCardie to Sankey, 9 Jan. 1932, ibid.   [106] Rowlatt to Schuster, 11 Jan. 1932, ibid.

[107] Memorandum, 6 Apr. 1932, ibid. Maugham wrote to Hanworth on 27 Feb. 1932: 'I hope you will keep a record for future generations of what in fact has taken place between the Government and the judges.' Hanworth Papers, Box C 949.

[108] Jack Mayer, on behalf of the Police Associations, added: 'if the judges rely on the sanctity of their contracts, so do the police.' Pollock, *Mr Justice McCardie*, 281.

[109] It consisted of Baldwin, Chamberlain, Samuel, J. H. Thomas, and Sankey. 'Situation very difficult': Sankey to Hanworth, 11 Feb. 1932, Hanworth Papers, Box C 949.

[110] Hanworth Memorandum, 6 Apr. 1932, LCO 2/1666.

[111] *Parliamentary Debates* (5th ser.), HC vol. 262, cols. 564–5 (25 Feb. 1932).

[112] Hanworth Memorandum, 6 Apr. 1932, LCO 2/1666. See also the views of the Chancery judges. Memorandum, 14 Mar. 1932, 'to correct the impression created by Mr Baldwin's answers', Hanworth Papers, Box C 949.

to the Master of the Rolls announcing, in a somewhat confused way, that 'if the government won't carry out their agreement and want to consult the Law Officers—I personally am disposed to refrain from paying any supertax . . .'.[113] From the War Office, Lord Hailsham offered to fight for the judges in Cabinet and produce his own memorandum.[114] Mr Justice Langton supposed, 'the real opposition springs from the Treasury Mandarins and not from the politicians', and suggested a round table with the Treasury.[115] Mr Justice Avory claimed that the Law Officers' opinions were 'influenced by political considerations' and 'an autocratic Attorney-General'.[116] Two weeks later, Avory was at it again. This time, he thought that there should be a public protest from the Bench; 'so long as we are in the category of servants of the Crown, it is quite unseemly that we should be adjudicating in any case where the Crown is a party, including the trial of crimes.'[117] Mr Justice Charles reserved the right to make a public protest,[118] as did Mr Justice Humphreys, who concluded perceptively that 'the politicians have triumphed and the last state of the judges is worse than the first.'[119] Lord Wright paused to 'wonder if we shall ever revert to £5,000'.[120]

At this point the dispute took two different tacks. The main body of the judges vacillated on whether the question of salaries should be linked with the judges' agreeing to sit longer hours and shorten the Long Vacation. By the spring of 1933, there were some judges—like Mr Justice Swift—who thought the judges should cut the Long Vacation voluntarily. A meeting of the judges on 30 March 1933 was reported to have seen the judges 'in a more chastened mood. All seemed to have realized the mischief of linking up the recommendation with regard to the Long Vacation with any resolution about the cuts.'[121] A small group of judges, however, was taking a second route. It proposed suing the Crown by way of Petition of Right. The three ringleaders in this were Clauson, Luxmoore, and Macnaghten.

The Government took the threat seriously. A Petition of Right—the method then in place for suing the Crown—would cause embarrassment. It would not be easy for the Attorney-General to deny his fiat—the required permission without which the case could not proceed. Who, however, would hear the case? Hanworth suggested the Judicial Committee of the Privy Council. Schuster speculated on how the Committee might be staffed. Reading might be a possible member. 'The other retired Lords of Appeal and Judges, who in theory would

---

[113] Macnaghten to Hanworth, 20 Feb. 1932, Hanworth Papers, Box C 949.
[114] Hailsham to Hanworth, 23 Feb. 1932, ibid.
[115] Langdon to Hanworth, 20 Feb. 1931, ibid.
[116] Avory to Hanworth, 28 Feb. 1931, ibid. The Attorney-General was Jowitt and the Solicitor-General was Inskip. Earlier on, Inskip had been sympathetic with the judges' cause.
[117] Avory to Hanworth, 18 Mar. 1932, ibid.
[118] Charles to Hanworth, 2 Mar. 1932, ibid.
[119] Humphreys to Hanworth, 28 Feb. 1932, ibid.
[120] Wright to Hanworth, Mar. 1932, ibid.
[121] Schuster to Inskip (by then Attorney-General), 1 Apr. 1933, LCO 2/1666.

be available are Sumner; Dunedin, Wrenbury, Sargant, and Rowlatt . . .'[122] Of these, Sargant is a sick man, Wrenbury is far too old for such a proceeding, and is in addition in very close touch with Clauson . . . You know the attitude that Sumner has always taken to any claim by the Crown.'[123]

Schuster wrote to the Attorney-General discussing the situation early in April. He thought it would not be possible to deny the fiat. While there was 'no reason to suppose that (the Law Officers') opinion was erroneous, . . . it is never possible to foresee the decision which may be reached by the Courts in a case of first impression . . .'. Should the Government lose, it would not be possible to have judicial salaries 'restored to the amount at which they stood before the Economy Act while the wages of the police, the salaries of the school teachers and the amount payable as unemployment benefit were still subject to reductions made under that Act'. Retrospective legislation, however, has 'always been open to criticism and is highly unpopular'. Thus, the Schuster solution was 'to deal with the matter immediately by legislation'.[124]

Sankey and Hailsham saw Macnaghten, who was relying on counsel's opinion and was prepared to slow down his Petition of Right but not to abandon it. Schuster thought Macnaghten 'was definitely unbalanced by the excitement of the last few days. Whenever we tried to talk simple business to him . . . he broke off into rhetoric and repeated scraps of eloquence which I recognized as taken from Hull's Opinion.'[125] Thus Schuster moved to develop (or to implement) the Government's plan. The next day he wrote to Sir William Graham-Harrison, the Parliamentary Counsel, explaining that 'The Cabinet are determined not to give way. On the other hand, they think it is scandalous that such a question should be tried before a judge whose interests must necessarily be involved in the proceedings before him.' Legislation must be prepared at once, and Schuster had by then concluded that, if a Bill were before Parliament when Macnaghten presented his petition, this would be sufficient ground for the Attorney-General to refuse his fiat.[126]

With the government legislation being drafted, Sankey and Hailsham met with Luxmoore and Clauson.[127] The latter were shown the outline of the Government Bill, which reaffirmed the independence of the judiciary, but included the possibility of salary reductions. The judges preferred one Clauson had drafted saying the judges were not in the service of His Majesty and therefore not covered either by the Act or the Order. Sankey told them that was out of the question. Hailsham had apparently exhausted his earlier sympathy for the judges and was tougher and warned them that the Government was determined, if there were doubts, to pass legislation saying the judges were subject to the

---

[122] Rowlatt had retired in April 1932 and been made a Privy Councillor.
[123] Ibid.   [124] Memorandum, Schuster to Inskip, 4 Apr. 1933, ibid.
[125] Schuster to Sankey, 6 Apr. 1933, ibid.
[126] Schuster to Graham-Harrison, 7 Apr. 1933, ibid.
[127] Sankey, memorandum, 31 May 1937, ibid.

cuts. Clauson and Luxmoore then asked for a Bill that would say that the Government could not cut the salary of an existing judge, in return for which the judges would all undertake to accept a voluntary cut. It was pointed out to them that they could not deliver on that promise in respect of all the judges and 'the state of mind and health of the Chief Justice is such that it is quite impossible to ask him to consider or do anything'.[128]

Once again, however, it was beginning to look as if the dispute had been smoothed over. The Lord Chancellor sent a memorandum to Cabinet, but attaching the memorandum by Clauson and Luxmoore, together with a letter from Macnaghten: 'I do want the lay members of the Cabinet to understand—if it be possible—that the temporary "cut" in the status of the judges is of no importance at all compared with the permanent "cut" in their constitutional status, which would be effected if it were admitted that the judges of the Supreme Court ought to be classed with the Civil Servants as "persons in His Majesty's Service".'[129]

As had become the pattern, there followed a series of disquieting events. The *Sunday Times* noted that the judges 'seemed to be squealing most' about the economy cuts which everyone faced, quoting an Under-Secretary of the Treasury speaking at Harrow.[130] Clauson demanded that the First Lord of the Treasury publicly rebuke the official, 'otherwise the position of those who desire to prevent an open breach between the judicial and executive branches of the Government will have been rendered impossible'.[131] Macnaghten, having refused to pay both income tax and super tax, attempted to embroil the Lord Chancellor in his dispute with the Inland Revenue, relying on his delay in the Petition of Right. Sankey was outraged and told Macnaghten in an October letter[132] he should feel free to bring his Petition of Right.

This caused Schuster to swing into action. Writing to Graham-Harrison, the draftsman, he warned of the danger of a Petition of Right and said that Sankey and Hailsham had agreed on the outline of a suitable Bill:

Begin with a recital, which should be as long and pompous as possible, asserting the independence and all the rest of it and negating any idea that the Economy Act or the Order in Council affected that in any way. I realize that this is extraordinarily difficult to do for I do not see how you can negative that which has never been asserted except by the Judges themselves.

Then declare that not-withstanding all this they are affected by the cut.[133]

---

[128] Ibid. The other leaders of the bench—the Master of the Rolls and the President of the Probate, Divorce, and Admiralty Division—refused to have anything to do with the Petition of Right.

[129] Ibid.   [130] 23 July 1933, ibid.

[131] Clauson to Sankey, 23 July 1933, ibid.

[132] Sankey to Macnaghten, 12 Oct. 1933, ibid. The Attorney-General was consulting with the Lord Chancellor about whether proceedings should be instituted against those judges who refused to pay their taxes. *Holmes–Laski Letters*, ed. Howe, ii. 1456.

[133] Schuster to Graham-Harrison, 26 Oct. 1933, LCO 2/1666.

In fact, the Petition of Right was not filed with the Home Office and the difficulties of drafting led the Government quietly to drop the Bill. Relations between executive and judiciary, however, continued to be tense. When Professor J. H. Morgan attacked the Government's position on judicial salaries in *The Times*,[134] Sankey and Hailsham composed a response, Schuster tightened it, and then the Attorney-General was instructed to find a KC MP to send it. It went to *The Times* in the name of T. J. O'Connor, KC, MP.[135] Moreover, Lord Chancellor Sankey's observations about the difficulties of drafting a Bill to ensure the independence of the judiciary led Lord Rankeillour to introduce his own Bill.

The Judiciary (Safeguarding) Bill, 1934, was described by Schuster as 'extremely silly'—'you will notice that all it says is that no reference in any statute is to affect these people unless there is an express reference.'[136] The Government hoped to be able largely to ignore the Bill, feeling, as Schuster put it, that 'the judges seem now to be alive to the expediency of no more discussion on the subject than can be helped'.[137] Yet the Bill generated support, and the usual arguments. It was alleged that the attempt to cut the salaries of judges had been 'a breach of unbroken Parliamentary privilege of 231 years'. High Court judges were on a different footing from civil servants and members of the armed forces.[138] They were not to be put in a category even with County Court judges and metropolitan magistrates.[139] On appointment to the bench they suffered great pecuniary sacrifices.[140]

The Bill received a Second Reading, and Sankey courteously suggested some changes to Rankeillour:

all of [the judges] are anxious about the constitutional position, but you know what amour propre is, and what they all feel most is being classed with other people. They do not regard County Court judges as His Majesty's judges, still less Stipendiary Magistrates. The thing that every one of them cares about most is, as they put it, that they were herded together with Civil Servants, teachers, policemen, and so forth. I think, therefore, it would be very helpful in healing the breach if you could see your way to confine your Bill to them.[141]

Amended, the Bill passed the House of Lords. Sankey was conciliatory towards the Bill, not because he approved of it, but because he had no wish further to offend the judges. 'The Lord Chancellor has shown polite neutrality.' Schuster felt the Government would ultimately need to substitute a Bill, because Rankeillour had passages about 'rights' and 'duties', as 'being in some mystical way a protection against socialism or fascism' although 'this seems rather outside

---

[134]   *The Times*, 29 Nov. 1933.   [135]   5 Dec. 1933, LCO 2/1666.
[136]   Schuster to W. R. L. Trickell, 8 Feb. 1934, LCO 2/1667.
[137]   Schuster to Sir Maurice Gwyer (Parliamentary Counsel), 13 Feb. 1934, ibid.
[138]   *Parliamentary Debates* (5th. ser.), HL vol. 90, col. 62 (23 Nov. 1933).
[139]   Ibid., vol. 91, cols. 222–7 (15 Mar. 1934).   [140]   Ibid., vol. 90, col. 1053 (1 Mar. 1934).
[141]   Sankey to Rankeillour, 6 Mar. 1934, LCO 2/1667.

the limits of the controversy on judicial salaries'. Schuster concluded that he found 'it very difficult to exaggerate the contempt which I feel for the Bill. If it has meaning at all . . . that meaning is mischievous.'[142] Schuster had no doubt that it was money, not constitutional principle, that was bothering the judges.

The Bill did not proceed to the House of Commons. The squalid incident blew over. It had not reflected well on the judges. They had appeared selfish and out of touch with reality. More importantly, in the long run, they had seemed confused about their constitutional role and how to protect it. The more they turned to the Cabinet and Parliament to protect their constitutional rights, the more they were established as creatures of statute. It was perhaps fortunate, in an ironic way, that Hewart's attack on Schuster—described in the previous chapter—occurred, to take minds away from judicial salaries.[143] In 1934, the judges' salaries were restored, and during the Second World War, Lord Simon, the Lord Chancellor, began to talk about raising them.

In terms of the historical perspective, however, what is striking is the amateur level of argument on both sides. Dicey had restated the English Constitution in such a way that Parliament seemed even more dominant in the English concept of the separation of powers than it had in the seventeenth and eighteenth centuries. What the battle about salaries reflected was two more minor aspects related to this. First, the judges—who, until the Utilitarian revolution in the mid-nineteenth century had been the second most important branch of government—had clearly become the third. This had the effect, second, of moving the debates away from power as such, towards status. Élites, conscious of ebbing power, have, throughout history, taken similar stands.

---

[142] Schuster to Inskip, enclosing memorandum by Napier, 20 Apr. 1934, ibid.

[143] Other, of course, than those of the judges. Roche and Maugham discovered that there was a quirk in the law by which income tax increased when they were promoted from the High Court to the Court of Appeal. Sankey warned Inskip (Attorney-General): 'Roche is never very easy to handle and is certain to resign if this claim is insisted upon. I imagine that Maugham will follow his example. It will then be impossible to obtain any new Lord Justices.' (Sankey to Inskip, 8 Nov. 1934, LCO 2/1678B).

Schuster negotiated with the Treasury (see Schuster to J. A. B. Ferguson, 11 Jan. 1935), and in July 1935 the situation was remedied by Statute. When Roche was later promoted to be a Lord of Appeal, he was taxed again and was outraged by the 'departure from the bargain'. Ibid.

4

Schuster and the Beginning of the End of Empire

As the judges increasingly sensed frustration at their declining status and role in the British Constitution, the irony was that at least for those members of the judiciary entitled to sit in the Judicial Committee of the Privy Council (Lords of Appeal, Lords Justices, and those who had held 'high judicial office'), the work presented was of increasing importance in terms of policy issues. Yet the judges seemed almost unaware of the constitutional challenge. The myth of Dicey had convinced them that technical competence was all; which judges sat and how written constitutions should be dealt with were largely irrelevant.

(a) The Judicial Committee: The Beginning of the End

It was during Schuster's term of office that the Judicial Committee of the Privy Council, at least as it was known in the later nineteenth century, began to come apart. There were a number of reasons for this. In retrospect the Hatherley–Selborne–Cairns plan to merge the Judicial Committee with the House of Lords had been one of the last serious possibilities of creating a court that would put the Old Dominions on a par with the Mother Country. That, however, had been torpedoed by a group of High Tories, anxious to maintain the mystique of the House of Lords.[1] What Britain itself was not prepared to use, the Dominions increasingly saw as second class. It certainly did not sit well with the increasing nationalism which grew in the Dominions as the nineteenth century turned into the twentieth.[2] Gallipoli and the Somme strengthened some blood ties, but by the 1920s, the Dominions were anxious to be seen as independent forces on the world stage.

Commonwealth relations were worked out at Imperial (later Commonwealth) Conferences. In the 1890s and up to 1905, Joseph Chamberlain still looked ideally for some form of political linkage, and failing that, at least some type of economic union. From 1905 onwards, the interest, generally manifested through Haldane, was in imperial defence.[3] Yet, as we have seen, the maintenance of judicial appeals to London was seen as an important cement in the fabric. By the 1920s, the idea of an imperial federation was dead. Imperial preference and imperial defence were still alive, but under attack. Together with the Dominions

---

[1] R. B. Stevens, 'The Final Appeal: Reform of the House of Lords and Privy Council, 1867–1876', *Law Quarterly Review*, 80 (1964), 343.

[2] Eddy and Schreuder, eds., *The Rise of Colonial Nationalism*, *passim*.

[3] D. C. Gordon, *The Dominion Partnership in Imperial Defence, 1870–1914* (Baltimore, 1965), *passim*.

Office and the India Office, the Lord Chancellor's Office hoped to keep appeals to the Judicial Committee alive and active, but the tide could not be turned back. There was a gradual decline in their importance.

The general pressures undermining the appeal were aggravated by nationalist tendencies in two nations that had not been taken into serious consideration (at least in appeal matters) before the First World War: India and the Irish Free State. The latter, in particular, raised concerns which were more emotional than logical. The 1921 Treaty had retained appeals to the Judicial Committee of the Privy Council, and to many—perhaps more so in England than in Eire—that right of appeal had to be protected to ensure the maintenance of the interests of the Protestant minority. It was a concern that, unfortunately, was to distort the debates on Commonwealth appeals during the 1920s.

There was, it is true, one last flurry of interest in a new Imperial Court, pushed by Australia and New Zealand during the First World War. As Schuster realized, however, there were at least three reasons why the interest would not prosper. First, there was the technical reason that no one could ever agree on who should pay for the Colonial judges, who would sit, permanently or semi-permanently in London. Second, the Dominions were not really interested in having their appeals heard by judges from other Dominions. Third, in the words Schuster put into the mouth of Lord Chancellor Finlay, the idea that English appeals should go to an Imperial Court was not acceptable. 'I believe that such a change would meet with very grave opposition in the United Kingdom itself. If Australian solicitors can sit, why not English? I am strongly opposed to such a scheme.' The Schuster–Finlay concern about the implications for a divided profession in England was, however, superfluous. Canada once again killed the scheme.[4]

Meanwhile, the Judicial Committee, despite all the rhetoric to the contrary, was doing a less than stellar job with its own actual decisions. *Webb* v *Outrim*,[5] decided in 1906, still rankled with the Australian judges.[6] In that case, Halsbury had refused to listen to any of the American precedents, going back to *Marbury* v *Madison*, on the issue of judicial review. Indeed judicial review was a concept that the Lord Chancellor found remarkably difficult to accept. 'This is a novelty to me. I thought an Act of Parliament was an Act of Parliament and you cannot go beyond it . . . I do not know what an unconstitutional act means.'[7] This strange approach to judicial review did not appeal to Canadians, either. The Halsbury view made nonsense of sections 91 and 92—the very basis of the Canadian constitution.

There were, moreover, important blunders by the Judicial Committee during

---

[4] LCO 2/2464. On the 1918 Imperial Conference and the Justice Minister of Canada (C. J. Doherty)'s role in killing the Imperial Court, see D. B. Swinfen, *Imperial Appeal: The Debate on the Appeal to the Privy Council, 1833–1986* (Manchester, 1987), 80–3. Loreburn said: 'We have not the right to play havoc with our judicial system in order to please a fancy.' Cited, ibid. 83.
[5] [1907] AC 81 (PC 1906).   [6] LCO 2/3464.   [7] [1907] AC 81 (PC 1906).

the 1920s—at least in political terms. In *Nadan* v *The King*,[8] the Judicial Committee re-confirmed the application of the Colonial Laws Validity Act with respect to the Canadian Criminal Code, striking part of the Code down. The decision had a nineteenth-century colonial ring to it. Then the Privy Council proceeded to mishandle *Wigg* v *Attorney-General of the Irish Free State*.[9] This so-called Transferred Civil Servants case was highly dubious from a legal point of view. After the decision, the Registrar of the Privy Council wrote to warn the Lord Chancellor that the Judicial Committee had misunderstood the meaning of 'lump sum allowance' as well as the meaning of a Treasury minute. The Lord Chancellor, Cave, then decided that legislation would not be an appropriate way to remedy the Privy Council advice (decision) lest it set a bad example to the Irish. Schuster therefore arranged for the Privy Council to rehear the case, since Haldane and Dunedin publicly in the House of Lords, and Lord Cave, on his death-bed, in a letter to the Prime Minister, all advised that the earlier opinion was wrong in law.[10] In short, a majority of the members of the Judicial Committee hearing the case had publicly admitted their decision was wrong. The case was referred back to the Judicial Committee under the 1833 legislation. The Privy Council, composed, it is true, rather differently, celebrated the rehearing by reaffirming its previous decision,[11] to the embarrassment of both the British and Irish governments. The two plaintiffs were paid in full; other members of the class had to prove their claims in a special tribunal.

There were other unfortunate Privy Council decisions in this period. In 1918, it had, in *In re Southern Rhodesia*,[12] given the British South Africa Company massive reparations to which many thought the Company was not entitled. In 1927, the Legislative Assembly of India, at least partly out of dissatisfaction with the decisions of the Privy Council, passed by only a single vote the motion in favour of paying the Indian members of the Judicial Committee.[13] In that same year, the Privy Council decided the Canada–Newfoundland Boundary dispute, awarding Labrador to Newfoundland. Once again there were doubts about the decision's soundness. Balfour noted, 'I am very uneasy about the Canadian–Newfoundland judgment which I am almost sure will get us into trouble.'[14] It did, even with the Quebecois, who normally, at that time, favoured appeals to the Privy Council.[15]

The Canadian press began sneering at the senility of the judges in the Judicial

---

    [8] [1926] AC 482 (PC).   [9] [1927] AC 674 (PC).
    [10] Heuston, *Lives of the Lord Chancellors, 1885–1940*, 440–3; Swinfen, *Imperial Appeal*, 104–7.
    [11] *In re Transferred Civil Servants (Ireland) Compensation* [1929] AC 242 (PC).
    [12] [1919] AC 217 (PC 1918). See generally C. Palley, *The Constitutional History and Law of Southern Rhodesia, 1885–1965* (Oxford, 1966), ch. 10.
    [13] Swinfen, *Imperial Appeal*, 107.
    [14] CAB 27/342. The uneasiness has continued. The Parti Quebecois has—in the 1990s—as part of its policy for post–independence Quebec, a plan to go to the International Court in the Hague to reclaim Labrador, taken, in its view, by the incompetence of the Privy Council. M. Richler, 'A Reporter at Large (Quebec)', *New Yorker*, 25 Sept. 1991, pp. 40, 81.
    [15] Swinfen, *Imperial Appeal*, 107.

Committee, and one MP at Westminster suggested they could neither see nor hear counsel.[16] Balfour, Lord President of the Council, emphasized 'the necessity from the Imperial Point of View of maintaining the prestige of the Judicial Committee'. It was a 'valuable bond of Empire'. He was concerned about the 'high average age' of the judges—the youngest was 63 and the oldest 89. In the light of such criticism, Atkinson was asked to retire in 1928[17] and was replaced by Atkin. The 1929 legislation created a new Lord of Appeal. In 1929, Lords Carson and Shaw retired, to be replaced and augmented by Lords Tomlin, Russell, and Thankerton—a trio of professional judges to replace two political law lords. In 1930, Macmillan replaced Sumner. As the 1930 Imperial Conference approached, Balfour warned:

There was a good deal of criticism of it [the Judicial Committee of the Privy Council] at the [1926] Imperial Conference, and . . . it then became perfectly clear that when the next Conference came around, the Judicial Committee would probably become the subject of a more serious attack. I very earnestly hope that before that period arrives its position will have been made as impregnable as the legal talent at our disposal, secured by adequate salaries, can possibly make it.[18]

Certainly the judges available to the Privy Council in 1930 were technically a considerable improvement on their predecessors of 1926.

Of course all the debates in the 1920s were, implicitly or explicitly, conducted in the shadow of the Irish Question. The Treaty of 1921 was a compromise and it satisfied few on either side. The Irish particularly feared the prejudices of three of the Law Lords—Carson, Sumner, and Cave—and Lloyd George agreed that their fears were justified.[19] Moreover, the Irish, who had no wish to have the appeal at all, felt they were constantly being given a conflicting message. While originally the Irish Free State had been compared to Canada, Haldane drew the analogy with South Africa, where special leave to appeal was rarely given. By the mid-1920s, an increasingly irritated Ireland was prepared to undermine Privy Council decisions by the simple expedient of reversing decisions by statute. Haldane and other Liberals announced that any Commonwealth country might terminate appeals to the Privy Council. Conservatives agreed in principle but argued that Eire was different.[20]

The friction over the Irish Treaty burst into flames for the first time at the Imperial Conference of 1926, and especially in the Inter-Imperial Relations Committee, where Eire got less support from Canada and South Africa than she

---

[16] Ibid.

[17] 'The Chancellor asked me to call on him. I did call. He said the scurrilous press of Quebec had abused the Privy Council and said the members were all old fogies, that I was the oldest of the old fogies and had better resign. Of course, I would not think of begging not to be dismissed, and answered him that I would resign if he wished it, and I did so.' Heuston, *Lives of the Lord Chancellors, 1885–1940*, 303–4.

[18] CAB/ 27/342.   [19] Swinfen, *Imperial Appeal*, 93.

[20] Swinfen, *Imperial Appeal*, 90–6. See also D. W. Harkness, *The Restless Dominion* (London, 1969), 112–14, 138–9, 165–6, 203–7, 251, 272.

had hoped. The brief to the UK delegation was clear. While a decision to abolish appeals by Canada as one of the 'old' Dominions was one thing, 'The Constitution of the Free State, unlike the Constitution of Other Dominions is the outcome of a special compact between the Free State and the British Governments, and special steps were taken to make it clear that the compact definitely included the right of the subject to petition for leave to appeal.'

This strong brief, which put over the issue to the 1930 Conference, was the work of the Dominions Office and the Lord Chancellor's Office,[21] and in the latter it was the work of Schuster and Cave. These two had taken a moderate draft of the brief to Ministers and transformed it into something much tougher. References to the 'wise' government of the Irish Free State were deleted, as was the statement that the 'new judges approved by the Free State Government appear to be excellent'. Gone was the observation that 'no instance has been brought to the notice of the British Government within the last two years in which it is even alleged that a supporter of the former regime has been denied justice by the Courts'. With respect to the 'betrayal' that abolishing appeals would represent, the brief originally noted that 'Such a point of view is no doubt unjustified; but that it exists is a fact which should, it is submitted, be taken into consideration.' Under Schuster's pen, this became: 'The existence of such cannot, it is submitted, be left out of consideration.' Gone altogether was the sentence, 'The maintenance of that right is of importance to the British Government, not because they regard it as necessary in the interests of the individual subject, but because they regard it as an answer to those who still protest that by the Articles of Agreement, the British government betrayed them to their enemies.'[22] With such a brief it was perhaps fortunate that the British representative was Lord Birkenhead, who was able to 'sweet talk' the Irish into holding the issue over until the 1930 Imperial Conference.

By the time of the 1930 Imperial Conference, a Labour Government was in power. It might be thought that the change in government would be helpful to the Irish cause. That was far from obvious. MacDonald, the Prime Minister, was already showing conservative tendencies and was anxious not to appear soft on the Irish. His Attorney-General, Jowitt, was, in so many ways, conservative and suspicious of the Catholic government in Eire. Fortunately, the Lord Chancellor, Sankey, actually believed in the equality of Commonwealth countries. Behind the scenes, however, there were various schemes developed, designed to retain appeals from Ireland on the most important issues. The most widely discussed was a variation of the Imperial Court of Appeal, so that imperial disputes with an international flavour would go to a tribunal which would provide services for the Commonwealth akin to those provided for the world community at large by the International Court in the Hague.[23] This led to a secret memorandum from

[21] LCO 2/3465.   [22] LCO 2/3465.

[23] See e.g. E. J. Harding (Dominions Office) to Schuster, 22 Aug. 1929; Wilf Malkin (Foreign Office) to Schuster, 23 Aug. 1928, LCO 2/3465.

Schuster, reluctantly conceding that such a tribunal might be necessary, but accepting that it would accelerate the demise of the regular work of the Privy Council. In short, as a ruse for protecting the 1921 Treaty, the Judicial Committee, as it was then known, might die an early death.[24] The irrationality of the history of this period is a reminder of the strength of emotions surrounding the whole Irish question.

The 1930 Imperial Conference went very much as expected. Schuster had suggested that if the unwanted Imperial Tribunal for the inter-imperial disputes were established, it might have to be peripatetic; there was also beginning to be a suggestion that the Judicial Committee of the Privy Council should move from capital to capital. Hanworth, the Master of the Rolls, suggested such a change to Sir John Simon. The latter, wrestling with the constitutional future of India as chair of the Simon Commission, was concerned about its impact on the Federal Court in India.[25] The Chief Justice of New Zealand (Sir Michael Myers) was shocked by such an idea: 'In his opinion this would be a retrograde step . . . he could think of no grander conception than that of appeal—because that was really what it was—to the King himself as the fountainhead of justice, and the one last remaining tangible link which he hoped might always remain between Great Britain and the Dominions overseas.'[26] The enthusiastic quality of the New Zealand view of the Privy Council continued over time, so that it is not surprising it is the only one of the Old Dominions, in the early 1990s, not to have abolished appeals to London.[27]

Ireland was determined to be the first to abolish appeals, and the 1930 Conference took its predicted form. The UK and Irish Delegates stated their positions firmly and unproductively. There was sympathy for the Irish position. When J. H. Thomas, the Labour Dominions Secretary, took the position traditionally espoused by the Tories, Guthrie, the Canadian delegate, protested: 'Mr Thomas, you say that the Irish Free State can do in this matter what Canada can do. You say that Canada can get rid of it if it wants. And your amazing conclusion is that the Irish Free State can't. Tell me, Mr Thomas, why?'[28] The truth was that, as with so much in relations between the British and Ireland, there was no logical answer. So the Imperial Conference ended with England and Ireland far apart, with the other Commonwealth countries embarrassed, and with an agreement in principle on an Imperial Tribunal, an agreement which was to die a quiet death.

The great hope for the future was Sankey's Statute of Westminster, which would spell out the formal independence of the Dominions. By this time, the Lord Chancellor's Office knew that the right of appeal from the Irish Free State

[24] 9 Aug. 1929, ibid.
[25] Simon to Hanworth, 31 Jan. 1930, Hanworth Papers, Box C 948.
[26] Secret Affairs Dispatch from Governor–General of New Zealand, 12 May 1930, LCO 2/3465.
[27] In 1991, six of the seven 'colonial' judges eligible to sit in the Privy Council were from New Zealand. The seventh was from the Bahamas.
[28] Cited Swinfen, *Imperial Appeal*, 121.

was of 'no advantage to anyone' and was 'slightly ridiculous',[29] but Thomas and MacDonald stuck to their guns. There was pressure to exempt Eire from the Statute of Westminster, and, when this was not done, J. H. Thomas still argued that the Statute did not free the Irish Free State from its obligation under the Articles of Agreement of 1921.[30] This was enough to beat back Conservative attacks in both Lords and Commons; and when in 1933, de Valera, the new Irish Prime Minister, passed legislation through the Dáil to abolish appeals, the then English Attorney-General, Sir Thomas Inskip, warned the Irish Government that they had no such right under the Statute of Westminster.[31] The Judicial Committee of the Privy Council, with Sankey presiding, in *Moore* v *Attorney-General of the Irish Free State* (1935),[32] however, held that they did.

The only other Dominion immediately to take advantage of the Statute of Westminster was Canada, with respect to criminal cases.[33] Yet the writing was on the wall. The Nationalists in South Africa were using the appeal as a way of attacking the United Party. Sometimes the attacks were couched in terms of legal knowledge ('it was impossible for judges who knew little of Roman–Dutch law to hear cases that had been dealt with by judges who had made a thorough study of Roman–Dutch law and had decided such cases on that basis'[34]). The agitation, however, continued and, with uncanny timing, the Judicial Committee of the Privy Council inflamed the situation in 1934 by appearing to go back on its stated position that it would take South African cases only if they involved an important principle of law. *Pearl Assurance Co.* v *Government of the Union*[35] did not fall into that category.

By 1935, the Nationalists had tabled a motion in Parliament to abolish appeals.[36] Jan Smuts, the United Party Prime Minister, was forced to agree that 'very careful consideration . . . was called for, largely owing to a change of attitude which had taken place in the Privy Council. To the astonishment of everybody the policy laid down by Lord Haldane many years ago, to the effect that the Privy Council would not entertain appeals in the ordinary course from Union courts, had been departed from in the case of the Pearl Assurance Company.'[37] Dr Malan for the Nationalists demanded that the 'ridiculous anomaly' (appeals to the Privy Council) be eliminated at once: 'There is attached to it the stigma of an inferiority complex.'[38] The UK High Commission found Smuts was only 'lukewarm' in his support of continuing appeals.[39] That was true; what Smuts was not prepared to do was to abolish appeals when the Nationalists were

---

[29] Cited Swinfen, *Imperial Appeal*, 126.   [30] Ibid.   [31] Ibid. 136.

[32] [1935] AC 484 (PC).

[33] Upheld in *British Coal Corporation* v *The King* [1935] AC 500 (PC). See Blom–Cooper and Drewry, *The Final Appeal*, 82–3. H. J. Stanley (High Commissioner in Pretoria) to Sir Edward Harding (Permanent Secretary, Dominions Office), 6 Nov. 1934, LCO 2/3465.

[34] Ibid.   [35] [1936] AC 570.

[36] W. H. Clark (High Commissioner in Pretoria) to J. H. Thomas, Dominions Secretary, 25 Feb. 1935, LCO 2/3665.

[37] Clark to Thomas, 11 Mar. 1935, p. 3, ibid.   [38] Ibid., p. 4.   [39] Ibid., p. 6.

using the issue solely for political purposes—but by 1936 Smuts agreed the disadvantages of appeals outweighed the advantages. The fact that there were so few appeals from South Africa perhaps explains why the appeal survived until abolished by the Nationalist government in 1950.

There was certainly no evidence that the rejuvenated Judicial Committee was wiser than its predecessor. As in the *Wigg* case, it sometimes seemed as if the British establishment had failed to notice that the Judicial Committee had separated from the Privy Council as such. When, in 1932, the Judicial Committee decided, in *Croft* v *Dunphy*,[40] that Canada had, under the 1867 Act, authority to extend its territorial waters to 12 miles for the purposes of interdicting bootleggers, there was deep concern. Lord Macmillan's opinion contained dicta which were deeply disturbing to both the British and Canadian governments, who were engaged in a series of arbitrations with the United States. When *The Times* published its report of the case in July, Sir Maurice Gwyer, the Treasury Solicitor, wrote to the legal adviser at the Foreign Office, Sir William Malkin, worried that Macmillan's opinion would legalize contiguous zones, to which Her Majesty's Government was opposed. The Canadian government representatives called on Gerald Fitzmaurice at the Foreign Office to register their concerns; and, during the long vacation, the Civil Service establishment responded.

On 25 August, there was a meeting of officials from the Foreign Office, the Dominions Office, the Office of the Treasury Solicitor, and the Privy Council Office, where it was decided that technically the judgment had not been issued; therefore, it was permissible for the Attorney-General to be heard before judgment was formally entered. By the time eight or nine permanent secretaries met on 27 September, the idea of a rehearing was ruled out because the decision had already been published in the *The Times Law Reports*. It was, however, agreed that the Attorney-General would write a letter to the Registrar of the Privy Council, a letter which was to be shown to Lord Macmillan. The letter (or letters) were drafted by the Treasury Solicitor, and in them, the Attorney-General was made to argue that he would have come to address the Privy Council if he had known a question of International Law was involved.

The Attorney-General then had a word with Lord Macmillan 'whose attitude had been very chilly'. Then Sir Charles Neish, the Registrar of the Privy Council, brought the Attorney-General's letter to the attention of Lord Macmillan. Macmillan responded that 'I should not of course object to altering a phrase of two, if that would give any comfort.' There the matter might have ended, but for the fact that the whole episode came to the attention of Lord Chancellor Sankey. He was outraged and wrote to Neish demanding a written explanation. The apologia was in fact provided by Schuster, who fortunately had not been at the meetings. ('It did not occur to me then that it could be suggested that the Interdepartmental Committee was called together for the

---

[40] [1933] AC 156 (PC 1932).

purpose of procuring an alteration in the judgment which had already been delivered.')

Sankey's letter to Neish was strong. It was a 'very serious matter . . . I cannot believe a Committee of Permanent Secretaries was sitting in Whitehall to suggest amendments . . . I cannot, and do not, believe, that the Executive or the Civil Servants would desire to interfere with a judgment delivered by the Privy Council.' Although the minutes of the Permanent Secretaries' meeting showed the Treasury Solicitor saying, 'I doubt if they (the Judicial Committee of the Privy Council) will omit it all, but they might be willing to tone it down', Schuster, as always, put a smooth face on everything. He repeated to the Lord Chancellor: 'The Treasury Solicitor informs me that the only question under consideration by the Interdepartmental Committee was the nature of the report, if any, to be made to the Attorney-General.' The Foreign Office consoled itself by having notes, critical of the passage in the opinion about contiguous zones, published in the *Law Quarterly Review* and the *British Yearbook of International Law*.[41] The provenance of this decision provides an appropriate introduction to a more detailed analysis of the Canadian connection.

(b) A Case Study of Canada

The British North America Act of 1867 (now known in Canada as the Constitution Act) was held to have left in place the appeal to the Judicial Committee of the Privy Council, an appeal which survived until 1949. One has to be aware of the danger—in looking at the broad sweep of the intervening years—of simplifying what the Privy Council wrought. The Canadian Constitution, like the US Constitution, has more than its share of subtleties and nuances.

Criticism of the Privy Council's handling of Canadian cases in those early years was based on competing notions of what might be called 'original intent' in the United States; or, looked at in the context of English legal culture, different approaches to statutory interpretation.[42] Most commentators felt the Privy Council had distorted the centralist intention of the confederators.[43] A later burst of criticism—from a group known as the Constitutionists—felt that the Privy Council had failed in its Canadian mission because it had failed to treat the British legislation as a Constitution but insisted on treating it like any other statute.[44] While these 'schools' of criticism often overlap, they reflect important and different jurisprudential approaches.

In this context, it is worth noting that by the mid-1870s, there were already

---

[41] The saga of *Croft v Dunphy* is taken from A. V. Lowe and J. R. Young, 'An Attempt to Rewrite a Judgment', 94 *Law Quarterly Review* (1978), 255–75. They rely on the following files: FO 371/15866–7, 371/16602–3, 372/2876, 372/2979; DO 35/147, 35/259.

[42] A. C. Cairns, 'The Judicial Committee and Its Critics', 4 *Canadian Journal of Political Science* (1971), 301–45.

[43] Ibid. 302.   [44] Ibid. 307.

efforts being made to end the appeal to London.[45] Looked at purely from a political point of view, what probably saved the appeal in these early years was an apparent change in the interpretation of the 1867 Act by the Privy Council. For the first dozen years of appeals, the Act was generally regarded as having been interpreted in a 'balanced' or 'neutral' way, with the Federalist view of the Supreme Court of Canada generally being accepted by the Privy Council. By the 1880s and 1890s, however, under the influence of Lord Watson,[46] there was a move generally perceived by most critics as being designed to protect Provincial powers at the expense of Dominion ones.[47]

Over the years, the Watson approach has been attributed to the English upper classes sympathy for States' Rights during the American Civil War, Dicey's use of the United States as a model of federalism, the Liberal interest in Municipal Reform and Home Rule, and the possibility that Watson and Davey had just absorbed their clients' (the Provinces') political posture while at the Bar and allowed it to guide them while on the Bench. Canadian scholars have tended to suggest that the Watson–Haldane approach reflected an anti-collectivist, pro-French-Canadian, or even a divide-and-rule approach.[48] Greenwood has now taken the last of these arguments and elaborated on it, suggesting that Watson was motivated by institutional self-interest. After undercutting the Supreme Court of Canada's approach, the Privy Council had to be retained as an apparently objective 'honest broker'.[49]

The Watson approach was continued by his disciple, Haldane.[50] A recent interpretation has suggested that Haldane, a Liberal imperialist and ever the idealizer, allowed his political assumptions to be transferred into judicial assumptions. In particular, Wexler has argued that Haldane's experience of imperial defence led him to a natural affinity for the Provinces, since he thought that while many Canadians would support Britain militarily, Canada would not. Wexler also argues that Haldane allowed his commitment to Irish Home Rule to colour his view of provincial power.[51] Whatever the reasons for this trend, it meant that, in

---

[45] C. G. Pierson, *Canada and the Privy Council* (London, 1960), 16–21.

[46] Stevens, *Law and Politics*, 179–80.

[47] Swinfen, *Imperial Appeal* 28–9. On this, see generally W. I. Jennings, 'Constitutional Interpretation: The Experience of Canada', 51 *Harvard Law Review* (Nov. 1937), 1–39. The harshest criticism of Watson's contributions probably comes in W. F. O'Connor, *Report Pursuant to Resolution of the Senate to the Honourable the Speaker by the Parliamentary Counsel Relating to the Enactment of the British North America Act, 1867, Any Lack of Consonance between its Terms and Judicial Construction of them and Cognate Matters* (Ottawa, 1939). For a critique of the O'Connor Committee's positions, see G. P. Browne, *The Judicial Committee and the British North America Act* (Toronto, 1967), 58 ff.

[48] These different views are reviewed in F. Murray Greenwood, 'Lord Watson, Institutional Self-Interest and the Decentralization of Canadian Federalism in the 1890s', 9 *University of British Columbia Law Review* (1974), 244, 256–7.

[49] Ibid.

[50] Stevens, *Law and Politics*, 200 n. Indeed, Haldane went further than Watson and developed the theory that trade and commerce power was available to the Dominion only in an emergency.

[51] Stephen Wexler, 'The Urge to Idealize: Viscount Haldane and the Constitution of Canada', 24 *McGill Law Journal* (1984), 608–50.

the future, any tampering with the Judicial Committee immediately involved the spectre of the politics of federal–provincial relations. While the Law Lords, sitting informally as the Judicial Committee of the Privy Council in a room off Downing Street and applying the formalistic, declaratory approach of English law, settled the great crises of constitutional law in the Dominion of Canada, there is little reason to believe this group of men knew much about the political disputes they were settling. Indeed, they probably knew little of Canadian politics—few members of the British Establishment did.[52] British judges had generally not visited Canada and had a patronizing view of Canadian judges and lawyers.[53] The English legal culture, however, revolving around the mechanistic implications of the declaratory theory, regarded all that as irrelevant. Staffing the Judicial Committee of the Privy Council with technically well-trained judges was the limit of imperial responsibility.

Of a significantly different stripe was Sankey—the English judge who was to become the favourite of the Constitutionists. Sankey, who became Lord Chancellor in 1929, did make a limited effort to return some power to the Dominion government, but, more importantly, unlike Watson and Haldane, Sankey broadened Loreburn's view that a constitution was not just another statute. In reversing the Supreme Court of Canada and holding that women could be appointed to the Canadian Senate, Sankey noted that 'the British North America Act planted in Canada a living tree capable of growth and expansion within its natural limits . . . Their Lordships do not conceive it to be the duty of this Board—it is certainly not their desire—to cut down the provisions of the Act by a narrow and technical construction, but rather to give it a large and liberal interpretation.'[54] Thus, Sankey was prepared to do what Haldane had not been, and in the context of the Statute of Westminster of 1931, which was largely his creation, he allowed Canada to abolish criminal appeals. Sankey also presided in the decision that held air navigation to be exclusively within the power of the Dominion, and shortly thereafter broadcasting was held to be exclusively a federal matter.[55]

The work—both in substance and style—of Watson and Haldane was, however, strongly ingrained and the urge to preserve appeals to the Privy Council

---

[52] For an analysis of the English view of Canada, see R. G. Moyles and D. Owram, *Imperial Dreams and Colonial Realities: British Views of Canada, 1880–1914* (Toronto, 1988).

[53] See e.g. Sir Almeric Fitzroy (Clerk of the Privy Council)'s surprised description of the Canadian Chief Justice, Sir Charles Fitzpatrick: 'Fitzpatrick is much above the usual type of colonial lawyer, a man of polished manners, intelligent address and not without distinct judicial virtue.' Fitzroy, *Memoirs*, ii. 490. In turn, Fitzpatrick had an appropriately deferential approach to the 'mother country's' judiciary. He claimed that 'amongst lawyers and Judges competent to speak on the subject there is but one voice, that where constitutional questions are concerned, an appeal to the Judicial Committee must be retained.' Sir Charles Fitzpatrick, 'The Constitution of Canada', 34 *Canadian Law Review* (1914), 1031.

[54] *Edwards v Attorney-General for Canada* [1930] AC 124, 136 (PC 1929).

[55] *British Coal Corporation v The King* [1935] AC 500 (PC); *In re Regulations and Control of Aeronautics in Canada* [1932] AC 54 (PC 1931); *In re Regulation and Control of Radio Communications in Canada* [1932] AC 304 (PC).

was attractive to a wide range of British politicians. When Ramsay MacDonald lost the premiership in 1935, and Sankey, much to his discomfort,[56] ceased to be Lord Chancellor, there was a move back towards a more formalistic approach to the interpretation of the 1867 legislation. That, in a system of *stare decisis* and conventional statutory construction, inevitably meant deferring to the pro-provincial slant of Watson and Haldane. Moreover, the new Chancellor, Lord Hailsham (the father of the recent Lord Chancellor) was not above packing the Judicial Committee to ensure that there was no 'law making', something which, because the legal culture denied the relevance of judicial predisposition, was made all too easy.[57]

The results were almost inevitable. 'It is possible, though it cannot be proved, that the desire of Mr. Ramsay MacDonald in 1935 to safeguard his son's political career, and the anxiety of Lord Hailsham to leave the lower office for the more exalted and better paid position on the Woolsack—circumstances which sent Lord Sankey into retirement—invalidated a large part of the Canadian "New Deal".'[58] Thus, when Canadian Prime Minister Bennett's Conservative government passed its 'New Deal' legislation in 1934 and 1935, the Privy Council solemnly struck down vital parts of it. For those Canadians who believed the Privy Council always favoured the *laissez-faire* over the collectivist approach, the decisions were proof positive.

During November 1936 the Judicial Committee heard five related appeals, and it gave judgment on them in 1937. Lord Atkin, who presided, and who was not an admirer of the Statute of Westminster,[59] announced that, unlike Sankey's 'living tree', '[w]hile the ship of state now sails on longer ventures and into foreign waters she still retains the watertight compartments which are an essential part of her original structure'. The result of the 'watertight compartments' was that, in a single day, the Judicial Committee struck down the efforts of the Ottawa government to implement the International Labour Organization conventions by providing a minimum-wage law and by limiting hours of work,[60] as well as the unemployment and social insurance legislation,[61] and federal marketing boards.[62] Only the relatively unimportant provisions with respect to unfair trade practices survived.[63] It is probable that Lord Wright dissented in some of these cases,[64] and most believe the swing vote was the retired King's Bench judge, Mr Justice Rowlatt, who was sitting to make up the quorum. He owed

---

[56] Stevens, *Law and Politics*, 227. As part of the political settlement in 1935, Ramsay MacDonald was replaced by Stanley Baldwin. MacDonald might have negotiated the continuance of Sankey as Lord Chancellor, 'but in fact MacDonald was anxious to secure a Cabinet post for his son, Malcolm. So he jettisoned Sankey.' Heuston, *Lives of the Lord Chancellors, 1885–1940*, 527.

[57] Ibid. 531.   [58] Jennings, 'Constitutional Interpretation', 36.

[59] G. M. Lewis, *Lord Atkin* (London, 1983), 110.

[60] *Attorney-General for Canada* v *Attorney-General for Ontario* [1937] AC 326, 354 (PC).

[61] Ibid.

[62] *Attorney-General for British Columbia* v *Attorney-General for Canada* [1937] AC 405 (PC).

[63] *Attorney-General for Ontario* v *Attorney-General for Canada* [1937] AC 405 (PC).

[64] Jennings, 'Constitutional Interpretation', 36.

his Privy Councillorship to the effort to pacify the judges after the National Recovery Act crisis. It was all high irony.[65]

While some writers have recently sought to take a more sympathetic view of the decisions on the ground that the Privy Council, in general, was merely following decisions of the Supreme Court of Canada,[66] this is, in the history of the Privy Council, disingenuous. It was Watson and Haldane who had mandated the Supreme Court of Canada to depart from a pro-federal to adopt a pro-provincial stance. That court was the prisoner of the Privy Council. The dispatches from the High Commission in Ottawa made it clear that the political outrage was widespread. The decisions were given in January 1937. The High Commissioner in Ottawa sent to the Dominions Office in London, in April, a report read carefully by the Lord Chancellor's Office, that there was a 'growing body of opinion in favour of the abolition of appeals to the Privy Council'. The most outspoken critic was M. C. H. Cahan, a former Secretary of State in the Bennett Cabinet who referred, in the Canadian House of Commons debate, to 'the futile efforts of this Committee of the Privy Council of the United Kingdom to revive and reassert reactionary policies'.[67]

By 1939, Cahan had introduced a Bill to abolish appeals to London, and he received almost universal support in the press.[68] Cahan vigorously attacked the Watson tradition in the Canadian House of Commons,[69] and he again received wide support. Cahan withdrew his Bill and the Government agreed to find time for more formal discussion the following year.[70] His career was watched carefully in the Lord Chancellor's Office. Even in the grimmest days of 1940, the Permanent Secretary in the Lord Chancellor's Office, Sir Claud Schuster, took a healthy interest in the Canadian election returns, writing to a London solicitor, 'I had also noted that Mr Cahan had been defeated. I hope I am not committing an indiscretion when I say that the news gave me a considerable amount of pleasure.'[71]

---

[65] Rowlatt was, incidentally, reported as having 'sat throughout the . . . hearings in his overcoat making neither note nor comment'. B. J. MacKinnon, cited in Pannick, *The Judges*, 16.

[66] Browne, *Judicial Committee*; Swinfen, *Imperial Appeal*, 152: 'In retrospect, it is difficult to understand why the Committee's decision with respect to these acts aroused so much ill feeling in Canada.' Pierson, *Canada and the Privy Council*, 68: 'Their rulings were not only good law, but they were made impartially in the light of constitutional history.' For a balanced view, see P. Freund, *The Supreme Court of the United States: Its Business, Purposes and Performance* (Cleveland, 1961), 107–8.

[67] F. L. C. Flood to Malcolm MacDonald (Secretary for Dominion Affairs), 21 Apr. 1937, LCO 2/3465.

[68] Stephen L. Holmes (High Commission in Ottawa) to MacDonald, 22 Feb. 1938, ibid. There was an increasing amount of press support for the Cahan Bill. The *Montreal Gazette* opposed abolition but it seems to have been the only newspaper to take that position. 7 Apr. 1937, ibid.

[69] High Commissioner to MacDonald, 26 Apr. 1938, ibid.

[70] Stephen Holmes to Lord Stanley (Dominions Secretary), 2 June 1938, ibid. The Lord Chancellor (Maugham) wanted to head off the inevitable by appointing more Canadian judges. Lord Stanley, the Dominion Secretary, thought that would look bad. Stanley to Maugham, 25 July 1938, ibid.

[71] Schuster to Quintin Iwi, 1 Apr. 1940, ibid.

The UK High Commission in Ottawa knew, however, that it was only a matter of time;[72] the reprieve was temporary. The O'Connor Report of 1939, commissioned by the Canadian Senate and concluding that the Privy Council had turned a primarily centralized constitution into a strongly federal one, led to a reference to the Supreme Court of Canada with respect to the power of the Dominion to abolish all appeals to the Privy Council. In January 1940, the Supreme Court held that Canada had such power under the Statute of Westminster.[73] During the Second World War, the domestic pressure in Canada to abolish appeals was reduced, and with half a million Canadian servicemen in Britain, the time was not ripe for abolition. Few, however, thought the arrangement would survive in the post-war period. To that period we now turn.

---

[72] 'The opinion has grown notably in the last two or three years that appeals to the Privy Council in constitutional cases have not proven an advantage to Canada, but have brought great disadvantage and harm. They have resulted in the weakening of Federal authority and the magnifying of the authority of the provinces entirely contrary to the intention of the framers of Confederation. This is partly responsible for the disunity that is manifest in Canada of late.' *Winnipeg Free Press*, 24 Jan. 1939, ibid.

[73] Stevens, *Law and Politics*, 202. For a study of the reference process, see J. McEvoy, 'Separation of Powers and the Reference Power: Is there a Right to Refuse?', 10 *Supreme Court Law Review* (1988), 429–68.

5

The Era of Napier and Coldstream: Numbers, Appointment, and Control of the Judges

The period under discussion includes the Coalition government during the Second World War, when Viscount Simon was Lord Chancellor; the Labour administration from 1945 to 1951, when Earl Jowitt was Lord Chancellor; and then the Conservative administration from 1951 onwards. During the early years of the last-named administration, Viscount Simonds was Lord Chancellor, to be replaced[1] in 1954 by David Maxwell Fyfe, Earl of Kilmuir. Kilmuir survived until the 'Night of the Long Knives' in 1962. Equally important were the permanent secretaries during the period under discussion: Sir Claud Schuster, who retired in 1944; Sir Albert Napier, who held the office until 1954; and thereafter, Sir George Coldstream.

To an outsider these years (1944–68) represented one of the most turbulent periods of English politics; although to an insider, the period seemed surprisingly serene. It was a period when the country appeared, from the outside, to be redefining its goals and its purposes. Internally, especially during the Labour administrations—but under Conservative administrations as well—the political establishment was faced with the need for a serious rethinking of what the judiciary was about. It did not occur.

As we have seen, the judges had been taken, or had taken themselves, out of many sensitive areas of adjudication by the 1930s. Even in other areas, the judges were increasingly relying on a highly formalistic attitude to decision-making[2] which stressed the mechanistic approach, emphasizing their claim that they had no control over the outcome of cases—a position that made it more difficult to allege that they were influenced by political or social views. If there were any doubt, as *Liversidge* v *Anderson*[3] made clear during the Second World War, they would side with the government. The declaratory theory of law made that all the easier.

After 1945, the Radical members of the Attlee government also made it clear they would allow no 'judicial sabotage' of social legislation.[4] At a time when a

---

[1] In 1954 Churchill asked Salisbury to tell Simonds he was no longer needed. Simonds was very hurt. A. Seldon, *Churchill's Indian Summer: The Conservative Government, 1951–1955* (London, 1981).

[2] Stevens, *Law and Politics*, pt. 3.

[3] [1942] AC 206. On this, see A. W. B. Simpson, 'The Judges and their Vigilant State', *1989 Denning Law Journal*, 145–67.

[4] Put in this graphic way by Aneurin Bevan, in refusing to allow appeals from National Health Service Tribunals to the courts for fear of 'judicial sabotage'. 425 *Parliamentary Debates* (5th ser.), HC

socialist government was emphasizing centralization and planning, what role the courts should play in controlling executive decisions was a delicate one. At least in terms of control of executive discretion, in *Franklin v Minister of Town and Country Planning*[5] in 1948, the House of Lords decided that control would have to be exercised through the legislature; the courts would take no part in maintaining even procedural due process. It was an approach which was to cause concern to those who had sympathized with *The New Despotism*.[6] It seemed to them as if the country had passed under the power of the Civil Service. It was not until around 1960, after a decade of Conservative governments, that the judges began to show interest again in controlling at least procedural due process where administrative decisions were concerned.[7]

There were other important and relevant changes during this period. Partly because the judiciary was getting much larger—in 1940, there were thirty-nine Supreme Court judges; in 1960, there were fifty-four—judicial administration was no longer on quite the same intimate basis. By the 1980s, the age of Thatcherism, things had changed still further. The Courts Act of 1971 not only modernized the court system, expanding the County Court judiciary to become Circuit judges, it seemed to shake off the obsession with keeping the higher judiciary small. The Supreme Court Act of 1981 not only authorized eighty High Court judges, the number of Supreme Court (Court of Appeal and High Court) judges was close to one hundred.

As judicial administration became more formalized, there was the fascinating sight of a judiciary being run by a government department. While Lord Hewart had become excitable on this issue in the 1930s, it was only in the years after 1945 that it became accepted—at least by the public—that the judges, in most of their functions, were public servants in a way that was little different from those public servants called civil servants. The judiciary—or at least some of its members—did not see itself in these terms. The issue of status, under the guise of independence, was very much alive.

The long-term impact of nineteenth-century court reforms also meant that the judges were less independent in the functioning of the court system. In the United States, in the federal system and normally in the state systems, the courts

---

vol. 425, col. 1983 (23 July 1946). A more moderate view was put by Sir Hartley Shawcross, the Attorney-General in the Attlee Administration. He declared that it was 'a most important principle of our constitutional practice that judges do not comment on the policy of Parliament, but administer the law, good or bad, as they find it. It is a traditional doctrine on which the independence of the judiciary rests. If once that doctrine were departed from, and judges permitted themselves to ventilate from the Bench the views they might hold on the policy of the legislature, it would be quite impossible to maintain the rule that the conduct of judges is not open to criticism or question.' *Parliamentary Debates* (5th ser.), HC vol. 474, col. 1762 (3 May 1950).

[5] [1948] AC 87 (1947).

[6] e.g. Allen, *Law and Orders*; G. W. Keeton, *The Passing of Parliament* (London, 1952).

[7] Stevens, *Law and Politics*, ch. 12. In 1989, Lord Ackner suggested the turning-point for the judiciary was *Ridge v Baldwin* [1964] AC 40 (1963). See *Parliamentary Debates*, HL vol. 505, cols. 1413–14 (7 Apr. 1989).

are run by the judges, sometimes by the Chief Justice himself, more often by a court administrator who reports to the Chief Justice. In England, the administration of the courts is largely done by the Civil Service—until the Courts Act of 1971 through the Lord Chancellor's Office, the Home Office and the Treasury; thereafter primarily by the Lord Chancellor's Department. The judges had relatively little by way of patronage or administrative responsibility. While various Masters of the Rolls and Lords Chief Justice have taken a leadership role, administrative input for the English judges is largely achieved by influence, irritation, and obstruction. Jowitt was, however, able to endear himself to the judges by condemning the Haldane Society's revival of the idea of a Ministry of Justice as a 'farrago of foolishness'.[8]

(a) The Number of Judges

Turning then to what might seem to be one of the more mechanical functions of the Civil Service, the task of the Lord Chancellor's Office is to provide an adequate number of judges. It has been a recurring theme. As the period opens, the accepted wisdom was that the Bench had to be kept small.[9]

The immediate squabbles were along demarcation lines. Lord Justice Bucknill argued for more Admiralty judges as litigation arose out of the collision of the Queen Mary with a naval vessel. The London Chamber of Commerce wanted the Commercial List merged with the Admiralty Division. Mr Justice Vaisey lobbied throughout 1947 on behalf of the Chancery Division, with a refrain that sounded suspiciously like the London mob in the eighteenth century: 'Give us back our sixth judge.' Beginning with a no-doubt inspired leader in *The Times* in January, the campaign ended with the appointment of Mr Justice Harman in December.[10] By 1948 it was the turn of the Court of Appeal to feel the shortages. Cases were taking longer to hear—the Diplock Case took a month.[11] When Lord Chancellor Jowitt warned Attlee, the Prime Minister, of the precarious situation—without enough Lords Justice to staff three divisions of the Court of Appeal—he received one of many 'Dear Bill' 'Yours Clem' letters of sympathy, devoid of promises.[12] At the same time, Jowitt refused to lend the Master of

---

[8] Jowitt to Morrison, 22 Dec. 1948, LCO 2/4115.

[9] One way of doing it was to restructure the High Court. As early as 1933, Schuster was arguing that the Probate, Divorce, and Admiralty Division should be merged with the King's Bench Division: 'There is, therefore, no reason for the continuance of a Division occupied with these three classes of subjects except that it happens to exist . . . There are many reasons why such a reconsideration should result in the absorption of the Probate Divorce and Admiralty Division in one great common law division, and even in the abolition of the demarcation between the three Divisions at present existing . . .' One thought was to have three or possibly four divisions, each with its own Chief Justice. 22 Feb. 1933, LCO 2/3828.

[10] LCO 2/3829. The situation was reviewed in 1956. Mr Justice Upjohn wrote to Lord Chancellor Kilmuir hoping to derail rumours that the number of judges in the Chancery Division was to be reduced to five. Upjohn to Kilmuir, 14 Dec. 1956, LCO 2/5917. Coldstream minuted that they 'could manage with one less'. 18 Dec. 1956, ibid.

[11] *Diplock, Wintle v. Diplock* [1948] Ch. 465 (CA).   [12] 23 May 1948, LCO 2/3847.

the Rolls, Lord Evershed, one of the Lords of Appeal.[13] The Court of Appeal had to manage with two-person divisions; while the Solicitor-General argued for the need for it to sit in four divisions.[14]

For trials in the High Court, meanwhile, a different type of crisis was brewing. The way around the judicial shortage there was to use Commissioners. They were increasingly used during the late 1940s—not only in divorce cases. By 1950, Jowitt admitted to the Attorney-General, Sir Hartley Shawcross, that there was a shortage of at least six judges on the King's Bench side.[15] Goddard had already warned of being badgered by the Bar Council about the system: 'a new and rather restive Bar Council'.[16] The issue came to a head in the Highnett Case, where Mr Commissioner Clark's handling of a criminal trial shocked the Court of Criminal Appeal.[17] Shawcross warned that there was 'a general feeling we are administering a kind of second class justice'. As Labour went to the country that year, Jowitt wrote to Lord Goddard, the Chief Justice, 'On the eve of what may prove to be my departure from office', saying it was time to get rid of the Commissioner system.[18] To his surprise, Labour was returned,[19] and the number of judges was indeed raised.[20]

(b) Choosing the Judges

Many commentators have generalized about the constitutional role of the Lord Chancellor; and then 'passed by on the other side'. Yet a reading of the Office papers over the years powerfully underlines the tensions involved in the peculiar

---

[13] Evershed, MR, to Jowitt, 20 July 1949; Jowitt to Evershed, 22 July 1949, ibid. At the same time, Napier was trying to decide how many of the Lords Justice should be from the Chancery Division. In 1946, Lord Greene, MR, had argued that at least three of the nine should be; particularly since, before 1938, at least four of the six were. The argument was that Chancery judges were not only for Chancery appeals, of which there were relatively few, but were also needed for revenue appeals, about half the County Court appeals, Workmen's Compensation Act cases, and appeals from the Divisional Court. LCO 2/3845.

[14] Soskice to Jowitt, 17 Oct. 1947, LCO 2/3822.

[15] Jowitt to Shawcross, 23 Feb. 1950; 1 Mar. 1950 ('completely uncontroversial'), LCO 2/3884.

[16] Goddard to Jowitt, 22 Jan. 1947, LCO 2/3830.

[17] Shawcross to Jowitt, 21 Feb. 1950; Jowitt to Shawcross, 23 Feb. 1950. For Goddard's suggestion that Clark be made a County Court judge, but still allowed to chair Sessions, see Goddard to Jowitt, 28 Feb. 1950, LCO 2/3887. Goddard also thought Roberts and Sharpe were 'not bad' Commissioners. Ibid.

[18] Jowitt to Goddard, 21 Feb. 1950, ibid.

[19] With respect to the election Shawcross thought the result 'very unsatisfactory . . . We shall have a grueling time in the new Parliament'; and he complained to Jowitt about a bad back (28 Feb. 1950). Jowitt replied (1 Mar. 1950): 'Take the advice of a very old and very lazy man, and cut out all unnecessary work'. LCO 2/3887.

[20] The process had begun in 1944, when the number (excluding the Lord Chief Justice and the President of the Probate, Divorce, and Admiralty Division) was raised to 32. It became 33 in 1949 and 39 in 1950. Goddard observed (Goddard to Jowitt, 5 Oct. 1950): 'If I may say so, I hope you will not consider any further appointments, or at any rate unless and until date fixing comes in. A team of 24 is quite as much as I can manage to drive satisfactorily, and we have neither the courts nor the accommodation for any more judges.'

constitutional structure of the Office, especially as exemplified in the choosing of judges. Napier appeared comfortable when he told the Canadians: 'The Lord Chancellor's selection is likely to be free from political influence owing to his special position as a Judge as well as being a Bencher of an Inn and having been a Barrister with a large practice'.[21] Yet seen from the inside, the pressures were far more complex; and the concept of non-political appointments a peculiar one. American states are currently trying to escape from the excesses of the election of judges, through the so-called Missouri Plan—the concept of a Judicial Commission dominated by judges and lawyers, which is supposed to ensure judicial independence. Yet why do both English and Americans assume that success in practice is synonymous with a predictability of independence?[22] Does it ensure judicial temperament?

Lord Jowitt was proud of the fact that he, as Labour Chancellor, had appointed only non-politicians to the Bench;[23] an approach to which Lord Simonds attempted to cling. It was Lord Kilmuir, in his effort to make the Common Law relevant, who announced that once again he would take political service into account.[24] What is the relationship between political activities and independence? If political service before appointment is to be treated as irrelevant, as many British commentators suggest should be the case, this would have deprived the Supreme Court of the United States of many of its most independent judges—using independence in the sense of judges who purported to adhere to doctrine and principle rather than to the political views of their appointers.

Jowitt, perhaps more than any other Lord Chancellor, sought to build consensus for his appointments, at least among the judges. While Schuster had allowed or even encouraged 'his' Lord Chancellors some discussion with the Master of the Rolls or other senior judges, Napier allowed Jowitt to claim to consult all the judges of the division concerned about new appointments. The mechanics of this could not have been easy, and while Simonds apparently tried to continue some kind of extensive consultation, Kilmuir was more casual, leading, at least on the issue of appointing QCs, to criticism in the press.[25] From this whole

---

[21] LCO 1/5909. For a study of the selection of English judges, see S. Shetreet, *Judges on Trial: A Study in the Appointment and Accountability of the English Judiciary* (Amsterdam, 1976), ch. 3.

[22] For a traditional explanation see T. C. Hartley and J. A. G. Griffith, *Government and the Law* (2nd edn. London, 1981), 181: 'One fact that promotes the independence of the superior judiciary is that they are all drawn from the bar after successful careers as barristers, a profession which tends to foster self-confidence and independence of mind.'

[23] Stevens, *Law and Politics*, 337.

[24] Ibid. 422. Even Jowitt had a different practice in choosing QCs (silks). He explained to the new Lord President, Lord Cooper, in 1947 that 'there were no written rules although there was now a closing date'. When all the applications were in they were divided by specialties, and if the Lord Chancellor did not know the person, he enquired of the judges before whom the barrister practised. He must have a 'good reputation for honesty and fair dealing' and a 'fairly extensive practice'. He took a 'much more lenient' attitude to MPs wishing to become silks. Jowitt to Cooper, 14 Jan. 1947, LCO 2/539.

[25] On 24 Feb. 1956, the *Daily Telegraph* claimed there were 'many silks with little work or income

period, however, comes the current tradition of consulting the Master of the Rolls and the Heads of Divisions.

In terms of numbers, soon after Labour took office in 1945, Jowitt was worrying Attlee about getting appropriate judge-power in the Court of Appeal. Lord Justice Tucker had just been appointed and Lord Justice Lawrence was away in Nuremberg. There were two slots. Jowitt was concerned that no one in the Court of Appeal knew Probate, Divorce, and Admiralty work. Jowitt noted that Bucknill was 'very highly thought of at the Bar and amongst his fellow judges . . . I think myself that Asquith would do better in the Court of Appeal than at *nisi prius* . . .'[26] I have a Canadian Appeal coming in the Privy Council shortly, and I must ask Greene (Master of the Rolls) to sit in order to get a sufficiently strong court. If there is any additional power in the Court of Appeal, we shall always be thankful to make use of it either in the Privy Council or in one of the other Divisions.'[27]

Napier reported that the Master of the Rolls would be happy to see either Bucknill or Asquith appointed.[28] Asquith was an enigma. Son of a Prime Minister, his appointment to the High Court Bench in 1938 came as something of a surprise, since he was not thought to have an extensive practice. Early in 1946, Jowitt, who had been in Asquith's father's chambers, wrote again to Attlee about promoting Asquith: 'The finest mind . . . on the other hand, he has shown a complete neglect of any sense of public duty. His conduct with regard to sittings is so bad that I am deeply concerned about it.' He was using the Equal Pay Committee as an excuse for not working. 'If he were to be appointed a member of the Court of Appeal, he would be one of a team, and under the tutelage of the Master of the Rolls he might be made to do some work . . . I recognize that his promotion would be regarded by the Bench and Bar as a reward for singularly unmeritorious services. On the other hand, I believe that he still has the best brain of any of the King's Bench judges . . . I should be thankful to get rid of him from the King's Bench Division, as would many, many of the senior judges.'[29]

The other names under consideration for the Court of Appeal were Wrottesley and Birkett. Jowitt reported that Wrottesley '. . . is hardworking and eminently competent. I do not put him down as a great lawyer, but he has good

---

. . . several years have elapsed since Lord Kilmuir was in close touch with the bar . . . unlike former chancellors he has tended to make appointments without consulting either Judges or Law Officers.' In a memorandum of the same day, Coldstream called it a 'damned pack of lies', pointing out that Kilmuir consulted 29 judges and silks. Coldstream to Kilmuir, 24 Feb. 1956, LCO 2/5345.

[26] The saying at the Bar was, 'The higher he went, the better he got.'

[27] Jowitt to Attlee, 19 Nov. 1945, LCO 2/3832. Jowitt also reported that Russell was resigning as a Lord of Appeal and suggesting Greene as a replacement. Ibid. Greene was not among the four law lords appointed in 1947 (Normand, Oaksey, Morton, MacDermott). He was, however, appointed in 1949.

[28] Napier, memorandum, 19 Nov. 1945, ibid.

[29] Jowitt to Attlee, 26 Jan. 1946, LCO 2/3822.

opinions from Bench and Bar alike.' Birkett, on the other hand, 'is a man of real distinction of mind, but very junior on the list of Judges . . . He is not a great lawyer . . . but he has a good mind, has rendered distinguished public service, and is a completely conscientious person.'[30] All three eventually made it to the Court of Appeal. Asquith in that very year; and his remarkable career led Churchill to offer him the Lord Chancellorship in 1951 for the not-very-substantial reason that Churchill had served in his father's Cabinet. Asquith declined the offer and Simonds, whom Churchill had never met, was given the Great Seal.

As the number of judges slowly increased and Goddard exhibited his skill at persuading the infirm to retire, there were more judges to be appointed. Napier was not as strong a Permanent Secretary as Schuster before him or Coldstream who succeeded him, and this left the voices of influence on the Lord Chancellor as the senior judge in the Chancery Division (Vaisey) and the Lord Chief Justice, Goddard; Lord Merriman, President of the Probate, Divorce, and Admiralty Division, carried less weight. When, for instance, the sixth slot was returned to the Chancery Division in 1947, Vaisey's first choice was Danckwerts and his second, Harman; he thought Upjohn and Andrew Clark too young.[31] Harman was, in fact, appointed.

When there were vacancies on the King's Bench in 1948, Jowitt's preferences were Hubert Parker, who had 'intellectual distinction'; Slade, although it was 'a bit doubtful whether he had the necessary balance'; and Anthony Hawke, Senior Treasury Counsel at the Old Bailey.[32] Writing to Shawcross a week later Jowitt said he planned to appoint Parker—the Treasury Devil— although he still liked Ashworth ('very good') and Pearson ('first rate').[33] Parker, however, replied that, as Treasury Devil, he was 'really part of government' and that he had 'just become fully useful in the Labour government's legislative policy. Another 12–18 months should result in the solution of these problems . . . the right course [is] to complete, as it were, the work.'[34] So Austin Jones went from the Divorce Division to the King's Bench, and, after Jowitt and the Office had con-

---

[30] Jowitt to Attlee, 26 Jan. 1946, LCO 2/3822. Birkett's promotion to the Court of Appeal was slow, at least as he perceived it. In 1948 Denning—junior to Birkett—was promoted and Lynskey (also junior) was offered the job. In 1949, Birkett confronted Jowitt about being passed over. He confided to his diary: 'I can see that my advancement has been held up because of my career as an advocate, my facility in public speaking, etc., which detracts from my reputation as a lawyer pure and simple . . . .I have a mind which I can apply to any case which comes before me, and in this respect have much more judgment than either Jowitt or Simon'. In 1950, he was finally made a Lord Justice. He quoted Johnson to his diary: 'The notice which you have been pleased to take of my labour, had it been early, had been kind, but it has been delayed till I am indifferent.' In the Court of Appeal he 'found the work dull, and its dullness increased as time went on'. He was, none the less, ultimately given a peerage. H. Montgomery Hyde, *Norman Birkett* (London, 1964), 541, 544, 546.

[31] Visit of Vaisey to Napier, 8 Oct. 1947, LCO 2/3829.

[32] There was also the possibility of transferring Finnemore and Austin Jones. Jowitt to Goddard, 7 Apr. 1948, LCO 2/3830.

[33] Jowitt to Shawcross, 16 Apr. 1948, ibid.

[34] Parker to Jowitt, 7 May 1948, ibid.

sidered appointing Holroyd Pearce, QC, from the Bar, Ormrod was promoted from the County Court. Later that year, when Singleton was appointed with a US judge to the Anglo-American Committee of Inquiry on Palestine, Napier was suggesting either LeQuesne or John Morris for the King's Bench.[35]

At times, however, Goddard lobbied hard for his protégés: in 1950 he strongly urged the appointment of Robert Hull, an Official Referee—a name that had been suggested a number of times over the years.[36] Meanwhile, spurred on by the proposed increase in the size of the judiciary, and by the entreaties of Manningham-Buller (Dilhorne), Shawcross argued the case of Gilbert Beyfus, QC, although with diffidence: 'You may well think, however, that other considerations apart from his age, put him out of the running.'[37] What these 'other considerations' were, we are not told, but Goddard liked him[38] and personally chafed against the alleged Jewish quota on the bench. Perhaps, as Adamson suggests, it was the rumour that reached the Lord Chancellor's Office that, after his birthday party at the Savoy, Beyfus had climbed a pillar. Some even suggested the Office was uncomfortable with his theatrical friends, his interest in greyhound racing, and the suicide of his solicitor cousin.[39]

The papers also reveal some of the thinking about appointments of Law Lords. Northern Ireland had been protesting, since the resignation of Carson in 1929, that it ought to be represented in the Lords. When the Appellate Jurisdiction Act of 1947 added two more Law Lords, the pressure mounted. Lobbying from the Northern Ireland Bar was directed at the Home Office and favoured MacDermott.[40] As the Bill became law, Jowitt wrote to O'Neill, the Ulster Prime Minister: 'I have no means of appraising the legal skill and acumen of the Northern Ireland bench.'[41] O'Neill's reply seemed to favour MacDermott, but the letter was unclear.[42] At this point the initiative passed to the perhaps unlikely voice of Professor J. L. Montrose of Queen's University, Belfast. He advised Shawcross, if he wanted to be political, to take Andrews, although he was not as good a lawyer as either Black or MacDermott. Of these two, Black was the better lawyer and Unionist. MacDermott, however, was 'strong in [the] power of seeing the law as a dynamic system', and his mind was still developing.[43] Napier read the Home Office reports and Montrose's letter, concluding that MacDermott was 'just good enough'.[44] Jowitt recommended MacDermott to Attlee.[45]

[35] Napier memorandum, Aug. 1947, LCO 2/2832. The other possible appointee to the Palestine Inquiry was, perhaps inevitably, Radcliffe.

[36] Goddard to Jowitt, 25 Feb. 1950, LCO 2/3887.

[37] Shawcross to Jowitt, 6 June 1950, LCO 2/4228.

[38] I. Adamson, *The Old Fox* (London, 1963), 273–4.   [39] Ibid. 144–5.

[40] Home Office to Napier, 17 Feb. 1947, LCO 2/3461.

[41] Jowitt to O'Neill, 19 Feb. 1947, ibid.   [42] O'Neill to Jowitt, 11 Mar. 1947, ibid.

[43] Montrose to Shawcross 26 Feb. 1947, ibid.   [44] Memorandum, 24 Mar. 1947, ibid.

[45] In fact, after his appointment, MacDermott sat less in London than other Law Lords because the Office refused to help him with expenses during term time. Jowitt to Attlee, 15 Mar. 1947, ibid.

If, as the Office papers suggest, it is the size of practice, temperament, legal skills and personal integrity that are paramount in choosing the judges, what does an 'independent judiciary' mean and why, with a responsible executive and no Bill of Rights or fundamental laws, is one needed?[46] How does the advice of the current judges or the influence of civil servants ensure judicial independence? While these questions raise wide issues, it is important to consider the narrower one, independent of whom? The Pope? That may sound slightly ludicrous, but in November 1949, as the Parliament Bill was being rejected a second time by the Lords and Nye Bevan was threatening to resign from the Cabinet because of cuts in social services,[47] as rationing was taking on even more draconian aspects, Pius XII was causing Lord Jowitt considerable concern.[48]

On 6 November, in a speech to a Catholic lawyers' conference in Rome, the Pope appeared to say that judges of the Roman Catholic faith should not grant civil divorces. On 17 November, Jowitt took the matter up with the Cabinet. He reported that there was only one Roman Catholic judge in the Probate, Divorce, and Admiralty Division, and that judge seemed to have no difficulties with exercising the divorce jurisdiction. Jowitt suggested, however, that the Labour government appoint no further Catholic judges to that Division and require from judges of the other Divisions—King's Bench judges heard divorce cases on circuit—'a clear statement they did not regard themselves as bound by the Pope's pronouncement'. As Jowitt said in a memorandum to the Cabinet, we must feel 'absolutely confident' that judges are abiding by their judicial oaths, since it was vital that 'justice is seen to be done'.[49]

In the Cabinet, Jowitt's concern about the Church of Rome touched some sympathetic chords. Chuter Ede, the Home Secretary, with whom the Lord Chancellor enjoyed working out cricket averages, sent Jowitt a copy of *American Freedom and Catholic Power*, published by a Unitarian publishing house in Boston.

---

[46] Abel-Smith and Stevens, *In Search of Justice*, ch. 6, 'The Judges and the Law'.

[47] Kenneth Harris, *Attlee* (London, 1982), 439–41.

[48] On balance, Lord Jowitt had little faith in foreigners. When a European Convention on Human Rights was suggested, Jowitt was appalled. While it was supported by the Foreign Office team—Bevin and Younger—it was 'opposed with passionate intensity by Lord Chancellor Jowitt, by the Colonial Secretary, James Griffiths, and by the Chancellor of the Exchequer, Sir Stafford Cripps'. Jowitt (Jowitt to Dalton, 3 Aug. 1950, LCO 2/5570) thought the scheme would undermine the English judiciary: 'We are not prepared to encourage our European friends to jeopardize our whole system of law, which we have laboriously built up over the centuries, in favour of some half-baked scheme to be administered by some unknown court.' Interestingly, Evershed, Goddard, and Shawcross agreed with Jowitt. So did Sir Stafford Cripps, but for other reasons. Human Rights would provide protections inconsistent with 'powers of economic control which were essential to the operation of a planned economy'. From Jowitt's point of view: 'It completely passes the wit of man to guess what results would be arrived at by a tribunal . . . drawn from various European States possessing completely different systems of law . . . Any student of our legal institutions . . . must recoil from this document with a feeling of horror.' The same reason led Jowitt to oppose the United Nations law on Human Rights.

This footnote is drawn from A. Lester, 'Fundamental Rights: The United Kingdom Isolated?', (Spring, 1984) *Public Law*, 46–72.

[49] CM (49), 17 Nov. 1949, LCO 2/4228.

Returned with the book three weeks later was a letter from Jowitt marked 'secret': 'I confess whilst not being in any sense an embittered Protestant that I cannot understand and have no sympathy with the Catholic point of view.' The pronouncement of the Bodily Assumption of the Virgin Mary 'fills me with despondency'. The result was that 'My own inclination for the time being is to try to avoid the appointment of Catholic judges.'[50] Ede responded that 'Like you, although brought up a Protestant, I have no feeling of bitterness on the religious issue. The recent pronouncement with regard to the duty of Catholic judges', however, gave him 'grave misgiving'. It was, indeed, 'Jesuitical'.[51]

Jowitt, however, was moving on the diplomatic front. He wrote directly to the British Minister to the Holy See, J.V.T.L.T. Perowne. Jowitt was anxious to know 'the extent to which [the Pope's] remarks could be regarded as binding upon members of his faith'. With what would seem some naïveté about Catholic doctrine, Jowitt asked, was the 'Pope's statement made *ex cathedra*?' It was a 'serious' problem since Greene, Lynskey, and Wallington were Roman Catholics. 'Our public is deeply disturbed.' J. S. Sumner Cocks of the British Legation talked to persons in the Rota and Holy Office and reported that only if the judge knew the parties were validly married in the eyes of God must he refuse to divorce them. The judge was under no obligation to inquire about this; at the same time the judge must be 'absolutely certain' that the parties 'had indeed been married in the eyes of God', and therefore this problem would occur rarely. Moreover the Pope had been talking about Italy, not the United Kingdom. Understandably Jowitt found the report 'very far from satisfactory. I can find nothing to allay misgivings which have been aroused by the earlier pronouncement.' In his secret letter to the British Minister he confided, 'I must soft-pedal on my appointment of Catholics, and for the time being I shall not appoint them without laying down a hard and fast rule which would cover myself for the future.'[52]

The Foreign Secretary, Ernest Bevin, had tried to cool Jowitt in the Cabinet and the Minister in the Vatican had obviously shared with the Foreign Office the Lord Chancellor's correspondence. In May 1950, Kenneth Younger, Minister at the Foreign Office, wrote to the Chancellor saying that the Foreign Secretary hoped there would be no ban on Catholic judges, while conceding the Pope's words were 'undeniably unsatisfactory'. The attached Foreign Office brief raised the jurisprudential (or theological) question: are Roman Catholic judges 'less independent than before' as a result of the Pope's remarks? The Foreign Office felt the Pope was talking about the Eastern Bloc, or possibly Italy, but he was certainly not thinking of the *status quo*.[53] Jowitt was not swayed by the honeyed words of the Foreign Office. The most he would say was that he hoped that he would not have to ban Catholics since he was currently thinking of appointing

[50] Jowitt to Ede, 1949, ibid.
[52] Jowitt to Perowne, 5 Dec. 1949, ibid.
[51] Ede to Jowitt, 13 Dec. 1949, ibid.
[53] Younger to Jowitt, 8 May 1950, ibid.

Robert Hull and Redmond Barry to the High Court Bench.[54] With perhaps a note of panic Younger urged Jowitt to go to see the Roman Catholic Archbishop of Westminster, since the Apostolic Delegate to England was ill.[55]

In fact, Jowitt wrote to Godfrey, telling him it was a matter of 'extreme urgency'. Under the new Act he was about to appoint a group of High Court judges and none of them would be Catholics unless he received satisfaction. This would be a pity, for 'Among the very short list of possible candidates is a well known and greatly esteemed KC of the Roman Catholic persuasion.'[56] The lines to Rome obviously hummed. Ten days later Godfrey reported: 'It can be stated that, leaving aside the question of the marriage-bond as it is before God and conscience, a Catholic judge can apply the civil law of divorce as it now stands in this realm.'[57] Ede complained 'at this method of obtaining a pronouncement on RC views'; but Barry was appointed to the Bench.[58] Meanwhile, Jowitt boasted to Ede that he had forced the Apostolic Delegate into a 'complete backdown'.[59]

Jowitt certainly took the marriage vow seriously. Indeed, *culpa in eligendo uxoris* was apparently inimical to independence. In 1947, two Chancery judges (Wynn-Parry and Romer) complained that they were not invited to garden parties at Buckingham Palace. The Lord Chamberlain's staff explained that they had both been guilty parties in divorce cases. Jowitt was shocked to discover this. He could explain Romer, who had been appointed by Lord Chancellor Maugham, but Jowitt himself had appointed Wynn-Parry. As the Lord Chancellor explained to the Lord Chamberlain, *Who's Who* did not reveal the vital information about a broken marriage, 'and it never occurred to me to ask him whether this had happened. If I had known it I do not say I should have regarded it as an absolute bar, but I would certainly have regarded it as a point which held very strongly against his appointment . . . I now ask every judge whom I have to appoint, "Is there anything about your private life you think you ought to tell me."'[60]

(c) Controlling the Judges

Independence is sometimes associated with tenure; but even here the law in action is more complex than the theory. In the 1940s and 1950s, for instance, there was a need for an internal early retirement programme, since the judiciary

---

[54] Jowitt to Younger, n.d., ibid.   [55] Younger to Jowitt, 22 May 1950, ibid.

[56] Jowitt to Godfrey, 23 May 1950, ibid.   [57] Godfrey to Jowitt, 31 May 1951, ibid.

[58] A note in the file from Napier said that when Barry was appointed he was shown the letter from the Apostolic Delegate. 9 July 1950, ibid.

[59] Jowitt to Ede, June 1950, ibid.

[60] Jowitt to Lord Chamberlain, 11 July 1947, LCO 2/4618. The matter was still worrying Jowitt's successor, Simonds, at least with respect to QCs. 'This is a matter in which the decision must to some extent depend on local conditions. But it is, I think, a matter of principle that a journey through the Divorce Court should not *ipso facto* be a bar to recommendation for silk.' Simonds to Napier, 29 Nov. 1953, LCO 2/5341.

had always opposed a mandatory retirement age. It was not until the Judicial Pensions Act of 1959 that a retirement age (of 75) was set for future High Court judges. No doubt there were many pressures for the change; and one can certainly sympathize with Lord Chancellors, their Permanent Secretaries, and Lords Chief Justice as they struggled to ease out those who were past their prime. Mr Justice Humphreys, whom Jowitt called a 'Grand Old Warhorse'[61] in 1947, went downhill. In 1950, the Chancellor wrote to the Chief Justice: 'I do feel the time has come when old Humphreys ought to go . . . I think it is a pity he should stay on when he is no longer quite as good as he was. But there is nothing I can do about it, and I do not suppose there is anything you can do about it either.'[62]

In 1947 the Chief's report to the Chancellor sounded like a list of walking wounded. Birkett was ill; and 'I do not think Croom-Johnson looks well'. 'I wrote to' Mr Justice Charles—a judge whose appointment Sir Claud Schuster as Permanent Secretary had opposed—'as nice a letter as I could, suggesting it might be in the interests of his health if he retired, but he hopes to continue . . .'. As early as 1942, Mr Justice Birkett described going on circuit with Mr Justice Charles. He 'smokes in the [assize] procession', 'belched from beer' in his assize sermon, and in Birkett's view Charles was 'a domineering, vulgar, unjust and decrepit old man, who is a blot on the administration of justice'.[63] The problem was somewhat different with Macnaghten, whom wags claimed had reached the High Court *per stirpes* rather than *per capita*, and whose most distinguished role on the Bench had been as a critic in the judicial salary dispute. 'I told him quite frankly,' wrote Goddard, 'that I thought his deafness, which had obviously increased, was such a handicap that retirement was desirable.'[64]

Of Charles and Macnaghten, Jowitt responded: 'You will be an even cleverer manager than I believe you to be if you can ever get either of them to resign.'[65] Were they independent—judicially? Charles, in fact, went the next month, while Macnaghten lobbied to be allowed to take the Liverpool and Manchester assizes—where his wife had family—meanwhile himself lobbying for Andrews to be a Northern Irish Lord of Appeal.[66] The Lord Chancellor capitulated—at least on the former issue: 'After all, he's a dear old (tho' a deaf old) thing.'[67] Jowitt and Goddard could both, however, take heart from the fact that by the spring of 1948, Mr Justice Atkinson and Lord Justice Wrottesley seemed ready to retire.

The Lord Chancellor's Office also had responsibilities of a schoolmasterly nature, which in another sense undercut notions of independence. Sometimes the boys had to be disciplined, sometimes prevented from fighting with one

---

[61] Jowitt to Goddard, 15 Apr. 1947, LCO 2/3830. Earlier in the year, while sick, he had been reported as anxious to get back to the Chalk Pit Murder. Jowitt to Goddard, 24 Feb. 1947, ibid.

[62] Jowitt to Goddard, 5 Oct. 1950, LCO 2/3889. He eventually retired at the age of 83.

[63] H. Montgomery Hyde, 'Diary of a Judge', *The Sunday Times*, 7 Apr. 1963. When Charles died in 1950, *The Times* obituary described him as 'the embodiment of genial good sense and straight dealing'. *The Times*, 4 May 1950.

[64] Goddard to Jowitt, 15 Jan. 1947, LCO 2/3830.

[65] Jowitt to Goddard, 15 Jan. 1947, ibid.

[66] Goddard to Jowitt, 23 Feb. 1947, ibid.

[67] Jowitt to Goddard, 24 Feb. 1947, ibid.

another, and sometimes to have their egos soothed. Generally serious waggings were reserved for the County Court—the civil servants drafted lectures to be sent to these judges. Lord Simonds, however, was prepared to dress down High Court judges.[68]

When Mr Justice Lloyd-Jacob wrote a somewhat confused letter to *The Times* about the peaceful uses of atomic power, urging all nations to punish other nations which used the hydrogen bomb,[69] Lord Hailsham, QC, who was to serve as Lord Chancellor during the 1970s and 1980s, was beside himself at the prospect of a High Court judge expressing himself publicly 'in the realm of controversial politics'. Hailsham wrote a vigorous letter to the Lord Chancellor.[70] In turn, Simonds minced no words in writing to Lloyd-Jacob:

I thought it (the letter) would be regarded as a deplorable incursion by a High Court judge into a realm of controversial politics, as indeed it is . . . A judge ought not to express his views in public on matters which are either political or controversial, and the subject-matter of your letter is both. In my opinion it was a breach of your duty as a judge to write the letter, and I am deeply sorry that you wrote it.[71]

Poor Lloyd-Jacob. His response was heartfelt:

I wrote it as a Christian, to my fellow Christians, with no thought of politics or controversy, believing that our nation is specifically entrusted with a duty of Christian leadership, desiring only that guidance might be given to us to live our lives aright and hoping that Convocation would lead us towards truth . . . I greatly regret that I so grievously misapprehended the scope of current political controversy. I did not suppose that any fellow countryman of mine of standing and knowledge would advocate treating atomic warfare as less reprehensible than gas or bacteriological warfare . . . to know that I have caused you worry and embarrassment is a wretched burden . . .[72]

Yet Kilmuir was prepared to be tougher than Simonds. 'After Mr Justice Hallett had been criticized for asking too many questions, Lord Kilmuir, the Lord Chancellor, sent for the Judge. It was arranged that he should continue to sit for a little while and then resign. That he did at the end of the summer term.'[73]

It is clear from reading the archives over the last one hundred years that County Court and now Circuit Court judges have continued to be treated with rather less deference than High Court judges. They have been removed without any constitutional fanfare. Before the establishment of the Top Salaries Committee, High Court judges were more humoured about their salaries than County Court judges.[74] Egos of High Court judges also received a more exten-

[68] For earlier efforts attempting to dress down Mr Justice McCardie for his remarks in a libel case arising out of the Amritsar Massacre, see LCO 2/961. McCardie was not repentant.

[69] *The Times*, 11 May 1954.   [70] Hailsham to Simonds, 14 May 1954, LCO 2/5923.

[71] Simonds to Lloyd-Jacob, 18 May 1954, ibid.   [72] 19 May 1954, ibid.

[73] Pannick, *The Judges*, 90, citing Lord Denning.

[74] For the County Court position, see e.g. LCO 12/54; for contrast, see e.g. LCO 2/3881, dealing with the High Court. Both deal with the post-1945 period. For the earlier period, see Ch. 3 above.

sive massage than those of the County Court. When a Soviet magazine criticized Mr Justice Birkett as 'the favourite judge of Lord Haw Haw',[75] there was talk of libel and contempt proceedings against Colletts, the bookstore which stocked the magazine. Napier wrote to the Foreign Office, which consulted the British Ambassador to Moscow, and (via Sir Alexander Cadogan) replied, 'Her Majesty's Ambassador does not think a protest to the Soviet Government would be effective.' Napier, however, insisted the protest be made.[76] When, however, in 1950, *Truth* opined that 'those appointed to the County Court bench seldom have very much, and not infrequently very little, work at the bar', a remark which led to a formal protest to the Office from the County Court Judges Association, Coldstream was cool: 'I showed the *Truth* paragraph to the Lord Chancellor, but he does not seem to have been so violently affected as the Judges at your meeting, and as a matter of fact, it did not appear to me quite as violent as I had expected.' The County Court judges were not pleased with the response.[77]

A similar dichotomy applied when resignations or reprimands were at issue. Judge Gaman provides a useful precedent. The good County Court judge, hearing undefended divorces in 1952, was particularly shocked by a case in which a woman had left her husband and had committed adultery at her mother's house. Indeed the judge was so outraged, that he opined, in a quote picked up by the press, 'the morals of West Hartlepool seem to be lower than any other place in the country.' The Mayor and Town Council of that Borough were outraged and the matter was not helped when Gaman explained that he was referring only to the 'bottom section' of inhabitants. Gaman, a product of Harrow and Oxford, apparently meant the lower classes[78] (although he later said he really meant the least moral), but unfortunately there was an area of West Hartlepool known as the Bottom Section, and its inhabitants—and the Town Clerk, the Boys Brigade, and the Salvation Army—were beside themselves.

The Mayor and Town Clerk wrote to the Lord Chancellor. Rieu, head of the County Court Division, asked for an explanation. Gaman explained that he was concerned about the 'moral laxity' and the 'attitude of women as well as men toward the marriage bonds. The restraining influence which such public opinion commonly exerts elsewhere seems to be largely lacking in West Hartlepool.' At the same time the Judge complained it was 'not fair of the paper to fasten on the quoted words'.[79] The Lord Chancellor's Office was not amused. 'No record of any previous complaint,' minuted Coldstream. The judge wrote a letter of apology to the Mayor. Both Coldstream and Lord Simonds said that was not

[75] 5 Aug. 1945, LCO 2/2967.

[76] 27 Sept. 1945, ibid.

[77] LCO 12/57.

[78] What the judge appears to have said was that 'Moral standards at the bottom end of the scale are a good deal higher on the average in Darlington, Stockton, Middlesbrough and the Durham mining areas than they are in West Hartlepool.' Gaman to Rieu, 1 Feb. 1952, LCO 12/76.

[79] Gaman to Rieu, 31 Jan. 1952, ibid.

sufficient,[80] and Gaman was required to apologize in open court.[81] Similar reprimands were meted out to other County Court judges who attracted unwelcome publicity,[82] and finally, in 1962, Coldstream sat down with them and told them exactly what they were entitled to say publicly.

(d) The Executive and the Judiciary

It is not possible, however, to write about this period or these issues without talking of the relations between the Office and the rising judicial star of the period, Sir Alfred Denning. He first came to the fore with his *Report on Divorce Jurisdiction*,[83] which led to the transfer of undefended divorce to the County Court judges, sitting as Special Commissioners.[84] The Report was bitterly opposed by the judges of the Probate, Divorce, and Admiralty Division, and especially by its President, Lord Merriman. Merriman complained that Denning had followed the recommendations of the Solicitors' Managing Clerks Association which were 'rubbish'.[85] George Coldstream, then the Deputy Permanent Secretary, warned that the President was on the verge of a breakdown.[86] Jowitt saw Merriman and warned him that the Cabinet backed Denning's plan. 'I found him ruffled, . . . and as you and I know, the President when ruffled is a bit of a handful.'[87] The President and the Divisional judges continued to obstruct both the jurisdictional and procedural changes, but ultimately most of the government's views prevailed.[88]

Relations between Merriman and Denning, however, remained cool. In January 1947, Jowitt wrote to Goddard about circuit arrangements:

Denning asks me if I can make any arrangement which will relieve him of meeting the President at Cardiff. He is so upset with Denning's report that relations between the two

---

[80] Lord Simonds said: 'Judge Gaman should apologise publicly. Nothing else will meet the case', ibid. He then signed a letter, drafted by Coldstream, dated 4 Feb. 1952.

[81] See *Northern Echo*, 14 Feb. 1952, ibid.

[82] See e.g the case of Judge Ingram Bell who wrote to *The Times* signing the letter 'A County Court Judge', arguing that part of the judge's salary should be tax free. LCO 12/78.

[83] *Committee on Procedure in Matrimonial Causes: Final Report*, Cmd. 7024 (1946).

[84] *Committee on Procedure in Matrimonial Causes: Interim Report*, Cmd. 6945 (1945).

[85] Memorandum, Coldstream to Napier, 26 Nov. 1946, LCO 2/3957. Denning observed: 'Thank goodness I did Divorce for only 18 months.' Lord Denning, *The Due Process of Law* (London, 1980), 189.

[86] 'Highly Confidential', Coldstream to Jowitt, 24 Oct. 1946, describing a 'somewhat painful' meeting with the President. 'Allowing for the fact that the President is highly strung, there is no question that his nerves are not in a state to undertake the kind of battle to which he now looks forward.' LCO 2/3951. For background see also Merriman to Jowitt, 4 Nov. 1946: 'In the past my ideas of the proper conduct of divorce cases has been attacked and ridiculed by certain of my superiors, not to mention my inferiors, in the judicial hierarchy of the Bench, in the House of Lords, and even in Press articles, and I have kept silent.' He warned, presciently, that the change would mean that the demand for solicitors' rights of audience could not be resisted, and there were 'dreadful examples . . . of the lengths to which some solicitors have been prepared to go in deceiving Counsel and the Court'. Ibid.

[87] Jowitt to Goddard, 7 Nov. 1946, ibid.   [88] See Ch. 6 below.

are very strained. This is in no way Denning's fault but apparently he had a meeting with Merriman lately at which the latter spoke in a way which makes Denning feel that living with him at Cardiff will be practically impossible.[89]

Goddard performed a sleight of hand; Jowitt commented that it was 'childish and deplorable tho' I can well understand Denning's point of view'.

A couple of years later, however, Denning began to fall out of favour, with the publication of his book of lectures, *Freedom under the Law*. Boggis-Rolfe in the Lord Chancellor's Office produced a list of 'errors' in the book, while Coldstream minuted that 'Denning J is wholly ignorant of the mechanism of administrative government.'[90] Jowitt wrote a personal letter to Denning. 'I always hold my thumbs, as the children say, when I hear that a judge has written a book and I am old-fashioned enough to think that the less they write the better.'[91] (It is little wonder the English judges have added little to jurisprudential debates.) Jowitt saw two dangers—that principles might be stated too broadly (for instance, Denning's comments on National Health Service liability) and that books might be 'controversial'. Denning did not fold as Lloyd-Jacob was to before Simonds, although he admitted that 'it grieves me much that you should find I have been at fault.' Denning, however, defended his remarks about the NHS; and as for his comments on appeals from tribunals, Denning, mimicking some of the views he was later to have about contracts, argued that this was so 'fundamental' that it was 'outside the realm of party politics'.[92] Denning's views about independence were different. Jowitt, however, continued to warn that 'One cannot be too careful about these things.'[93]

Jowitt's successor, Lord Simonds, was a good deal more careful with Lord Denning, as he by then had become. Not only were there spats between the two in both court and legislature,[94] but behind the scenes it was clear Simonds did

---

[89] 15 Jan. 1947, LCO 2/3830.

[90] Coldstream thought Denning did not understand that civil servants frequently disagreed with their ministers; and Ministers and officials who were in danger of exceeding their powers were frequently restrained by lawyers in the Department, although 'the quality of the legal Civil Service is admittedly exceedingly uneven'. LCO 2/4617.

[91] 7 Dec. 1949, ibid.　　　[92] 12 Dec. 1949, ibid.

[93] 13 Dec. 1949. Jowitt added: 'I congratulate myself on realizing that sitting in the Divisional Court you used to be wasting your sweetness on the desert air', a reference to his promotion to the Court of Appeal in 1948. Ibid.

[94] Simonds, as the High Priest of substantive formalism, clashed frequently with Denning. When Denning sought to embrace the mischief rule of interpretation and suggested that appeal courts should look to the purpose of legislation when a lacuna was discovered, Simonds was beside himself: 'The part which is played in the judicial interpretation of a statute by reference to the circumstances of its passing is too well known to need restatement: it is sufficient to say that the general proposition that it is the duty of the court to find out the intention of Parliament—and not only of Parliament but of Ministers also—cannot by any means be supported. The duty of the court is to interpret the words that the legislature has used; those words may be ambiguous, but, even if they are, the power and duty of the court to travel outside them on a voyage of discovery are strictly limited . . . What the legislature has not written, the court must not write. This proposition, which restates in a new form the view expressed by the Lord Justice . . . cannot be supported. It appears to me to be a naked usurpation of the legislative function under the thin disguise of interpretation. And it is the less

not trust Denning's judgment. It is true that when Fisher, the Archbishop of Canterbury, wrote to say he had been told he should have a judge to chair the Committee on Laity Representation in Convocation and he thought Denning would be right ('keen Churchman . . . he may be a little impetuous . . . a keen reformer'), Simonds replied 'I can think of no judge better than Denning.'[95] In matters of state, however, more delicate issues were at stake.

When the Foreign Office asked the Lord Chancellor's Office for a judge who might write an article for the *United Nations Yearbook on Human Rights*, Denis Dobson at the Lord Chancellor's Office suggested Denning. His superior, Coldstream, noted, 'Denning LJ might well be approached . . . but perhaps you should get specific authority from the Lord Chancellor.' Lord Simonds and Sir Frank Newsam, the Permanent Secretary at the Home Office, did not think Denning was a good idea; so Birkett, for whom the Lord Chancellor's Office had done a number of favours in the foreign field, was substituted. As Hoare at the Home Office wrote to Dobson: 'There is little likelihood of any contribution by Lord Justice Birkett going off the rails; and if it does, in some particular aspect, our relations with the judge are such that we should have no difficulty in asking him to reconsider some particular passage.'

The Foreign Office had set out by proudly proclaiming that, unlike other contributions in the *Yearbook*, the British contribution was 'independent of government'. Inroads were, however, appearing. Dobson wrote to Birkett saying the article should be 'objective in tone', but it should be tactful.[96] At this point, however, the Colonial Office began to be nervous, since a Colonial judge serving in Malaya—Terrell—had recently been held to be in the position of a civil servant rather than a judge and there was a fear he might appeal. Sir Kenneth Roberts-Wray, Legal Adviser at the Colonial Office, urged that Birkett should

---

justifiable when it is guess work with what material the legislature would, if it had discovered the gap, have filled it in. If a gap is disclosed, the remedy lies in an amending Act.' *Magor & St Mellons RDC v Newport Corp.* [1952] AC 189, 191 (1951).

It was also Denning, in one of his moves to expand the rights of third-party beneficiaries, who spurred Simonds to a vigorous restatement of the role of the House in common law appeals: 'For to me heterodoxy, or, as some might say, heresy, is not the more attractive because it is dignified by the name of reform. Nor will I easily be led by an undiscerning zeal for some abstract kind of justice to ignore our first duty, which is to administer justice according to law, the law which is established for us by Act of Parliament or the binding authority of precedent. The law is developed by the application of old principles to new circumstances. Therein lies its genius. Its reform by the abrogation of these principles is the task not of the courts of law but of Parliament. . . . I would cast no doubt upon the doctrine of stare decisis, without which law is at hazard.' *Midlands Silicones, Ltd. v Scruttons, Ltd.* [1962] AC 446, 467–9 (1961).

[95] Simonds to Fisher, 3 Dec. 1953. Jowitt had lent Mr Justice Lloyd-Jacob for the Committee on Ecclesiastical Courts, LCO 2/5912.

[96] 'While it is natural to suppose that a fair-minded reader of such an article would be led to the conclusion that the independence of the judiciary is far better safeguarded in this country than in some others, the Foreign Office, who are responsible for submitting the article to the UNO, are anxious that it should avoid direct comparisons with the systems prevailing in other countries.' LCO 2/5911.

not deal with removal other than by Parliament;[97] Dobson put it to the judge rather differently: 'in the present circumstances you will probably think it better not to make any reference to the Colonial judiciary.'[98] When Birkett sent in the paper, the Home Office was comfortable; Sir Kenneth Roberts-Wray was still nervous. The *Terrell* case[99] had decided that the Act of Settlement did not apply in Malaya, and Roberts-Wray produced a rather long and tortured page on the subject.[100] Birkett was warned that the Colonial Office would be adding a long footnote. Ever gracious, Birkett incorporated the Colonial Office reservation as part of his own text and was rewarded by a letter from Selwyn Lloyd, the Foreign Secretary, thanking him for the article: 'it will . . . bring home to its readers that the United Kingdom and its Colonies possess one of the most precious of Human Rights, a really independent judiciary.'[101]

There are further surprises in the Lord Chancellor's Office papers—even after the warning about the English absence of any natural inclination towards the separation of powers.[102] The Lord Chief Justice was actively lobbied by the Lord Chancellor and Attorney-General on judicial policy. In 1947 Jowitt wrote to Goddard, who had been appointed Lord Chief Justice early in the Attlee administration and was developing a reputation as a 'strong judge':[103] 'I do sincerely hope that the judges will not be lenient to these bandits [who] carry arms [to] shoot at the police . . . I may be written down as a Colonel Blimp, but you know I do take the view, which I think you share, that we have got rather soft and woolly in dealing with really serious crime.'[104] In the light of what is now known about Lord Goddard, there was little danger of this urging falling on deaf ears. Two years later, Lord Goddard sentenced Derek Bentley to hang.[105]

In 1950 Shawcross, the Attorney-General, was more specific, although in a more liberal direction. When the Court of Criminal Appeal decided that, unless counsel intended to call the accused, cross-examination of the police might not include questions on how the confession was obtained, the Attorney-General complained to the Chief Justice. Goddard agreed that the Court, composed of judges in his division, had gone too far and promised to raise the matter at the Council of Judges, the annual or semi-annual meeting of High Court judges.[106]

[97] Dobson to Birkett, 24 June 1953, LCO 2/5911.
[98] 30 June 1953, ibid.
[99] *Terrell* v *Secretary of State for the Colonies* [1953] QB 482.
[100] Roberts-Wray to Theisiger, 24 Oct. 1953, LCO 2/5811.   [101] Ibid.
[102] In the Attlee administration, the Law Officers and the Lord Chancellor had problems of communication, and even in 1950 were still trying to ensure that the Lord Chancellor would be informed before important legal issues were referred to Cabinet by the Attorney-General. There had apparently been several instances of failures to inform. The problem was solved by the Lord Chancellor being furnished with opinions of the Law Officers, apparently for the first time. Shawcross to Attlee, 19 Apr. 1950, LCO 2/3633. See also LCO 2/4309.
[103] Ibid.
[104] LCO 2/3830.
[105] David Yallop, *To Encourage the Others* (London, 1971), *passim*.

Such pressures exist in the United States; they would—ideally at least—be exercised in a more circumspect way. Certainly these incidents throw an interesting light on the complacency of the position of Professor John Griffith:

In spite of the reduced political role of the courts in Britain, it is still of the greatest importance for the judiciary to be independent of the Government. This is one aspect of the doctrine of the separation of powers that is accepted in the British constitution. The reasons for this are obvious: the principles of the rule of law and equality before the law demand that justice should be administered impartially—'without fear and favour'—and this would be jeopardized if the courts were, as is the case in most one-party regimes, subject to pressure by the Government.[107]

In these exchanges did the separation of powers exist; were the judges independent? The answer needs careful unpacking. The nature of English government is such that overt pressures on the judges are rarely observed. Covert pressures are more common. The Jowitt–Shawcross–Goddard interaction reflects one level. The urging of judges to be 'tough' and the judicial assumptions about the probity of the police are symbiotic relationships at this level. The English system, however, can put English judges more obviously in the political vortex when their responsibilities are moved outside the regular courts. To this issue we now turn.

---

[106] Shawcross to Jowitt, 19 Apr. 1950, LCO 2/6672. For another example of civil servants trying to correct the errors of the courts, see the complaint by Judge Maude at the Old Bailey, concerned about the way his leniency in a bigamy case had been handled by the Court of Criminal Appeal: 'What I guess must have happened was that, as it wasn't Jimmy Cassels particular case, he had not digested the matter and that when Goddard took it out of Gorman's hands and made a mess of it, Gorman hadn't got the courage to put it right.' Coldstream minuted: 'It is quite clear the Lord Chief Justice went right off the rails.' LCO 2/5102.

[107] Hartley and Griffith, *Government and the Law*, 175.

6

The Era of Napier and Coldstream: The Use of the Judiciary

(a) The Uses of Ignorance, Impartiality, and Independence

Independence of the judiciary is often used to signify, from a public service point of view, impartiality and, from a constitutional viewpoint, an absence of discretion. This latter notion was revitalized by Dicey into the idea of individual judges being free of control by executive and legislative. This Anglicized view of the Rule of Law, together with the long tradition of politicians accepting the declaratory theory of law meant that English judges were accorded a high rating on any independence scale. Such a political asset, however, was always prone to be misused by politicians. The right of the executive to use a judge outside his regular duties is regarded as a delicate one in the United States. Many thought it wrong for Justice Jackson to be involved at Nuremberg, and even worse for Chief Justice Warren to chair the Commission investigating the Kennedy assassination. The absence of any vigorous commitment to the separation of powers has made such assumptions rather vaguer within the British constitution. Judges have always been summoned to the opening of Parliament and indeed still are. Private Bills were referred to them for advice in the eighteenth century; although, after it became possible in 1833 to refer matters to the Judicial Committee of the Privy Council for advisory opinions, it was assumed that judges would be spared undertaking executive chores. For a while that was borne out by political history.

Until well into this century the Houses of Parliament behaved much like the US Congress, which basically uses the committee system to investigate controversial issues and to develop policies. As late as the Marconi Scandal[1] in 1914, the investigation was carried out by House of Commons' committees. As the English courts and judges were seen to be less an element in the political process and rather to be 'above politics', the use of judges—and some would say the misuse of judicial independence and impartiality—developed rapidly.[2] As the courts were increasingly excluded from many areas of social legislation and as the importance of political connections declined as a basis for judicial appointments,

---

[1] G. R. Searle, *Corruption in British Politics, 1895–1930* (Oxford, 1987), ch. 8.

[2] It is arguable that, in the last decade, there has been something of a reversal of the trend in the sense that the House of Commons' Committees have become increasingly active. Indeed, in some areas, there could even be the possibility of conflict between legislative and judicial inquiries. For instance, in 1991, the collapse of BCCI was being investigated both by the Treasury Committee of the House of Commons and a Committee chaired by Lord Justice Bingham.

the temptation to push the independent and impartial judge outside the courts
was increased. The first serious use of judges in this way had been the special Act
of Parliament to investigate the Parnell Forgeries in 1888. The process gradually
accelerated, although until the First World War, judges were generally used to
chair technical committees and commissions.

The trend was accelerated by statute; the Tribunals of Inquiry Act of 1921
stimulated the use of judges to investigate specific incidents.[3] Already the Royal
Commission on the Coal Industry (1919) trumpeted the way for a rather
different political role for the judges; for here was a Chancery judge (Sankey)
concluding that 'the present system of ownership and working in the coal industry stands condemned, and some other system must be substituted for it, either
nationalization or a method of unification by national purchase and/or joint
control.'[4] The conclusions made it logical to bring Sankey into the second
Labour Government as Lord Chancellor.

Between 1945 and 1965 over a third of Royal Commissions and Departmental
Committees were chaired by judges; and if practising lawyers are included the
percentage rises to almost a half. It was the era of consensus politics, or, as Sir
Alan Herbert somewhat uncharitably suggested, 'government by Radcliffery'—in
honour of Cyril Radcliffe and the extensive use of his judicial talent to chair
committees.[5] In the Jowitt years there appears to have been little by way of
complaint about the use of the judges—at least at a philosophical or political
level. The issue was generally addressed at a housekeeping level. The files are
replete with requests from Lord Greene, the Master of the Rolls, to the
Chancellor, pleading a shortage of judges in the Court of Appeal and requesting
that Evershed and Cohen be released from chairing their Commissions.[6] Or the
Chancellor would be found writing to the Prime Minister complaining of a
shortage of Lords of Appeal because Oaksey had been siphoned off for 'the
Police Enquiry'.[7]

It was not that the politicians or civil servants were unaware of what they
were doing. The Civil Service voice was clear as Sir William Armstrong, permanent secretary at the Treasury, wrote in the summer of 1950 to Boggis-Rolfe at
the Lord Chancellor's Office, explaining that the Chancellor of the Exchequer
wanted a Royal Commission on Taxation. It was 'essential to have a strong
Chairman of acknowledged impartiality and high intellectual ability. This suggests irrestibly to him the appointment of a judge, preferably one with revenue

---

[3] See generally, memorandum from Theisiger to Coldstream, 2 Jan. 1952, LCO 2/5904.

[4] Cmnd. 359 (1919), Recommendation 9. See also Heuston, *Lives of the Lord Chancellors,
1885–1940*, 504–5; C. L. Mowat, *Britain between the Wars, 1918–1940* (London, 1962), 31 f.

[5] T. J. Cartwright, *Royal Commissions and Departmental Committees in Britain* (London, 1975), 69.
For details of the commissions and committees see ibid., app. B. For a generally critical view, see
Griffith, *Politics of the Judiciary*, ch 2. For a recent popular view, see J. Paxman, *Friends in High Places:
Who Runs Britain?* (London, 1990), ch. 4.

[6] Greene to Jowitt, 13 May 1948, LCO 2/3847.   [7] Jowitt to Attlee, May 1948, ibid.

or commercial experience.'[8] Boggis-Rolfe sent on this advice to Coldstream and the Chancellor: 'Apart from the time the Chairmanship would require, the inquiry is essentially of a political nature'; he nevertheless recommended that a judge be spared.[9] There then followed a marvellous 'hash session' at which the virtues and vices of various of Her Majesty's judges were noted;[10] from a jurisprudential point of view, particularly interesting was Jowitt's observation to Sir Stafford Cripps, Chancellor of the Exchequer, that Donovan would be excellent, 'but he has been so recently appointed that I doubt if he has yet achieved the public regard for impartiality'.[11] It took time in the priesthood to acquire the aura of objectivity, impartiality, and thus independence. In the end Radcliffe was appointed.

Not that Radcliffe had been on the Bench all that long; but apparently he had objectivity and impartiality even when at the Bar. The most famous example of this was his well-known work in India at the time of Independence. Lord Mountbatten, the Viceroy, requested a 'suitable incumbent' to be Chair of an Arbitral Tribunal. The ideal qualifications were someone not over 60, preferably about 55, who must be a Privy Councillor who had no experience of India.[12] Jowitt felt Radcliffe, who was still at the Bar, 'has in a pre-eminent degree all the qualities that are needed for this great task'. He was offered the job and accepted it subject to 'certain considerations' relating to salary, post-tax receipts, and family travel.[13] The problem was that the political scene was constantly changing.[14] Mountbatten actually made Radcliffe Chairman of the Boundary Commission rather than the Arbitral Tribunal. Radcliffe noted drily that 'it was not until after I had seen [the Prime Minister] that I discovered the Arbitral Tribunal was not the same thing as the Boundary Commission.'[15] The Government backed out of its promise of a Privy Counsellorship; and it is said that Radcliffe left England

[8] Armstrong to Boggis-Rolfe, 18 July 1950, ibid.

[9] Boggis-Rolfe to Coldstream and Jowitt, n.d., ibid.

[10] Jowitt would have liked Romer, but the Chancery Division was 'too busy'. Radcliffe would be 'great'. He also suggested Malcolm Eve, QC. Jowitt to Cripps, 21 July 1950. Evershed, more cautiously, agreed a judge should be spared in this case because the subject matter was 'law-related'. He thought most puisne judges were not household names, and he doubted 'whether these names carry enough weight'. He suggested either Somervell or Cohen from the Court of Appeal. Vaisey to Jowitt, 25 July 1950. Jowitt thought that Somervell might not be satisfactory because of his 'political provenance' (he had been Attorney-General). Jowitt to Vaisey, 25 July 1950. The chairmanship was therefore offered to Cohen. Ibid.

[11] Ibid.

[12] John Higgins, 'Partition in India', in M. Sissons and P. French, eds., *Age of Austerity* (London, 1963), 200.

[13] He was earning at least £60,000 per annum at the Bar and, by taking the job, he might lose the tax-free status of his post-retirement earnings. Jowitt urged he be made a Privy Counsellor, that his family be given special treatment and that he have a living allowance of £5,000 p.a. Jowitt to Listowel, 13 June 1947, LCO 2/3234.

[14] After Radcliffe accepted, Lord Listowel, the Secretary of State for India, noted 'a peaceful partition [would] largely depend on the effectiveness of the arbitral machinery.' Listowel to Jowitt, 16 June 1947, ibid.

[15] Radcliffe (in Delhi) to Jowitt, n.d., ibid.

after a half-hour's briefing clutching two maps.[16] Such was impartiality and the spirit of independence.

The intellectual tone of the debate about the 'outside' use of the judges was, however, about to be raised. As the Labour government gradually disintegrated in the late summer of 1951, Hilary Marquand, the Minister of Health, was having serious problems with the British Medical Association (BMA) whose members, especially the General Practitioners, were on the verge of a strike. Marquand wrote to Jowitt explaining his urgent need for a judge to head the Commission on remuneration in the National Health Service. The BMA had threatened that, if the doctors were not given a Lord of Appeal, they would mount an anti-government campaign: 'Knowing your general views about the release of Lords of Appeal for tasks of this kind I strongly resisted . . .', wrote Marquand, but the medical profession wanted an answer within five days.[17]

Jowitt really had no policy on the use of judges; he had just gone along supplying them while extolling the virtues of judicial 'impartiality' and 'independence'. When Marquand wrote his letter, Jowitt was addressing the Australian Bar, reminding its members that the task of the judge was 'deciding what the law is . . . not what social and political conditions do today require'.[18] The permanent officials in the Lord Chancellor's Office were not happy with Marquand's request and strengthened Jowitt's resolve not to release a Lord of Appeal,[19] but agreed by telephone to release a High Court judge. Some members of the BMA Council wanted to know which judge was to be appointed, others said they would be satisfied if they were told the judge's field.[20] As the days ticked away, the BMA made it clear it would like Mr Justice Gorman while the Lord Chancellor was thinking of Mr Justice Lloyd-Jacob. By 21 October, Marquand was both explaining what he needed—an adjudicator to determine 'the size of the central pool . . . having regard to changes in the value of money since 1939', and warning that the BMA was 'incredibly suspicious of the Government'.[21] So were the voters; the General Election produced the first purely Conservative majority since the 1920s.

There is evidence that the permanent officials thought that the new Tory government would be less casual in its use of judges than Jowitt had been. The reverse in fact was to be the case, although the new Chancellor, Simonds, a professional judge himself, was clearly uncomfortable with this casual stance. Napier, for instance, warned Coldstream that the new Minister of Health (Crookshank)

---

[16] Stevens, *Law and Politics*, 446.   [17] Marquand to Jowitt, 2 Sept. 1951, LCO 2/5802.

[18] Stevens, *Law and Politics*, 338–9.

[19] Napier argued that 'with a clear conscience you can say no Lord of Appeal can be spared'. The Privy Council was sitting in two Divisions, one of which was hearing Australian appeals and had therefore to be staffed by five Lords of Appeal. Meanwhile the House of Lords was hearing *Kemsley* v *Foot*, the Gold Bar case, and the *Fitzwilliam Estates* case, and these all required five Law Lords. Napier to Jowitt, 26 Sept. 1951, LCO 2/5902. Jowitt informed Marquand no Lord of Appeal was available on 2 Oct. 1951, ibid.

[20] Russell-Smith to Napier, 5 Oct. 1951, ibid.   [21] Marquand to Jowitt, 21 Oct. 1951, ibid.

intended to continue with a judicial adjudicator and that he preferred Lloyd-Jacob.[22] It was at this point that Simonds showed his colours: 'I must confess that I feel uneasy about bringing the judiciary into this dispute, but if you [Crookshank] and the Chancellor of the Exchequer both think that we cannot go back on the decision to refer the dispute to an independent adjudicator, I must do my best to find a judge.'[23] He insisted, however, that before a judge was provided, both sides had to agree to accept the judge's decision.

Battle lines were hardening. Simonds asked Danckwerts to do the job. Danckwerts accepted, noting that 'as I know nothing whatever about the matter, at any rate I come to it with an open mind.'[24] Simonds reminded Crookshank that Danckwerts 'knows nothing whatsoever about the subject in dispute which is, I think, a decided advantage'.[25] Such statements sound odd in the light of modern studies of the psychology of decision-making; the statements, however, clearly represented the basic view of the English judicial establishment. Ignorance, impartiality, and independence were seen largely as synonymous.

(b) The Classic Case: The Restrictive Practices Court

That same month—December 1951—the next shot was fired. Peter Thorneycroft, President of the Board of Trade, wrote to the Lord Chancellor to say that he would be introducing a Monopolies and Restrictive Practices Bill in February 1952, and he wanted a High Court judge as Chairman of the Commission. Thorneycroft reported that the Home Secretary (Sir David Maxwell Fyfe, the future Chancellor, Lord Kilmuir) and the Attorney-General agreed that a High Court judge was 'essential' and that a mere barrister would not 'command the same public confidence and approval as that of a judge'. The politicians explained that 'from the standpoint of political presentation, [the High Court judge] would add greatly to the exposition of the Government's case', while agreeing the 'work would not be wholly judicial in the ordinary sense'. Thorneycroft requested a High Court judge 'who would be qualified to under-take what I may call the administrative side of the work as well as the quasi-judicial'. In particular he needed a young judge who had had administrative experience during the Second World War; he thought Devlin, Parker, and Pearson 'peculiarly suitable'.[26]

Simonds was no more enthusiastic than the permanent officials in the office. In another office memorandum,[27] from Theisiger to Coldstream, the

---

[22] Napier to Coldstream, 13 Nov. 1951, ibid.
[23] Simonds to Crookshank, 15 Nov. 1951, ibid.
[24] Danckwerts to Simonds, 1 Dec. 1951, ibid.
[25] Simonds to Crookshank, 3 Dec. 1951, ibid.
[26] Thorneycroft to Simonds 21 Dec., 1951, LCO 2/5904.
[27] Another memorandum reported that, in 1948, Lord Justice Cohen had been invited to become Chair of the Monopolies Commission when it was established; and Jowitt approved. Cohen, how-ever, refused the appointment not only because he was worried about his shareholdings, which could

constitutional position was reviewed from the War of the Roses, through Coke and James I, to Birkenhead. The conclusion was:

The extra-judicial functions of the judiciary may therefore be defined as either advising the Crown as a body or as presiding over a special tribunal which, by its very nature, would not last very long, or as presiding over a Commission while carrying on their ordinary judicial functions.

The proposal to second a King's Bench Judge to the Monopolies Commission falls into none of these categories. The Commission does not advise the Crown but the Executive in the shape of the President of the Board of Trade. He would be seconded probably for several years, unlike the short emergency procedure of special tribunals. He would not be able to carry out his judicial functions at the same time and special provision would have to be made either for a further Judge to be appointed to the King's Bench Division (if he was to be maintained on the strength) or for him to continue to hold his judicial style and title and receive his salary.

It would appear that the latter is contemplated. Thus, the style and title of a High Court Judge is really to be used by the Chairman of the Monopolies Commission merely to enhance its dignity and to promote public confidence while, and for the same reasons, the person selected for that position is to be chosen from the judiciary. It cannot therefore, in my opinion, be considered as a Judge performing extra-judicial functions, but as special dignity being required for this particular Commission.[28]

Behind the scenes efforts were made to soothe Simonds' concerns.[29] The Home Secretary sent the Chancellor a memorandum, explaining he could not find a national figure:

For this reason I was attracted by the suggestion of seconding a judge for a limited period. I entirely appreciate the difficulties of that period being long. He would then cease to be a judge in all but a name to which he was doubtfully entitled. What I had in mind, however, was seconding a younger judge with experience of commercial work, who would return to his judicial duties. I realize that even that period might make him less familiar with the recent movements of the law, but I cannot feel that it would be too great a strain for such a man to get into his stride again, or that this experience should debar him from promotion . . .[30]

---

lead to conflicts of interest, and because his pension was threatened, but also because he believed the prestige of the Bench would be undermined if a judge transferred to other work, particularly a job subject to dismissal by the President of the Board of Trade. Napier to Coldstream, 31 Dec. 1951, ibid.

[28] Theisiger to Coldstream, 2 Jan. 1952, ibid.

[29] See David Maxwell Fyfe (Home Secretary) to Simonds, 16 Jan. 1952, ibid.:

'My dear Gavin, Thank you very much for your letter and note. If it were not that I am very worried about the Monopolies Commission, I should have accepted your view out of hand. I am, however, the fons et origo of what I hope may be prevented from becoming an evil.

'I have therefore ventured to put on paper the background of the suggestion. Fred Grant, the tax silk, has been a part time member at my suggestion. He told me that the time wasted by the Chairman's lack of training was appalling. On the other hand the selection of someone who was a second-class silk or a County Court Judge or even an Official Referee would not meet the requirement of confidence.

'It is a problem in which your help will be invaluable.'

[30] Ibid.

The picket in the Office was the Deputy Permanent Secretary, George Coldstream. He was not impressed by the Home Secretary's advocacy:[31]

> The Home Secretary's memorandum is mainly directed to the difficulty of finding a suitable individual. He does not attempt to deal with the important point of principle, viz: whether it is right to ask the judiciary to descend into the arena of public affairs. The position is, of course, made worse by the Home Secretary's proposal that the Judge should be seconded for a limited period.
>
> The Monopolies Commission is in truth an instrument of Government policy . . . I feel convinced that the proposal should still be rejected. One does not know what invitations have already been offered to, and rejected by, persons prominent in public life . . .[32]
>
> If a member of the Judiciary has to be chosen, in the last resort, I would suggest approaching one of the senior Judges who is unlikely to end up in the House of Lords. It is hardly for me to suggest names, but perhaps Wynn-Parry and Lynskey, JJ might be in this class, though either might go to the Court of Appeal (Lynskey, of course, has already refused). But it would have to be on the footing that they would continue by statutory provision, to earn their pensions, and perhaps it would be wise to offer them Peerages as well, so that at the end of the day they would be available to sit, as trace-horses, in the House of Lords.

The Office, having demolished the Maxwell Fyfe arguments—at least to its own satisfaction—at this point was prepared finally to reject the request from the President of the Board of Trade.[33] No High Court judge was provided.

[31] Coldstream to Simonds, 17 Jan. 1952, ibid.

[32] At this point Coldstream speculated that although Sir John Anderson had turned it down—a fact admitted by Maxwell Fyfe—Sir Malcolm Eve or Lord Llewelyn might take it. Ibid.

[33] Simonds to Thorneycroft, 18 Jan. 1952. 'The request is without precedent in that a Judge so appointed will cease to be a Judge for an indefinite term which may extend to the whole of his working life. On the rare occasion when a judge has been asked to do work other than that to which he has been appointed, for example to preside over a Royal Commission, or over a Tribunal of Enquiry (as was Porter J. over the Budget Leakage Enquiry, or Lynskey J. over the "contact men" enquiry), or, as in my own case, to act as Chairman of a tribunal such as the National Arbitration Tribunal, the work has been of a temporary nature and it has been assumed that the Judge will, when he has finished his job, return to his proper work on the Bench . . . In these cases it can properly be said that Mr Justice X is the Chairman of the Commission or Tribunal as the case may be.

'It is far otherwise when a Judge is invited to take such an office as Chairman of the Monopolies Commission, which is a full-time job and may last for twelve years. It becomes then a mere fiction to say that Mr Justice X is Chairman of the Commission. All that can truly be said is that the Chairman of the Commission is a gentleman who used to be Mr Justice X; and I should myself think it objectionable that, ceasing to be a Judge and with a limited prospect of becoming one again, he should retain the title of Mr Justice X. His work has ceased to be judicial in the strict sense of the word and that quality should not be ascribed to it by giving him a title which he should no longer bear. The fact that he is liable to be dismissed from his office by the Board of Trade is a clear indication of its character.

'Another important consideration is this. When a man is appointed a Judge his life is in a sense dedicated to that work. He does not and ought not to contemplate that any other occupation is open to him: he may, it is true, hope for promotion to the Court of Appeal or to the House of Lords, and so far he may be said to be not impervious to the considerations which affect the minds of those who seek promotion, though I have never heard anyone dare to suggest of any of His Majesty's Judges that his judicial conduct was influenced by any other consideration than his judicial oath . . . If it is superior in these respects, then there will be, or may appear to be, just the evil thing which is by all means to be avoided—the possibility of subservience of the Judge to the Executive in order that he

By February 1952 the permanent officials of the Office and the Board were closeted together, haggling over names of possible QCs to chair the Commission. There were to be three permanent members of the Commission and the Chairman was to be a lawyer.[34] The issue of a judicial chairman, however, did not die. As the Commission continued its work, various business groups lobbied against its reports, which were alleged to be arbitrary, discretionary, and biased[35]—the antithesis of the alleged attributes of the independent English judiciary. In 1954, *The Times* joined in the attacks on the 'injustice' of Monopolies Commission procedures and called for a judicial tribunal,[36] and the issue became almost a crusade for Sir Harry Pilkington, the President of the Federation of British Industries; an 'independent' judge, he argued, had to be appointed. While Peter Thorneycroft remained President of the Board of Trade, by 1955 he had a more sympathetic Lord Chancellor, Kilmuir, who, as Sir David Maxwell Fyfe, had advocated just such a solution.

While Thorneycroft explained to Kilmuir that businessmen wanted an adversarial rather than an inquisitorial system,[37] the Lord Chancellor's permanent civil servants warned that they saw little wrong with the then current arrangement and that 'public interest questions are not justiciable issues such as are appropriate for determination by a truly judicial body: the function is more nearly executive or administrative.'[38] The officials' concern led to a meeting between the

---

may obtain some reward. It has been suggested that the Judge appointed to the office of Chairman of the Monopolies Commission should be regarded as "seconded" for a period of years and, further, that the period should not be more than three years. But, whatever his promotion or demotion be called, my objection remains. Nor do I think it at all likely that, if he made a success of it, he would not be pressed to continue in office for a further term. And I must add that, whether he was 'seconded' for three years only or for a longer term, it would almost certainly militate against his chance of judicial promotion, a fact which, surely known to him, would deter him from accepting the office unless it was attended by some other substantial advantage. I am now dealing with a single request concerning a single office, but I think that this is merely a somewhat glaring case of a tendency which is today conspicuous of asking that Judges should undertake extra judicial work. It is a compliment to the Judiciary which I have no doubt is well deserved that a tribunal, commission or what you will, should at once be credited with fairness and impartiality if its president is a Judge, but I would dispense with the compliment in order to preserve their dedicated and independent position.' Ibid.

[34] The Lord Chancellor suggested Frederick Grant, QC, who was already a member; and the name of Robert Hull, QC, by then the Chairman of the Transport Tribunal, surfaced. 13 Feb. 1952. For some reason neither of the English 'silks' seemed to fly and attention then turned to a Scottish silk, R. P. Morrison, but his name, although approved by Simonds, faded when he insisted on a pension. Thorneycroft to Simonds, 28 Feb. 1952. Then, nearly a year later, Sir Lionel Heald wrote to the Chancellor to say the job had been offered to Scott Cairns, QC. Heald to Simonds, 12 Jan. 1952. That was news to Simonds. Heald asked the very questions expected: what were his 'future prospects'; if the appointment turned out well would it not make him a better puisne later on. Simonds agreed Cairns was 'fair minded', and he approved. Minute, 20 Nov. 1953. That did not stop a Tory MP writing to the President of the Board of Trade, 'shocked' at the appointment of a Liberal who was 'very hostile to the Conservative party on all occasions' and hated by business. Malcolm McCorquodale to Thorneycroft, 18 Nov. 1953. Ibid.

[35] Stevens and Yamey, *The Restrictive Practices Court*, 12–13.

[36] *The Times*, Leader, 20 Oct. 1954.

[37] Thorneycroft to Kilmuir, 27 Oct. 1956, LCO 2/6239.

[38] Dobson to Coldstream, 3 Nov. 1954; Coldstream to Kilmuir, 15 Nov. 1954, ibid.

Chairman of the Monopolies Commission (Scott Cairns, QC), the Lord
Chancellor, and the Attorney-General (by then Sir Reginald Manningham-
Buller), to see how far the so-called 'inquisitorial' methods were, in fact, necessary, and how far legal findings could be separated from findings of fact.[39] A
further meeting on the subject included the officials and, despite the Bar's interest in a judicial solution, all agreed that the existing procedures were
satisfactory.[40]

The political pressures in the Conservative Party, however, were too strong to
tolerate the status quo. In July the Lord Chancellor and Solicitor-General were
waited upon by Sir Lionel Heald (a former Attorney-General) and J. E. Simon
(later a Lord of Appeal) and a group of other Conservative MPs. Kilmuir found
himself defending the Commission, arguing it was more effective than the
American solution; Simon in particular, was strongly for some kind of Sherman
Act.[41] By then, however, the general *Report on Collective Discrimination* by the
Monopolies Commission had been published, with the majority suggesting the
outlawing of certain practices.[42]

A Cabinet Committee was at once established and, in its second meeting,
came up with a solution: registration of agreements, followed by an investigation
by a tribunal—the nature of which was left open—which would evaluate the
agreements by standards which, somehow or other, would be developed.[43]
Thorneycroft's team at the Board of Trade set to work to devise such standards
and to produce a tribunal. At the Conservative Party Conference in the early
autumn there was a groundswell for using High Court judges to staff the tribunal. Politically the call was for power to be transferred from the Civil Service
and tribunals to the judiciary.[44] The Cabinet Office warned that 'the prescription
of criteria for use by the High Court may well be objectionable on principle.'[45]
Such concern, however, paled into insignificance when contrasted with the agitation which seized the officials in the Lord Chancellor's Office.

Dobson minuted Coldstream: 'The whole nonsense had been caused by the
agitation about tribunals . . . a High Court Judge . . . is ill suited to decide the
sort of cases that will be at issue here.' The suggestion that appeals should go to
the Court of Appeal was 'horrifying'.[46] Later that same day Kilmuir was presented with a paper from Sir George Coldstream that was worthy of Sir
Humphrey Appleby. It recorded that all the civil servants involved at the

---

[39] Some thought the problem was that Scott Cairns was too tough in cross-examination.
Coldstream to Kilmuir, 18 Feb. 1955, ibid. The three met on 21 Feb. 1955.
[40] 28 Mar. 1955, ibid.   [41] 12 July 1955, ibid.
[42] Monopolies and Restrictive Practices Commission, *Report on Collective Discrimination*, Cmnd.
9504 (1955).
[43] First meeting, 5 July 1955; second meeting, 11 July 1955, LCO 2/6241.
[44] In the Cabinet Office it was faithfully recorded that 'the most difficult problem will no doubt
be to prescribe criteria on which the High Court (or a tribunal) can judge whether particular restrictive agreements are harmful to the economic and social welfare of the country.' F. A. Binney to Lord
Chancellor's Office, 11 Oct. 1955, ibid.
[45] Ibid.   [46] Dobson to Coldstream, 12 Oct. 1955, ibid.

Cabinet Office and the Board of Trade—Sir Harold Lunt, Sir Thomas Padmore, and Sir Edward Bridges—agreed with Coldstream and Dobson that Thorneycroft's proposals were 'thoroughly unsound' and should be remitted to the official level. Coldstream was also concerned that Thorneycroft had already approached Evershed and Devlin. It was all 'Highly improper. No Minister, still less an official, ought ever to approach one of Her Majesty's judges on a matter relating to the jurisdiction of the court without the prior concurrence of the Lord Chancellor, or, in his absence, of his Permanent Secretary.' The separation of powers apparently gave priority to civil servants over most politicians in dealing with the judiciary. Coldstream also warned that the Law Lords would probably oppose the scheme; the threat was that the judges in the legislature would side with the civil servants to protect the independence of the High Court judges.[47]

Three weeks later Coldstream was still complaining that objective criteria could not be devised. 'I have assumed it would be wrong to require the courts to pronounce on issues of economic policy.' He was, however, sensing that the tide of battle might be ebbing. The only justification for letting the courts loose was the 'wretched state of business in the Chancery Division'. The least harmful way out in that direction would be to emulate the Railway and Canal Commission, where the courts supervised a regulatory commission.[48] The same day, it was reported that the issue 'has proved even more difficult than anticipated'.[49] The Attorney-General ruled 'out the possibility of using the High Court to decide cases arising under the proposed legislation since it would be wrong to give the Court a jurisdiction which would carry with it administrative powers in a matter of policy which are properly the responsibility of ministers'.[50] In the light of this Kilmuir argued for a commission.

Once again, however, the Federation of British Industry insisted on a court: 'The more judicial it is, the greater is likely to be respect for its jurisdiction.'[51] In the Federation's eyes, independence was essential. The enthusiasm was not shared by Her Majesty's judges. While Mr Justice Vaisey announced to the Lord Chancellor that 'I consider it to be our duty to do what Parliament asks of us, relying upon it, and you, to keep us so far as possible out of political controversy,'[52] the majority of the Chancery judges had 'grave objections'. 'It seems to the Chancery judges inevitable that "the political element" must play a part in the deliberations of the Court as proposed to be constituted and objection is taken to making a judge merely a member, although the presiding member with

---

[47] Coldstream to Kilmuir, 12 Oct. 1955, ibid.

[48] Coldstream to Kilmuir, 3 Nov. 1955, ibid. That became the basis of the instructions from the Board of Trade to Parliamentary Counsel. LCO 2/6242.

[49] 'The general conclusion reached by the Attorney-General is that it is virtually impossible to define the justiciable issue without reference to economic considerations.' Binney to Kilmuir, 3 Nov. 1955, LCO 2/2641.

[50] Ibid.   [51] Graham Hayman to Thorneycroft, 2 Feb. 1956, ibid.

[52] Vaisey to Kilmuir, 26 Mar. 1956, LCO 2/6242.

a casting vote, of such a court.' Some Chancery judges favoured using the regular courts, 'but some of them feel in addition that the whole principle of bringing a High Court judge into the matter which on any footing must have a political flavour' was a mistake.[53] The logic of the Chancery Division's position helps explain the ambivalent attitude to administrative law taken by the English judiciary during this period.

In the Queen's Bench Division, where business was brisker, there was no support for a Restrictive Practices Court, and Lord Goddard was forced to call an additional Council of Judges.[54] Only Mr Justice Devlin dissented from his brethren. 'I do not see why the working of the judicial part of it should lead to any exceptional difficulty and I welcome the decision that issues of great importance between the Government and individuals should be determined by the High Court,' Devlin wrote.[55] Kilmuir purred: 'You put exactly my view on a subject which has worried me a great deal.'[56] Devlin replied with even greater enthusiasm:

I feel that the idea you are using in the bill,—the combination of the judiciary with those experienced in other sorts of administration,—might with the aid of a new and flexible procedure develop into the right way of dealing with the whole problem of the Government's legal relation to the citizen. What will then be needed is the creation of a new jurisprudence and a Hardwicke or a Mansfield or a Marshall to do it. Tom Denning would do it superbly. I should like to see the Exchequer Division revived with him at the head of it; . . .

If it (the High Court) is going to play its full part in the future life of the nation, it must not barricade itself within its existing functions, even though an adaptation may contain an element of risk. At least that is what I believe, but clearly it is not at all the general view of the judges. If this experiment failed,—not necessarily a breakdown but a failure to produce convincing results,—the stand-patters will be confirmed and it will be very difficult again to use the High Court for the solution of any new problems.[57]

At this point, Devlin read a speech by Kilmuir about the renewed role of the common law:

The law is not to be compared to a venerable antique, to be taken down, dusted, admired and put back on the shelf; rather it is like an old but still vigorous tree—firmly rooted in history; but still putting out new shoots, taking new grafts and from time to time dropping dead wood . . . law is not an end in itself. It is a means whereby the State can develop and regulate in an orderly and just manner the social system which it desires.

For this reason Kilmuir believed 'the law should be brought in to help in the solution of the great problem of the modern State'.[58] After reading the speech Devlin responded: 'I am very glad to feel you will be (barring some Socialist

---

[53] Meeting of Chancery judges, 2 Mar. 1956, LCO 2/6242.
[54] Goddard to Kilmuir, 2 Mar. 1956, ibid.   [55] Devlin to Kilmuir, 7 Mar. 1956, ibid.
[56] Kilmuir to Devlin, 8 Mar. 1956, ibid.   [57] Devlin to Kilmuir, 12 Mar. 1956, LCO 2/6244.
[58] For these, and related observations, see Stevens, *Law and Politics*, 421.

intermissions!) Lord Chancellor for the next twenty years or more and that you think as you do.'[59]

(c) Restrictive Practices: The Public Doubts

The civil service and judicial doubts about the justiciability of the proposed solution became part of the public consciousness as Parliament began debating the restrictive trade practices legislation. The aspect of justiciability which was at issue was whether the problem to be solved was one which was apt for a judicial solution—in the sense of the submission of the problem to what was essentially a new division of the High Court.[60] The dispute emphasized the difference between the American and British view of the separation of powers. In the United States, the emphasis is on drawing a clear distinction between the responsibilities of Legislative, Executive, and Judiciary. In Britain, the issue is looked at from the other end of the telescope. Rather than looking at decision-making as a spectrum, an effort is made to categorize each decision as inherently judicial, executive, or legislative in character. Even for a system skilled at verbal distinctions, this proves a daunting intellectual challenge. Historically it has resulted in an artificially narrow view of the judicial.

Politically the issue of justiciability was at the core of the dispute on the Restrictive Practices legislation. The Labour Party insisted strongly that the task given to the court was not justiciable. Its real political objection may well have been its belief that the Bill was a sham, and MP's hostility to the use of the judges may have been because the judges were suspected of economic illiberalism; but the battle was fought out on the aspect of justiciability, with the Labour Party voicing the objections argued by the civil servants in the Lord Chancellor's Office. Could the issues in the Bill be made sufficiently clear to be submitted to

---

[59] Devlin to Kilmuir, 19 Mar. 1956, LCO 2/6244.

[60] The effect of the lay judges on the issue of justiciability is difficult to analyse. The presence of such members of the Court drew the argument from the Opposition that if the issue were justiciable, there was no need to have them, and if were not justiciable, there was no point in handing the issue to a body disguised as a court. See e.g. speech of R. Jenkins, *Parliamentary Debates* (5th ser.), HC vol. 551, col 433 (12 Apr. 1956). The Lord Chancellor's answer to that was that 'clause 20 [now section 21] defines closely the conditions which the Court is to take into account, and does not leave it to the Court to determine the economic and commercial policy of the country . . . The Government do not deny that some element of economic judgment will be demanded of the Court, and that is why it will be a mixed one, and the expertise and experience of practical affairs of the lay members will contribute to its judgments.' Speech of Lord Kilmuir, *Parliamentary Debates* (5th ser.), HL vol. 198, cols. 18–19 (26 June 1956). See also speech of Lord Mancroft, ibid., col. 964 (11 July 1956).

Nevertheless, the government refused to designate the laymen as 'assessors', which is what the Labour Party insisted they should be called. Government speakers argued that 'we are much more likely to get people of the high quality which we require . . . if they are given the status of lay members rather than tacked on as technical assessors . . .'. Speech of D. Walker-Smith, *Parliamentary Debates* (5th ser.), HC vol. 552, cols. 2309–10 (17 May 1956). In the 1964 debates on the Resale Prices Bill, however, Edward Heath constantly referred to the lay judges as assessors; e.g. ibid., vol. 691, col 272 (10 Mar. 1964).

a court? In other words, could the policies involved be made subject to legal standards? This was the basic dispute with which Parliament wrestled.

The Labour Party was in favour of implementing the recommendations of the majority made in the Monopolies Commission *Report on Collective Discrimination*[61] and declaring certain restrictive practices to be illegal, and in this it received some support from the press.[62] An outright prohibition, it was insisted, would provide an ideal legal standard which might easily be applied to the facts of any particular case. The Labour Party, therefore, argued that the establishment of the Restrictive Practices Court was unnecessary. Labour members purported to be incensed because they alleged that, from party political speeches, it was clear that the Government had committed itself to a judicial solution and then sought—unsuccessfully in their view—to make the issues justiciable.[63] The chief spokesman for the Opposition was Sir Lynn Ungoed-Thomas, a former Labour Solicitor-General, and later a High Court judge. He had fundamental objections to the use of a court for deciding such issues:

The function of a court is not that which is mentioned in the Bill; it is entirely different, namely, to interpret and administer law, and not to make it. The Bill hands over to this court governmental and parliamentary power. All judgments are founded upon law or upon facts, but in this case the decision which really matters will be a decision founded neither upon law nor upon fact. It will be a political and economic decision.[64]

The Government spokesmen, while willing to admit that the new court involved certain innovations, were at pains to argue that there was nothing extraordinary in the function it was expected to perform and that such a function was basically no different from those traditionally performed by the courts. It was pointed out that the courts had, on many occasions, to determine what amounted to the public interest, particularly in cases involving contracts alleged to be in restraint of trade.[65] The courts were also said to be involved with economic issues when they were granting or revoking patents;[66] and much prominence was accorded to the Railways and Canals Commission in which laymen had sat with judges to determine whether certain contracts of carriage were 'just and reasonable'.[67]

---

[61] e.g. speech of Sir L. Ungoed-Thomas, ibid., vol. 549, col 2027 (6 Mar. 1956); speech of M. Turner-Samuels, ibid., col. 2021; speech of D. Jay, ibid., col. 1946.

[62] *The Economist*, 176 (1955), 9; 177 (1955), 640; 178 (1956), 501.

[63] Speech of Sir L. Ungoed-Thomas, *Parliamentary Debates* (5th ser.), HC vol. 551, col. 407 (12 Apr. 1956).

[64] Speech of Sir L. Ungoed-Thomas, ibid., vol. 549, cols. 2029–30 (6 Mar. 1956).

[65] Speech of P. Thorneycroft, ibid., vol. 551, cols. 417–20 (12 Apr. 1956).

[66] Speech of Sir L. Heald, ibid., col. 425.

[67] Speakers who cited this example obviously had not read the speech of Lord Bramwell in *Manchester, Sheffield and Lincolnshire Rly.* v *Brown*, 8 App. Cas. 703, 716 f. (1833), an appeal under sect. 7 of the Railway and Canal Act, 1854 (17 & 18 Vict., c. 31): 'Here is a contract made by a fishmonger and a carrier of fish who know their business, and whether it is just and reasonable is to be settled by me who am neither fishmonger nor carrier, nor with any knowledge of their business . . . It seems to me perfectly idle, and I cannot understand how it could have been supposed

These instances were summed up by Derek Walker-Smith, as junior to Peter Thorneycroft. He insisted that the process proposed was in no way alien to the traditional judicial process:

It is just not true to say that Parliament alone is concerned with economic and social matters and that the Court has no part in them. The courts deal with many social and economic matters under the guidance of principles laid down by Parliament. There are many examples in the spheres of landlord and tenant and of public health. The distinction is not between the kind of subject dealt with. The true distinction is between the level at which that subject is dealt with. Parliament is not in a position to examine, control, or to judge the individual levels of economic activity. It is a doctrine which has proved true in many fields.[68]

It all sounded a little as if the difference between the legislative and the judicial was the difference between wholesale and retail. The argument did not begin to distinguish between executive discretion and judicial discretion. Yet it was on these main themes that the Government based its case: that the courts had handled such questions before, were fully competent to handle questions of reasonableness, and that the issue had been made justiciable by reducing it to an individual level.[69]

The opposition would have none of this. Of the argument that judges often had to decide questions of reasonableness, and this was essentially what they were required to do in this new court, Sir Lynn Ungoed-Thomas replied:

It has been said that the courts are accustomed to deciding whether a thing is reasonable or not; of course they are. Whenever they assess damages they assess what is a reasonable amount. That argument begs the question, which is the ambit within which reasonableness

necessary, that it should be referred to a judge to say whether an agreement between carriers, of whose business he knows nothing, and fishmongers, of whose business he knows nothing, is reasonable or not. If it is a question it is one of fact.'

The lineal descendant of this commission was still concerned with questions of the reasonableness of tariffs; it was by then known as the Transport Tribunal. It operated in much the same way as the new court, being a court of record, with lay members, presided over by a High Court Judge or a Judge of the Court of Session. Like the Restrictive Practices Court, its decisions were final on questions of fact, but appeals to the ordinary appeal courts were allowed on points of law. See O. Kahn-Freund, *The Law of Inland Transport* (3rd edn. 1956), ch. 4. The powers of the Transport Tribunal were considerably reduced by the Transport Act, 1962.

   [68] *Parliamentary Debates* (5th ser.), HC vol. 549, col. 2042 (6 Mar. 1956).

   [69] Rather surprisingly, the most coherent defence of the process on constitutional grounds is provided by a Fabian pamphlet published some years later: 'It is difficult to see what is objectionable in Parliament delegating the duty of decision. What it has done in effect is to set up a kind of Grand Jury, which decides each case. Inevitably economic and political factors influence its decisions. But it is applying a firm framework of principles that Parliament itself has laid down. So far from being a loss, it is in fact a gain that these—after all fairly narrow—economic issues have been taken out of day to day politics. It has to be recognised that in normal circumstances it is not easy to get contentious legislation that may adversely affect specific industries introduced by any Government.

'The way in which the Act insulates the decisions taken from pressure groups, lobbying, and the anxieties of day to day politics should be recognised as an important advantage. If need be Parliament is still in a position to intervene, as it did in the case of the cotton judgment; the only right it has given up is the right to shelve the matter.' P. Hutber, *Wanted, a Monopoly Policy* (London, 1960), 25–6.

has to be exercised. If it is within a justiciable issue, then the courts of law exercise reasonableness, but no one will suggest that because there is an exercise of reasonableness in Budget decisions therefore Budget decisions are things which ought to be submitted to a court of law.[70]

Nor would the former Solicitor-General concede that justiciability had anything to do with the fact that problems were dealt with individually. Justiciability

depends not upon reasonableness or unreasonableness, or upon whether or not it is an individual case, but essentially upon the nature of the issue that has to be considered by the body that we set up. We know that the function of the court of law is to apply the general rules of law to the facts of a particular case. The rules and the definition are there and the Court interprets the definition as part of its function in applying it to the facts of the case. The law, therefore, applies equally to everybody. It is an essential part of the rule of law that we have in this country that there is a general rule which courts of law apply indiscriminately to the facts of the particular case.[71]

He concluded his argument by declaring:

This is not really a matter suitable for judicial decision according to the rules and the ordinary way in which we conduct matters in the courts of law in this country at all. It is a matter of a decision to be made from the greatest accumulation of knowledge and experience which is available, and the greatest accumulation of knowledge and experience available in this country is only available, in the last resort, to the Minister. It is essentially a governmental decision.[72]

Moreover, it was argued that it was unfair to force judges into deciding cases where their predispositions would be likely to become obvious:[73]

We do not, by submitting what are essentially political matters to the decision of a court turn them into legal matters. We cannot convert a political matter into a legal matter merely by asking the opinion of a judge about it. It is, in fact, the height of folly to drag the judges into these matters. It is not pleasant when we have cases, such as the famous trade union cases, which impinge upon politics. They are not welcome cases, but they are quite inevitable on occasion, and what are we doing here is to drag the judges into the vast field of political and economic matters.[74]

It would be wrong, however, to assume that opposition to the use of the judiciary for this new task was confined to the Parliamentary Labour Party. *The Economist*, while welcoming the Bill, was extremely chary of the idea of using the judges. It feared not only their economic illiberalism, but also their method of reasoning: 'the idea that a decision should change if the climate of opinion changes, even though other things remain the same, is not an idea that will be

---

[70] *Parliamentary Debates* (5th ser.), HC vol. 551, col. 404 (12 Apr. 1956).
[71] Speech of Sir L. Ungoed-Thomas, ibid.   [72] Ibid., col. 410.
[73] 'The duty ought never to be placed on the judiciary of giving a decision on what, in effect, is not a justiciable issue but a question of economic and political policy.' Speech of E. Fletcher, ibid., col. 423 (12 Apr. 1956).
[74] Speech of Sir L. Ungoed-Thomas, ibid., vol. 549, col. 2033 (6 Mar. 1956).

easily digestible by trained legal minds'.[75] As the Bill progressed, *The Times* cast considerable doubt on the wisdom of using the judges. It took the view that the judiciary might be compromised:

Close thought must be given to the probable effect on the judiciary itself. Will judges who have been watched in the new tribunals weighing these highly controversial questions of expediency, however closely their terms of reference are limited, carry back to the Queen's Bench or Chancery quite the same unassailable reputation for detachment from political considerations that they have hitherto enjoyed?

More important, however, *The Times* agreed with the Labour Party that parts, at least, of the Bill were not justiciable.[76]

These concerns clearly affected Mr Justice Devlin, the first President of the Restrictive Practices Court. In the first case, *The Chemists Federation Agreement (No. 2)*,[77] Devlin announced:

[We] have to consider the fundamental question whether it is contrary to the public interest that sales of medicine should be effected only through chemists . . . But since this is the first judgment delivered under the Act, it is as well that we should make clear that we are not, in our view, in any way required to answer this question as a matter of policy. We are not to consider whether competition in the sale of medicine is desirable or undesirable, whether drug stores are a suitable outlet for them or whether chemists should have such a monopoly, or whether the Chemist's Federation is a good or a bad thing. Such questions of general policy are settled by this Act.

In the third case, Mr Justice Upjohn made a similar point:[78]

We are not called upon to say whether a stop-loss scheme such as this is fair and reasonable, nor whether it is likely to be for the general economic advantage of the community. The legislature has performed that task and has decided that in general such schemes are to be deemed to be contrary to the public interest.

Moreover, the theme that the separation of powers in England revolved around the function and not the functionary continued to be the basis of establishment thinking. When, for instance, in 1962 the Royal Commission on the Press recommended a court to investigate press mergers, it cautioned:

The adoption of this system, however, imposes one firm necessity. A court of law cannot be asked to adjudicate at large upon broad issues of public advantage without being brought too much into the political arena, and the criteria of public interest to be applied would have to be stated by Parliament with sufficient precision to create justiciable issues which were capable of decision according to evidence.[79]

---

[75] *The Economist*, 176 (1955), 205.
[76] Cited, speech of D. Wade, *Parliamentary Debates* (5th ser.), HC vol. 552, col. 668 (3 May 1956).
[77] [1958] LR I RP 75, 103.
[78] In *The Blanket Manufacturers' Agreement* [1959] LR I RP 208, 254.
[79] *Report*, Cmnd. 1811 (1962), para. 342.

Whatever the reasons, one of the ironies of constitutional development since this has been that the proposed press model was not adopted; and with respect to monopolies and restrictive practices, while the Restrictive Practices Court is still in existence, it has little work. The Fair Trading Act of 1973 strengthened still further the busy Monopolies Commission (by then renamed the Monopolies and Mergers Commission),[80] and Mrs Thatcher's Competition Act of 1980 gave additional investigatory power to the administrative Office of Fair Trading itself.[81] The wheel had come full circle; two quasi-independent bodies are exercising wide discretion in order to enforce political policies. The attempted judicial solution had largely fallen into desuetude.

(d) Another Spoke in the Wheel: The Lord Chancellor's Office and Committees

The issue of independence of the judiciary, especially in the judges' work as commission and committee chairs, is tied into another aspect of committee work: the Lord Chancellor's Office's role within committees, particularly specialized ones. One can get some sense of the Department's effective control of the process of legal reform from looking at the work of its representatives on committees.[82] (It generally had a member on legal committees as well as staffing them.) The minutes of the Rushcliffe Committee, which led to the Legal Aid and Advice Scheme, make it clear that Napier's interjections were significant in guiding the scheme in the directions which still shape it today. Indeed, it is also clear from the Lord Chancellor's Office papers that Rushcliffe owed his appointment as Chair of the Committee to the feeling that he could be controlled by the Office.

Napier, in the Committee, opposed the idea of a body interposed between the Law Society as administrator of the Scheme and the Government—a kind of Legal Services Corporation—although he had to agree to an Advisory Committee. Meanwhile Schuster (by then Lord Schuster), as a member of the Rushcliffe Committee, managed to persuade his colleagues that there was no need for a new system of criminal legal aid (both he and Napier misleadingly said they had not heard any criticism of the Poor Person's Procedure); and neither thought it necessary to inform the accused of their right to such aid. The Office opposed—not entirely successfully—the right of appeal from the denial of a legal aid certificate; and it was adamant the Office should not review denials of aid. At the same time they saw no reason why the Office should not run the scheme, providing the Lord Chancellor could not be asked detailed questions. The Office was also responsible for the compromise that provided for the State's recovering costs from the other party when an assisted litigant won, but not vice versa.[83]

---

[80] R. Whish, *Competition Law* (2nd edn. London, 1989), ch. 3.
[81] Ibid., ch. 4.   [82] LCO 2/3900.
[83] Schuster agreed it was unfair, but he could see no way out of the difficulty. He was strongly opposed to leaving the judge to decide about recovery. Major W. T. C. Skyrme, the secretary,

A sense of the relative power within the Department may be gained by look-ing at the Cabinet Committee on the Reform of Legal Procedure established by Clement Attlee when Labour was returned to power in 1945. Jowitt, the Lord Chancellor, was not trusted by many members of the Labour Administration of 1945;[84] and he wrote a secret memorandum, setting out his views on the reform of the legal system, in November of that year, which, in retrospect, confirms many of the concerns of his colleagues. His three main thoughts were that divorce—even uncontested petitions—should be kept out of the hands of County Court judges lest their diversity in decisions would produce the confu-sion he saw in the USA; he was concerned about the implementation of Rushcliffe; and while he thought that there ought to be a Royal Commission on the Cost of Litigation, it would not be fair to the profession, which was just recovering from the War.[85] Some of the members of the Cabinet Committee were, in Jowitt's eyes, 'safe', but sceptics like Nye Bevan were not likely to be sympathetic to the judiciary or the profession.

The Cabinet Committee on the Reform of Legal Procedure was staffed by Coldstream from the Lord Chancellor's Office and Topham from the Cabinet Office. The Prime Minister said the priority was to deal with the huge divorce problem. Bevan argued for the simple solution: just transfer the jurisdiction to the County Courts—a view shared, generally, by the Labour Party; while most other reformers—including Goddard, the Lord Chief Justice—thought that at least undefended divorces should go there. Lord Merriman, President of the Probate, Divorce, and Admiralty Division, however, was strongly opposed. He wanted a Commission of Conciliation and Enquiry, consisting of barristers and social workers, which would sit in camera, supervised by High Court judges. Merriman had half convinced Jowitt and fully convinced both Archbishops this was the way to go. There was no way but to establish a committee; and the Cabinet Committee agreed.[86]

There were delays. The Lord Chancellor's Office wanted Lord Lindsay as Chairman, and a legally oriented committee. The haggling over names, and the evaluation of members of the Bar, make fascinating reading. Coldstream man-aged to veto names so that there was no more than one Labour MP, and had his way on most issues, but Shawcross, the Attorney-General, had his way on the chairmanship, which went to Mr Justice Denning.[87] Denning, at that time, was

minuted that the issue of the recovery of costs gave rise to heated debate throughout 'the whole of our deliberations'. 21 Nov. 1945, ibid.

[84] Stevens, *Law and Politics*, 335–41.

[85] The other members of the Cabinet Committee were Shawcross (Attorney-General), Soskice (Solicitor-General), Thompson (Lord Advocate), Ede (Home Secretary), Bevan (Health), Wilkinson (Education), and Silkin (Town and Country Planning). CAB 134/657. Jowitt, in a memorandum to the Cabinet (24 Nov. 1945) also argued there was 'real urgency' about codification.

[86] LCO 2/3946.

[87] The creation of the Committee was revealing. Coldstream wrote (2 May 1946) to Sir Thomas Lund, Secretary of the Law Society, asking if Littlewood (later President of the Law Society) was 'too conservative'. Lund replied that Littlewood was 'not your man' (Lund to Coldstream, 10 May 1946).

regarded as superb by the Office and worked his committee ferociously. Its *Interim Report*, calling for County Court judges to be used as Special Commissioners for hearing undefended cases, was ready by October—a five-month sprint.[88] Merriman was beside himself. He told Coldstream that County Court judges undermined 'the safety of the marriage tie'. As Coldstream noted: 'The President thereupon sent for Denning J., and told him that he considered that his proposals amounted to selling the fort, and that he wished to make plain he opposed root and branch.' By November, however, Lord Goddard had come out in favour of using the County Court judges and the Cabinet decided to go with Denning.[89] Coldstream planted a parliamentary question in the Lords and arranged to have the Lord Chief Justice, as well as Lords Simon and Wright, there to support the Government.[90]

The final Denning Report, recommending changes in many of the divorce procedures, which the Chairman found 'archaic', was no more attractive to Merriman. Denning had failed to invite Merriman to appear before the Committee a second time. 'I take serious exception to this method of proceeding,' said Merriman. According to a memorandum from Coldstream, Merriman was only prepared to accept twelve of forty recommendations. Merriman wrote that although Denning had spent two years in the Probate, Divorce, and Admiralty Division, he 'seemed to have learned very little'. While the Government accepted the Report, the President stalled. In December, the Chancellor set up the Hodson Committee, comprised of two High Court judges and Coldstream, to implement the Report. The Division used it as a blocking device. Coldstream urged Jowitt to warn Merriman that political pressure was mounting; and to tell Hodson that his Committee was there to implement the Denning recommendations, not judge their merits.[91] To cut a long story short, Merriman was ultimately overruled by Jowitt and all but one of the Denning Committee's recommendations were implemented. Denning—and Coldstream— had won.[92] On this occasion, the judiciary had been effectively used to procure substantive law reform through executive committees.

He was vetoed. Ellen Wilkinson, the Minister of Education, wanted a woman. Coldstream suggested Mrs Lane. Judge Engelbach (12 May 1946) thought Mrs Lane did her cases 'pleasantly' but 'certainly not with outstanding ability'. Another Mrs Lane was appointed. Coldstream vetoed any Matrimonial Registrars or divorce practitioners. Ibid.

[88] LCO 2/3951.

[89] 7 Nov. 1946, ibid. Merriman was 'bitterly hostile'. The Archbishop of Canterbury wrote to the Lord Chancellor expressing the fear that 'some of the County Court judges would become to be known as lax and superficial with disastrous results.' 7 Nov. 1946, ibid.

[90] Ibid. Lord Reading asked the question. Coldstream to Jowitt, 2 Nov. 1946, ibid.

[91] LCO 2/3957.

[92] The Bar and solicitors supported the recommendations. There were two parliamentary questions and Gerald Gardiner was pushing on behalf of the Haldane Society, ibid. The mechanics of having County Court judges sit as Divorce judges are collected in 2/3953. It led to the appointment of two more County Court judges in London. Coldstream told the judges to wear black robes and, ideally, morning coats. They were to be given clothing coupons, but had to buy the clothes themselves. In July 1947, the office relented, and paid half the cost of the robes.

With the divorce issue out of the way the Cabinet Committee turned its attention to litigation in general.[93] While some Cabinet members clearly hankered for a radical approach, involving the very nature of the adversary tradition, Jowitt and the Lord Chancellor's Office played the cautious role. Jowitt was only prepared to tinker with the status quo. He wanted the Bar preserved in its traditional form. He was opposed to any Continental influences. To protect the High Court Bench and the barristers' traditional role, he persuaded the Cabinet Committee that what was needed was two committees—one on the High Court and one on the County Court—thereby ensuring that the existing structure and monopolies would not be threatened. Indeed, the Lord Chief Justice (Goddard) and the Master of the Rolls (Greene) saw little point in having a committee on the High Court at all; and certainly did not want any non-lawyers on it. Jowitt put his conscience at rest by appointing a committee with non-lawyers, but making Raymond Evershed chair, since 'I know from previous correspondence that he does not want to do anything so drastic as to substitute for our procedure something analogous to French procedure.'

'The previous correspondence' was important. In the waning days of the Churchill administration, in 1945, Evershed had written to Viscount Simon, the outgoing Chancellor, arguing that the supremacy of the Rule of Law in England 'is largely bound up with the immense prestige and personal position accorded to the judges'. There were at least four reasons for this. First, the judges were chosen from a 'cloistered' and 'aristocratic' profession. Second, the judge was 'the complete master of the trial'. Third, the strict rules of procedure 'make the proceedings not only solemn (if not Olympian) but secure a real impartiality'. Fourth 'the rules as to dress (wigs and gowns) plus the rules of common law and precedent have made the law something of a mystery'.

From all this, Evershed drew certain conclusions. First, 'if very far reaching reforms were made so as to make our procedures more like the Continental, the result might well be to impair the position of the judges. *Per Contra*, if it is desired to maintain the personal position of the judges certain limitations to the scope of the reforms which are possible have got to be realized.' First and foremost there should be no fusion of the professions: the distinction between barristers and solicitors was sacrosanct. Second, Evershed was 'inclined to think that a complete codification of our law plus the abolition of our rules of precedent would tend to make our law simpler and therefore cheaper. On the other hand, it would tend to make it less certain and authoritative and it would tend to derogate seriously from the supremacy of our Courts.' Finally, Evershed thought 'that a complete and radical change of our whole system so as to make it conform more to the "centralized" system would or could greatly cheapen our law . . . But in considering such a change, the main thing to bear in mind is, I believe, the effect such a change might have on the position of Judges.' Such was the

[93] LCO 2/4012.

provenance of the Evershed Committee.[94] Its conservative assumptions were to shape English legal culture for the remainder of the century.

In fact Lord Evershed was, in the context of most members of the Bench, liberal; and he was aided by Gerald Gardiner, QC—whom Jowitt had tried to keep off the Committee[95]—and Mr Justice Upjohn,[96] but much of the power in the Committee lay in the hands of Coldstream.[97] He was able to cool the urge of Professor T. H. Marshall—one of the unwanted laymen—to investigate the French system so that courts might consider cutting down on oral evidence and have the Committee review the rules of evidence with a view to lowering the cost of litigation. Geoffrey Crowther, the economist, favoured the formal abolition of the distinction between barristers and solicitors.[98] Even Evershed, as he originally drafted the Report, had a recommendation that the Bar Council— rather than the Inns of Court—be made the controlling force at the Bar, with barristers, like solicitors, taking out practising certificates. Upjohn and Gardiner[99] saw this as an implied criticism of the Inns, and the ideas were dropped.[100] Had they not been, the recommendations of the Rawlinson Committee would have been unnecessary.[101]

It would be wrong, of course, to assume that the Lord Chancellor's Office always managed to control committees and commissions. The Beeching Committee, which led to the Courts Act of 1971, in some ways got away from the Lord Chancellor's Department; although Derek Oulton was secretary of the Committee and later on, in the Department, implemented the Report. That document, against the opposition of the Bar, rationalized the court structure; and the objections of the judges to permanent or semi-permanent courts of general jurisdiction outside London were finally overcome. The idea that 'more means worse'—a notion that had kept the bench artificially small—was finally abandoned. Beeching, however, was almost unique among laymen; he was not intimidated by lawyers or judges. Of the Bar's evidence he said the Bar 'really wanted nothing to change, but things simply to improve'.[102]

Coldstream (a member of the Committee), who had retired from the Lord Chancellor's Office, would ask hard questions; but he could not control Beeching. Judges were not able to get away with their usual platitudes.[103]

---

[94] Evershed Memorandum, dated 27 July 1945, LCO 2/3827.

[95] The 'robust' Summons for Directions was largely his work, ibid. In retrospect, the Summons has not justified its robust reputation.

[96] He sold the idea of shorter vacations for the judges. Ibid.

[97] See e.g. his letter to Evershed, 15 Feb.1952, ibid.

[98] See dissents of these members. *Final Report of the Committee on Supreme Court Practice and Procedure*, Cmnd. 8878 (1953), 317.

[99] See their letters of 1 Apr. 1953, LCO 2/3827.

[100] Evershed still urged the Chancellor to do something about counsel's fees. Letter, 20 May 1953, ibid.

[101] *The Times*, 25 Apr. 1986.   [102] Hearing, 18 July 1967, LCO 7/1.

[103] In fairness, Beeching did pressure the Bar Council on the shortage of counsel and the implications for increase in the number of provincial chambers. Ibid. Derek Oulton was the secretary. Under Beeching's guidance he put hard questions to the Bar. Ibid.

Denning appeared and was much in favour of reforming the Chancery Division, but was somewhat defensive about the Queen's Bench Division.[104] Indeed, as Beeching pressed on, Denning increasingly mouthed traditional judicial views. While he was in favour of permanent courts in the provinces,[105] and while he thought blurring the distinction between the High Court and County Court acceptable, he also thought it important that the High Court be kept small ('I am sorry we have got so many [judges] as we have at the moment') and equally important that its judges go on circuit ('The impact on a community is very great if you go into these outlying districts . . .').[106] To this latter remark, made in oral evidence, Beeching replied: 'Except that you are discouraging crime where it does not happen . . .'.[107] When asked about lay magistrates, Denning said he enjoyed sitting with them in Quarter Sessions and thought 'their views were worth just as much as mine'. This led to the obvious Beeching response: 'Do you think High Court judges ought to have them in that case?' His Lordship was not amused.

It is perhaps not surprising that it was the Beeching Committee which led to the Courts Act of 1971 and the transformation of the old Lord Chancellor's Office into the modern Lord Chancellor's Department—a very different animal. More important, Beeching was able to push through a restructuring of the courts which Bench and Bar had successfully thwarted for the previous one hundred years. Like the trains, Beeching made the courts run on time. The Courts Act, 1971 was a perfect vehicle for ensuring the effective hearing of cases. Enough courts and judges were to be provided for the ever-increasing number of criminal cases waiting to be heard. What was lacking was a serious analysis of whether these cases had been allocated to the right level of judge. History controlled that; and it was a history which was probably out of touch with modern needs. Together with the expansive Widgery Committee on Legal Aid, it has been said that the Courts Act provided 'the perfect eco-system for lawyers'. An important part of the Lord Chancellor's Department's work since these two events has involved attempting to cut the costs of Legal Aid, funded as the result of the Widgery Report, and operating within a court structure enshrined in the Beeching Report.

[104] The memorandum of the Lord Chief Justice, Parker, was relatively open-minded (LCO 755); that of the High Court judges less so (LCO 7/66).

[105] LCO 7/56/A: 'There is a strong case for merging the Divisions of the High Court.'

[106] He was then asked by Mr L. Cannon: 'In view of the fact that we have so few judges, is this not extremely wasteful just for the sake of whatever marginal effect it has in impressing people of the sanctity of the Law?' To this Denning replied: 'I can see the force of that from the point of view of administration and efficiency . . . But there are intangibles beyond.' Ibid.

[107] Beeching noted: 'I think you are trying to have it both ways. If you had a very few judges in order to preserve the respect for and the quality of the High Court judges, I do not think you can afford to have them spending their time relatively unproductively in very small centres.' Denning's view was that if the number of High Court judges were increased very much, not only would quality decline, but it would be impossible 'to get a common uniformity of approach on matters of principle on problems that arise'. Ibid.

7

Judicial Salaries from the 1940s to the 1980s

We have already examined the claims of the High Court judges to protect their fiscal and constitutional position during 'the Long Weekend' which embraced England between the First and Second World Wars.[1] Yet, intellectually, far more interesting were the efforts under the Attlee (1945–51) and Churchill (1951–5) administrations to examine the extent to which judicial independence was dependent upon fiscal independence. During a period when the rhetoric of equality was strong, the High Court and Appeal judges in particular raised fascinating issues of economic comparability. In a nation where a Churchill administration produced a Beveridge Report and the 1944 Education Act, while Labour produced a policy of nationalization and the National Health Service, there might seem to be ideal opportunities for unpacking the concept of judicial independence. In fact, the arguments about judicial salaries were treated much like any other pay claims.

The issue of judicial salaries, especially before the passage of the Administration of Justice Act, 1973—which provided an extra-parliamentary method of raising High Court salaries—highlighted the relationship between legislature, executive, and judiciary. To the judges, fiscal independence was an integral part of judicial independence. High Court salaries had been set at £5,000 in 1832, while the County Court salaries had been raised to £2,000 in 1937. During the Second World War, Viscount Simon, Churchill's Lord Chancellor, suggested an increase in High Court salaries to £7,000. The issue was raised in November 1944;[2] and by February 1945, Simon was pressing Sir John Anderson, Chancellor of the Exchequer, for an answer before everyone's energy was absorbed by the Yalta Conference.[3] The answer was 'no', but with the War over, Goddard, the new Lord Chief Justice, raised the issue again with the Labour Chancellor who had appointed him, Jowitt.[4]

(a) The Labour Years, 1945–1951

The more vigorous cry in fact came from the County Court judges. At their meeting in February 1946, they voted that the 'ratio between the remuneration

---

[1] See Ch. 2 above.

[2] Napier memorandum, 15 Dec. 1944. The only salary not to be increased was that of the Master of the Rolls. Greene, MR, hastened to write to Simon: 'You will not, I know, misunderstand me. I am concerned not for myself but for the future holders of my office . . . the office of Master of the Rolls [is] increasingly unattractive.' Greene to Simon, 15 Nov. 1944, LCO 2/6691.

[3] Simon to Anderson, 23 Feb. 1954, ibid.   [4] Memorandum from Napier, 21 Dec. 1945, ibid.

of County Court and High Court judges needs reconsideration . . . [I]n country districts, [the County Court judge] is the permanent representative of the judiciary in the eyes of the ordinary citizen. From this point of view it is important that his status and prestige, which must to a considerable extent depend on his salary, should not be conspicuously below that of a High Court judge.' The increase in the salaries of lawyers in government also raised issues of comparability and constitutionalism:

The fact that the salaries of these solicitors [to Government Departments] have been raised to a higher level than those of County Court judges might well lead to the inference that the lawyers who serve the Executive Government are regarded as discharging a more important function than that of the judiciary. It would . . . be especially regrettable that this inference should be drawn in view of the fact that in recent times the powers of the Executive over the life of the community have been greatly enlarged.[5]

The complaints of the High Court judges were different. Odd as it may sound in retrospect, much of the debate revolved around the daily tax-free allowance of £7.10, paid to judges on circuit in addition to their actual expenses. Originally paid as part of the package organized by Selborne in the 1880s to make the judges feel better about the so-called Winter Assizes, it was intended to cover the cost of entertaining the local gentry. Its purpose after 1945 was seen primarily as a tax-free addition to judicial salaries. Lord Justice Asquith wrote somewhat pathetically to Jowitt in April 1946, from the straitened ambience of Brooks's: 'The only way in which Queen's Bench Division judges have been able to balance their budgets during the War has been by going circuit.' Chancery judges were denied 'this bonus'. 'I've lived from hand to mouth during the War.' Asquith had sold his King's Bench robes but could not afford Court of Appeal ones. In order to match the £5,000 p.a. in 1832, Asquith claimed that High Court judges would have to be paid £70,000 in 1946 values.[6] Jowitt was unmoved; he pointed out he was having no difficulty in attracting the best people to the Bench; and restated his view that the County Court judges had the better claim.[7]

Jowitt was, nevertheless, toying with the idea that £500 of a High Court judge's salary should be treated as tax-free expenses;[8] but the Inland Revenue stood firm that they could only allow judicial expenses incurred 'wholly, exclusively and necessarily in the performance of their duties'.[9] Moreover, many judges, led by Lord Greene, held it was dishonourable to 'fiddle' with expenses when the 'moral claim' of the judges was 'outstanding'.[10] Following an article by Schuster on judicial salaries in *The Sunday Times* in December 1947,[11] however, the Inland Revenue did allow deductions for judges' studies and law libraries at

---

[5] Memorandum contained in a letter from Judge Davies to Napier, 27 Dec. 1945, LCO 12/54.
[6] Asquith to Jowitt, 3 Apr. 1946, LCO 2/6691.
[7] Jowitt to Asquith, 8 Apr. 1946, ibid.   [8] Napier to Padmore, 25 Apr. 1947, ibid.
[9] E. G. Grigg to Napier, 27 Nov. 1947; Vaisey to Napier, 3 Dec. 1947, ibid.
[10] Greene to Napier, 23 Jan. 1948, 11 Feb. 1948.   [11] *Sunday Times*, 28 Dec. 1947.

home.[12] Lurking in the background was the fear that if salaries were seriously adjusted the judges would lose the 'perk' of not being taxed on fees earned at the Bar but paid after they went to the Bench.

The Scottish High Court judges competed with their English brethren in terms of dissatisfaction. Lord President Cooper wrote to one of the Scottish law lords, Lord Normand: 'I am amazed at the almost mutinous spirit which seems to prevail even among the less demonstrative of my brethren.'[13] Two days later the Lord President was reporting that Lord Sorn had spent no less than £25 of his own money while sitting for a week. 'The Scottish Bench is rapidly being depressed to a level far below that of a managerial position.'[14] Lord Normand hastened to see Sir George Coldstream, only to be told that nothing could be done at that time.[15]

Meanwhile, County Court judges continued to complain about their salaries and the differential with the High Court. Judge Pugh, the Secretary of the County Court judges, called on Jowitt in December 1947 to tell him that salaries were 'so low as to interfere, in the case of one or two judges on the County Court Bench, with the proper discharge of their duties'.[16] By spring 1949, there were threats, since morale was so bad, that some 'judges will take some individual steps to ventilate their grievances publicly':

If judges are to live in mean houses, wear cheap clothes . . . not only would their work suffer by reason of their mental discomfort but the present high estimation in which the judiciary is everywhere held would also suffer. If the members of the judiciary are not regarded with respect, their impartiality will, such is human nature, come to be doubted . . .

Either the judges of the County Courts will be considered as people of inferior importance financially to dentists, town clerks, city engineers, medical specialists and a host of others holding government appointments or your Lordship's successors may be constrained to fill the County Court bench with failures at the Bar to whom even £2,000 a year is a fortune.[17]

With the Chorley Report on the salaries of senior civil servants published,[18] the Lord Chancellor's Office began pushing for higher judicial salaries. Jowitt claimed in Cabinet that two persons had refused offers of High Court judgeships and that he could recruit only 'burnt-out' barristers for the County Court.[19] In February 1949, Napier saw Sir Edward Bridges, Permanent Secretary of the Treasury, asking for at least another £1,000 for both High Court (£6,000) and

---

[12] £40 and £75, respectively, 3 Apr. 1948, LCO 2/6691.
[13] Cooper to Normand, 16 Jan. 1948, LCO 2/3885.
[14] Cooper to Normand, 18 Jan. 1948, ibid.   [15] 19 Mar. 1948, ibid.
[16] Memorandum from Napier, 15 Dec. 1947, LCO 12/54.
[17] Memorandum from three County Court judges, contained in letter from Pugh to Napier, 22 Feb. 1949, ibid.
[18] *Report of the Committee on Higher Civil Service Remuneration*, Cmnd. 7635 (1948).
[19] LCO 2/3881; LCO 2/4609, referring to CM (50).

County Court (£3,000) judges.[20] Treasury officials were not noted for their enthusiasm for increases in judicial salaries—particularly for the High Court judges, whose salaries exceeded their own—but Bridges did suggest that if Sir Raymond Evershed, in his report on High Court procedure, called for increases in judicial efficiency and not too many new judges, a case for the increases could be made in the 1949–50 session.[21]

Something, however, always seemed to come up, especially with regard to High Court salaries. A wild card was the Scottish judges. They, in an uncharacteristically uncanny act, had, in 1887, given up their circuit expenses for an all-in salary of £3,700. In March 1949, they threatened a public statement. Lord President Cooper warned, 'his colleagues could no longer be restrained'.[22] Meanwhile the politicians were even less enthusiastic than the Treasury officials about a general salary increase for judges. Although the Financial Secretary to the Treasury said in the House of Commons that a Bill would be forthcoming in the session, in May the Cabinet decided not to proceed.[23] Jowitt continued to lobby Herbert Morrison, who remained 'rather apprehensive about the political aspects of the Bill'.[24] Napier continued to lobby the Treasury and believed that he had its agreement to the increases if the Evershed Report would shorten the long vacation, increase the length of the judicial day, and call for a maximum of three new High Court judges.[25]

The rank and file of the Labour Party was, however, letting its views be known. Reginald Paget, QC, MP, wrote to Morrison that he did 'not feel that it is possible to justify in the country that £5 is too much for a railwayman and £5,000 too little for a judge. Nor do I think that the argument that the Evershed Committee will propose more work for judges and that they should therefore have their salaries raised, is very convincing. It involves the proposition that £5,000 is only adequate for a part-time job.'[26] While Shawcross, the Attorney-General, argued that Paget was 'emotional and of quite unsound judgment',[27] the Parliamentary Labour Party warned Attlee that it must be consulted before any increase was suggested.[28]

The warnings continued. Morrison's office noted that 'there will be serious trouble if and when the Bill gets to the floor of the House';[29] and later in the Session the Parliamentary Party reiterated that the claims were 'completely out of step with the general policies urged on the lower income groups'.[30] On the other side of the argument, *The Times* thundered that judges needed the rises

---

[20] 23 Feb. 1949. For details, see LCO 2/3881 and LCO 12/54.
[21] Bridges to Napier, 28 Feb. 1949, LCO 2/3881.
[22] Normand to Napier, 9 Mar. 1949, ibid. Napier had already minuted that the English and Scottish judges should be dealt with together. LCO 2/3885.
[23] 16 May 1949, LCO 2/3881.
[24] Jowitt to Morrison, 20 May 1949; Morrison to Attlee, 30 May 1949, ibid.
[25] Minute by Napier, 20 May 1949, ibid.   [26] Paget to Morrison, 30 May 1949, ibid.
[27] Shawcross to Jowitt, 31 May 1949, ibid.   [28] PLP to Attlee, 31 May 1949, ibid.
[29] Morrison to Attlee, 8 June 1949, ibid.   [30] PLP to Attlee, 7 July 1949, ibid.

because of the 'importance of (their) status', to ensure 'independence', and to provide 'control of the bureaucracy'.[31] Asquith, by then comfortably established in the Court of Appeal, made much of the discrimination against appeal judges who could not collect tax-free circuit allowances;[32] and both Shawcross and Jowitt used Mr Justice Lynskey's refusal to be promoted from King's Bench to the Court of Appeal as further evidence of the inadequacy of salaries.[33] Thus the Lord Chancellor's Office attempted to proceed with its plan to raise High Court salaries to £6,000 and County Court salaries to £3,000. The Treasury warned the Office that 'it is very important that the knowledge that we are thinking in some detail about improving judicial salaries and pensions should not be generally known'.[34]

The hopes were soon dashed. Opposition from the back benches was considerable, and after the Permanent Secretaries decided not to press for their recommended awards under the Chorley Report, the limited enthusiasm for the increase in judicial salaries on the part of the Civil Service evaporated.[35] Shawcross continued to argue for at least a car pool for judges: 'Often they cannot obtain, and I think really cannot afford, taxis and one quite frequently sees them standing in queues for buses outside the courts or the Old Bailey, mixing with the jurors and witnesses in cases they are in the course of trying.'[36]

Even that did not move the Lord Chancellor: 'Wilfrid Greene, when Master of the Rolls, took a strong view that he could not accept a car from the pool to drive him between the Law Courts and Waterloo because it would be a present from the Executive, offered without Parliamentary authority.'[37] Even the County Court judges, while announcing that their 'plight' was 'worse', realized that, with the collapse of the pound, any increases would have to wait until after the 1950 Election.[38]

Even after the Election, the Labour Government, with a small majority, hesitated to act. Jowitt suggested to Gaitskell, the new Chancellor of the Exchequer, that there ought to be a committee on judges' pensions. Gaitskell dismissed this as 'totally impracticable', pointing out that even a suggestion of pensions for the widows of judges had 'provoked considerable controversy'. Gaitskell did, however, offer a deal: if Jowitt would abandon a pay claim for High Court judges,

---

[31] *The Times*, 28 May 1949.

[32] Asquith to Jowitt, 4 and 13 June 1949, LCO 2/3881. This led Napier to minute, 'The [circuit] allowances must be too high.' Ibid.

[33] Shawcross also noted that some judges were worse off than NHS specialists. Shawcross to Morrison, 31 May 1949. In his letter to Attlee, Jowitt also noted that he was having difficulties attracting people to the Bench. 'I still believe our ancestors were wise in placing judges above financial difficulties.' Jowitt to Attlee, 9 July 1949, ibid.

[34] Crombie to Napier, 26 July 1949, ibid.

[35] Memorandum, Napier to Jowitt, 22 Sept. 1949. In vain did Jowitt report to Attlee that Evershed had recommended shorter vacations (by three weeks), a longer day (by one half-hour), and only four more King's Bench judges. LCO 2/3881.

[36] Shawcross to Jowitt, 18 Nov. 1949, ibid.　　　　[37] Jowitt to Shawcross, 23 Nov. 1949, ibid.

[38] Meeting with County Court judges, 5 Dec. 1949, LCO 2/3881 and LCO 12/54.

Gaitskell would consider a pay claim for the County Court judges.[39] It was a deal that Jowitt accepted;[40] although High Court judges were by then openly calling for a general tax-free allowance.[41] No sooner had Jowitt agreed to this deal than he found the Treasury had two further caveats with respect to County Court judges: £2,750 was better than £3,000, since the Sheriff Substitutes, the rough equivalent of County Court judges in Scotland, could be paid no more than £2,750 without triggering a pay claim from the Scottish Lords of Session; and, emulating the structure of paying the Sheriff Substitutes, the Treasury proposed a step system of salary increases for the County Court judges, based on longevity.[42] The Lord Chancellor's Office was amused by neither arrangement. When Judge Pugh asked why progress was so slow, Napier replied that '[T]he progress would have been much quicker but for the Union with Scotland.'[43] Meanwhile, Napier explained to Padmore at the Treasury that a step system of salaries would make successful counsel even more reluctant to take judgeships, since the executive would have control over promotion.[44]

Indeed, until the end of the Labour administration, there was bickering about these two issues. C. C. Cunningham, the Permanent Secretary at the Scottish Office, and Hector McNeil, the Scottish Minister, could see no reason at all why Scottish High Court judges should not be paid at the same rate as the English; nor did they see why Sheriff Substitutes should be discriminated against *vis-à-vis* County Court judges.[45] The Treasury was not entirely dissatisfied to have a split in the ranks; its memorandum to Cabinet merely noted that there could be no pay increases for the English High Court lest it start a pay claim among the Scots.[46] There was still disagreement between the Lord Chancellor's Office and the Treasury on the issue of the salary and grading of County Court judges. Gaitskell wanted £2,750 on appointment and £3,000 after five years.[47] Once again Jowitt caved in and agreed;[48] and the final Cabinet paper called for such a step—as well as increases for Sheriff Substitutes, expenses for all Scottish judges, and an additional £500 for Northern Ireland High Court judges.[49] After Cabinet, however, the steps disappeared; all County Court judges were to get £2,800. Ministers had felt that litigants would worry if their cases were heard by

[39] Gaitskell to Jowitt, 11 Dec. 1950, LCO 2/4610. In the first draft of the response to Gaitskell, the Office wrote: 'I cannot think it desirable that a judge should ride on the same bus as jurors.' In the next draft it was replaced with: 'Judge has to take home books.'

[40] Jowitt to Gaitskell, 15 Dec. 1950, ibid.

[41] Sir Raymond Evershed said it was 'absurd and all wrong that Her Majesty's judges on circuit should have the privilege of a reasonable profit and living free beside'. All should have a tax-free allowance to maintain their 'dignity of position'. Evershed to Jowitt, 18 Dec. 1950, ibid.

[42] Coldstream to Napier, 25 Jan. 1951; Napier to Padmore (Treasury), 12 Feb. 1951, ibid.

[43] Napier to Pugh, 19 Mar. 1951, ibid.   [44] Napier to Padmore, 12 Feb. 1951, ibid.

[45] C. C. Cunningham to Treasury, 21 Apr. 1951; McNeil to Gaitskell, 14 June 1951, LCO 2/4610; 2/4611.

[46] The Scottish judges were, however, to be given expenses. Memorandum, 1 May 1951, LCO 2/4610.

[47] Simon to Jowitt, 12 June 1951, LCO 2/4611.   [48] Jowitt to Gaitskell, 16 June 1951, ibid.

[49] 6 July 1951, ibid.

a judge at the bottom of the scale.[50] Nothing more, however, happened before Labour went out of power.

(b) The Conservative Administration, 1951–1964

With the return of the Conservatives, the judges had in Churchill a leader who shared their view of the mystical importance of the judiciary. Unfortunately, in Simonds they had a Lord Chancellor who was a neophyte in the political jungle. Simonds was upset when there was no mention of increasing judicial salaries in the Speech from the Throne.[51] He then wrote a letter, beginning 'Pray forgive me for bothering you,' to R. A. Butler, the new Chancellor of the Exchequer. Its message was, however, direct: even in the then-current economic circumstances something must be done for the judges.[52] At one of his earliest Cabinet meetings, Churchill announced that an increase for County Court judges was 'non-controversial'.[53] Within days a Bill was published, pushing County Court salaries to £2,800, with the judges giving up their *per diem* payments for hearing divorce cases.[54] This increase became law in the Judicial Offices (Salaries) Act. In 1957, County Court judges' salaries were increased to £3,750, in the Judicial Offices (Salaries and Pensions) Act. More importantly, the latter statute gave the government the power to raise County Court salaries by delegated legislation, subject to Parliamentary Resolution.[55]

The issue of High Court judges' salaries, meanwhile, remained unsettled. At the beginning of the Churchill administration, the Scottish Office reminded the Lord Chancellor's Office that the Scottish High Court judges expected parity with the English High Court judges,[56] noting that 'the relatively small number of judges have been singled out for adverse discrimination in this matter, and no attempt has ever been made by any Government to justify this adverse discrimination.' Scottish judges thus felt an 'acute sense of injustice'.[57] Scottish lobbying did not stop. In the Cabinet meeting of 8 November, Churchill apparently mentioned that he was in favour of tax-free allowances for High Court judges.[58]

---

[50] The Cabinet met on 16 July 1951. For details of that meeting, see CM 52(51); also LCO 2/4614. Gaitskell explained that Scottish judges were paid less because Scottish barristers earned less. LCO 2/4614.

[51] Memorandum, files, 2 Nov. 1951, LCO 2/4611.

[52] Simonds to Butler, 6 Nov. 1951, ibid.

[53] He also expressed the hope that a way would be found to give High Court judges 'expenses'. CP 5(51)2.

[54] One of the big issues was whether stipendiary magistrates should have the same salary as County Court judges, as they had until 1947. As they pointed out in a memorandum, they were chosen from the 'same stratum' in the legal profession. LCO 2/4611.

[55] Perhaps remarkably, the procedure for salary increases passed unopposed. *Parliamentary Debates*, (5th ser.), HC vol. 573, cols. 211 f. (9 July 1957).

[56] Lewis (Scottish Office) to Boggis-Rolfe, 20 Nov. 1951, ibid.

[57] 15 Dec. 1951. In response, the Lord Chancellor wrote that 'The problem of the judges' salaries in England is vexing me very much at present.' Simonds to Cooper, 18 Dec. 1951, ibid.

[58] LCO 2/4614. For details of the Cabinet meeting, see LCO 2/5908.

Within the week the Scottish Office had wind of the 'mention' and announced 'it seems clear that the Scottish judges would have to share in any scheme of this kind . . . '.[59] There were problems with this, even in England. If the judges were paid a taxi allowance of 10s. or 15s. a day, there would be pressure to end the tax-free status of non-accountable circuit allowances which, for High Court judges, averaged £840 p.a. A childless judge would have to earn £9,280 gross p.a. to earn the equivalent. Giving up the £7.10 circuit *per diem* would be 'a large sacrifice', and even a 30s. taxi allowance would only produce the equivalent of £6,020 p.a.[60] Coldstream soon decided that both the idea of a reduction in circuit expenses and that of a London taxi allowance were dead.[61]

There followed a further period of bickering. Many judges wanted part of their salaries tax-free. The Lord Chancellor's Office suggested £100 tax-free allowance. The Inland Revenue said that what was not tolerated in commerce would certainly not be tolerated in Government;[62] and the Revenue was adamant that the maintenance of privacy and a good position in society was not 'wholly, exclusively and necessarily' incurred in fulfilling their judicial duties. Once again the Scottish question queered the pitch. Coldstream minuted that he was not sending a copy of the latest Treasury proposals 'to the Scottish Office till I get from them the facts about the walking habits of Scottish judges'.[63] The Scottish Office nevertheless got wind of the proposals, and its civil servants, without consulting their ministers, took a Civil Service union position: 'The High Court judges, at any rate in Scotland, can hardly argue that the risk of contamination to which they are exposed by having to travel to court in their own cars, or by public transport, or on their own feet, is such as to imperil their standing in Society or their impartiality on the Bench. All sorts of people, including civil servants, have to submit to such risk.'[64] In short, ten of the fourteen Scottish High Court judges walked to work.

There was something ironic about the whole situation. In these years, it had become customary to refer to the judges in hushed tones of awe. The Lord Mayor's dinner for the judges set the tone for these eulogies. In 1949 the judges were told that 'if British judges were ever biased at all, it was always in favour of the accused,'[65] and in the following year the Lord Mayor affirmed that 'our judiciary today stood unchallenged by friend and foe and remained the bulwark of our nation and a guarantee of peace.'[66] On the question of sentencing, the Lord Mayor asserted in 1952 that the judges 'maintained, with glorious continuity, the

[59] 13 Nov. 1951, LCO 2/4613.

[60] Mr Justice Bryne, on circuit for 230 days, was paid £1,720. Mr Justice Lynskey was paid £11,137.10s. Boggis-Rolfe memorandum, 7 June 1952, LCO 2/4613.

[61] Boggis-Rolfe to files, 9 June 1952, ibid.

[62] 10 Jan. 1952, ibid. Mr Justice Devlin asked for a set of Halsbury's Laws to use in the country at the weekend. Boggis-Rolfe said no—9 May 1952, ibid.

[63] 25 May 1952, ibid.   [64] Memorandum from C. C. Cunningham, 7 June 1952, ibid.

[65] *Law Times*, 208 (15 July 1949), 46.   [66] Ibid. 210 (14 July 1950), 31.

high standards which they, and they alone in the world, had created'.[67] The Lord Mayor for 1953, Sir Rupert de la Bere, was prepared to go even further, and expressed the view that 'Her Majesty's judges had a greater understanding of human nature than any other body of men in the world.'[68] By 1956 judges were said not only to protect and understand society but even to be rebuilding its 'moral barriers'.[69]

The Lord Chancellor's Office, however, continued to wrestle with what was special about the judges. Napier noted in a letter to the Treasury: 'The uniqueness of the position of the judges may be very difficult to express, but I believe profoundly that it exists and that it is of great importance to the country.'[70] In this he was supported at least by the Scottish judges. The Lord Advocate (Lord Clyde) wrote to the Lord Chancellor, exclaiming that it was 'most unsuitable for a High Court Judge to travel in a public conveyance'—and arguing for a £500 tax-free allowance for all.[71] The Prime Minister joined the emotional mêlée. Churchill wrote to Simonds saying he knew that two judges had resigned to go back to the Bar, and all the judges should be given £1,500 or £2,000 tax-free.[72] Simonds in some embarrassment explained that two judges had asked about resignation—Mr Justice Donovan to go back to the Bar[73] and Lord Justice Upjohn to head a Foundation[74]—but had been dissuaded.[75]

By August 1952, the Chancellor of the Exchequer was waxing lyrical in his communications with the Lord Chancellor. There was no right time for a salary increase; but £7,000 for High Court Judges—'it would be impolitic to make such a large increase even for so special a class as the judiciary.' All he could say was that tax-free payments would be worse. Where would it end?[76] Meanwhile, the Lord Chancellor's Office worked on a Secret memorandum about the role of the judges. Its tone and content were important because it emphasized the relationship between status and independence. The memorandum began by noting that the 'maintenance of a strong and independent judiciary, which was one of the main issues in the seventeenth century conflict between Crown and Parliament has, by the wisdom of our ancestors, been secured in two ways: tenure and absence of financial worries'. It closed by citing Birkenhead: 'The judges, though independent of the Government, are far from being independent of Parliament. They are the precision instruments for carrying out the will of Parliament.'[77] For some, that might sound an odd concept of judicial independence.

---

[67] Ibid. 214 (11 July 1952), 26.   [68] Ibid. 216 (17 July 1953), 374.
[69] Ibid. 222 (20 July 1956), 40.
[70] Napier to Treasury, 12 June 1952, LCO 2/4613.
[71] Clyde to Simonds, 13 June 1952, ibid. Clyde's letter followed a letter of outrage from the Lord Justice General (Cooper) to the Lord Advocate making it clear that the Scottish judges 'were in a state of Indignation' after 32 years of negotiation and the offer of 'big money' for doctors. Cooper to Clyde, 4 Apr. 1952, LCO 2/4612.
[72] Churchill to Simonds, 28 June 1952, LCO 2/4613.
[73] LCO 2/6354 (closed until 2004).   [74] LCO 2/6355 (closed until 2002).
[75] Simonds to Churchill, 30 June 1952, LCO 2/4613.
[76] Butler to Simonds, 11 Aug. 1952, LCO 2/5906.   [77] LCO 2/5906.

By the autumn of 1952, Churchill in Cabinet was back to his idea of a tax-free allowance for judges in view of their 'uniqueness' and the 'unrivalled reputation of the High Court bench'. They were, he said, in an immortal phrase, 'a National asset the Conservative Party should feel honoured to uphold'. Like the Prime Minister, £2,000 of their salaries should be tax-free.[78] The Inland Revenue protested, arguing that this would favour independently wealthy judges and, at the very least, only a slice of the salary should be tax-free.[79] The Treasury was no happier, but Churchill made it clear he wanted to lead the fight, and Simonds produced a new memorandum saying that 'never since Stuart times was it so important that the Bench should be vigilant, fearless and strong'.[80] There was compromising behind the scenes, and at the 25 November Cabinet meeting a Bill was agreed with a £1,000 tax-free allowance for High Court judges. Immediately the Treasury said the circuit allowances must go,[81] a move that did not appeal to the Lord Chief Justice.[82]

The Treasury remained unhappy, and there were worries that the arrangement would be demanded by all judges.[83] The Prime Minister, however, saw the Leader of the Opposition,[84] and on 26 February 1953, the Cabinet agreed to a Second Reading.[85] An emotional brief was prepared for Churchill, calling the judges an 'essential feature of the British way of life' who were 'the envy and admiration of the world' and were to be rewarded with a 'bold new method of giving' increases.[86] There was more talk of the danger of the judges using public transport. Although Churchill was the chief Government spokesman, the Second Reading went badly, not, surprisingly, because of hostility from Labour, but, surprisingly, because of the opposition of the Tory back-benches. Crookshank, the Leader of the House, agreed to delay the debate, and Butler advised the Lord Chancellor that nothing should be done until after the Budget.[87]

The press reflected the political spectrum opposed to the proposal. The views of some were to be expected. The *Tribune*, under the title 'Judges Screw', saw it as a case of jobs for the boys.[88] The *New Statesman*, inaccurately, thought Churchill was in the hands of the Lord Chancellor and the Lord Chief Justice.[89]

---

[78] Cabinet, 21 Oct. 1952, ibid. See also 2/5908.

[79] The Lord Chancellor's Office implied there were no independently wealthy judges. The Inland Revenue pointed out that this was not so. One judge had £12,000 of outside income and the £2,000 tax-free allowance would push his income (£5,000 plus £12,000) to the equivalent of £82,900. Padmore to Napier, 7 Nov. 1952, LCO 2/5906. It was therefore agreed that the £2,000 would be taken in a band £1,500–£3,500. On the remainder, tax would be paid. Secret memorandum, 11 Nov. 1952, ibid.

[80] Oct. 1952, ibid.   [81] Padmore to Napier, 27 Nov. 1952, ibid.

[82] Although he agreed to review them. 2 Dec. 1952, ibid.

[83] 'It is not suggested that the judicial qualities needed in a High Court judge on the one hand and a County Court judge on the other are any different in essence: the matter is one of degree.' Memorandum, Coldstream, 27 Jan. 1953, ibid.

[84] Butler to Churchill, 17 Feb. 1953 (on meeting with Attlee), ibid.   [85] LCO 2/5908.

[86] Bruce Fraser (Treasury) to Coldstream, 7 Mar. 1953, ibid.

[87] 27 Mar. 1953 (the debate had been on the 26 Mar.), ibid.   [88] 21 Mar. 1953.

[89] 21 Mar. 1953.

Yet newspapers from the *Herald*,[90] through the *Manchester Guardian*[91] and *The Sunday Times*,[92] to the *Daily Telegraph*,[93] while favouring a salary increase, uniformly attacked the tax-free approach.[94] Only *The Times* approved both the increase and the method.[95]

The Times, after noting that the High Court judges had received no increase since 1832, thundered: 'There are practically no rich men nowadays—as the subjects of King William IV understood riches—and it is far beyond the capacity of public funds to endow the present judges with the opulence that their predecessors enjoyed a century ago. But it is of first-rate importance that they should continue to be men of substance and security. The vast moral authority of the law in this country is bound up in the public mind with the visible adjunct of the men who dispense the Queen's justice.'[96] Ten days later, *The Times* returned to the theme: 'The dignity of the bench must be upheld by a certain way of living, which must extend as much to the judges' home lives as, for example, to the manner in which they travel to and from the courts.'[97]

The overall reaction of the press was, however, hostile. Poor Simonds could not understand what had hit him. Writing to Derek Walker Smith, the Chair of the 1922 Committee, he protested that 'we as a party have a great opportunity of asserting this principle (the privileges of the judiciary) by saying that, in relation to income tax, we would do for the judges what we would not do for any other section of the community.' Those who challenged the Bill forgot 'the wisdom of our ancestors who remembered the Stuart times'.[98] R. A. Butler, Chancellor of the Exchequer, had only one piece of advice for Simonds: avoid the 1922 Committee.[99]

By April 1953, Coldstream was suggesting a basic salary increase: to £8,000 for the English High Court and £6,000 for Ulster and Scotland.[100] In fact, he had wanted a base of £10,000, but with 6*d.* off the super-tax, the Treasury pressed for £8,000. By May, it was still £6,000 for Scotland, but Ulster was down to £5,750. While all judges should get £150 tax-free, 'anything which savours of treating the judges differently from the general body of taxpayers is impracticable on political grounds.'[101] By May, however, the Cabinet, led by the Chancellor of the Exchequer, had agreed to double the base judicial salary to £10,000.[102]

Simonds eventually appeared before the 1922 Committee. He did reasonably

[90] 16 Mar. 1953.   [91] 14 Mar. 1953.   [92] 22 Mar. 1953.   [93] 16 Mar. 1953.
[94] See also *The Economist*, 21 Mar. 1953.   [95] 23 Mar. 1953.
[96] *The Times*, 14 Mar. 1953.
[97] *The Times*, 24 Mar. 1953. See on all this, B. Wootton, *The Social Foundations of Wage Policy* (2nd edn. London, 1962), 128–9. The only other support appeared to come from the *Solicitors' Journal*, which concluded that the income was 'not in the same class as the inflationary wage increases to which we have become accustomed'. *Solicitors' Journal*, 97 (21 Mar. 1953), 197.
[98] Simonds to Walker Smith, 17 Apr. 1953, LCO 2/5906.
[99] Butler to Simonds, 27 Apr. 1953, ibid.   [100] 1 May 1953, LCO 2/5907.
[101] Coldstream to Napier and Simonds, 28 Apr. 1953, ibid.
[102] CC (53) 30th meeting, 5 May 1953, ibid.; see also 14 May 1953, LCO 2/5908.

well. One member wrote: 'In 10 years time we may be able to say that it was thanks to the judges' determination to increase their spending money that the dead wall of egalitarian reward was first breached and then done away with in a new and brighter age.' Yet the hostility of the back-benchers was still there. They argued that the non-contributory pensions really made the existing salaries worth £8,864. Moreover, as one back-bencher complained to the Lord Chancellor: '[Y]ou referred to the harrowing sight of a judge going in a car while his wife had to do her shopping on foot. Many hard-working professional and salaried men have just such a jaundicing experience . . . Few of them have pensions on the scale awarded to judges. Many of them have to go to their place of work, strap-hanging.'[103]

Relations, meanwhile, between the Lord Chancellor's Office and the Treasury were, at times, chilly. Coldstream warned Napier: 'I don't want to be unfair, but the ordinary run of Treasury official are pretty lukewarm about all this.'[104] Napier, perhaps unwisely, told the Treasury of the judicial doubts: 'the judges consider themselves as the innocent victims of ministerial blundering, and they are left guessing how serious may be the damage to their prospects.'[105] Bridges at the Treasury was testy. The Treasury had been busy with the Coronation, and the judges had better forget about a bill in the then-current Session; and 'if the judges do regard themselves as the innocent victims of ministerial blundering, the Chancellor of the Exchequer is not to be regarded as one of those who made the blunder. If rather more heed had been paid to his views, the present unhappy situation might have been avoided.'[106]

In June 1953, however, the Chancellor of the Exchequer did send over a Bill raising English High Court judges to £8,000 with proportional increases for their Celtic brethren.[107] At once the Scottish Office said if the Scottish judges did not get the full £3,000 they would open up a debate in Parliament on differentials.[108] Meanwhile the Inland Revenue said that if the judges were to receive a £150 'taxi' allowance, it would be taxable,[109] and Coldstream said the only way to make it tax-free would be to say so in the Bill and that would be 'unattractive politically'. Thus Coldstream on his own contacted Godfrey Davis, Ltd. about the possibility of a judicial motor pool to ferry the judges to and from the London rail termini. As he reported to Simonds, 'I find the car proposal rather attractive . . . apart from state and dignity, there is the additional and powerful reason that scrambling to and from work in public conveyances undoubtedly detracts from a man's efficiency.'[110] The Treasury, however, was unenthusiastic and urged the proposal be dropped and the High Court judges be

---

[103] F. J. Erroll to Simonds, 14 May 1953, LCO 2/5907.
[104] Coldstream to Napier, 11 June 1953, ibid.
[105] Napier to Bridges, 12 June 1953, ibid.   [106] Bridges to Napier, 17 June 1953, ibid.
[107] Chancellor of the Exchequer to Lord Chancellor, 20 June 1953, ibid.
[108] David Milne (Scottish Office) to Padmore (Treasury), 30 June 1953, ibid.
[109] Padmore to Napier, 2 July 1953, ibid.
[110] Coldstream to Simonds, 6 and 9 July 1953, ibid.

given £8,500.[111] Before the Treasury communicated this offer, however, Simonds offered to settle for £8,000;[1.2] an offer Butler hastened to accept.[113] Within a couple of weeks the Cabinet approved a base increase of £3,000 all around.[114]

The vital issues were by then whether the rise would be retroactive and whether the judges would have to give up circuit allowances before the new salary scale went through. The Permanent Secretary opined that it would be a 'real disaster' if the bill failed again; and there 'will be plenty of sniping from the left-wingers'.[115] The Office busied itself with minutiae. After all there were the real expenses to be taken care of. Napier explained to Parliamentary Counsel that 'the High Court judge as Commissioner of Assize is not an individual but a circus.' Thus there had to be 'allowances of so much per day for the board and lodging of the circus at each town where they perform'.[116]

The Prime Minister again agreed to introduce the Second Reading.[117] The judges continued to suspect the worst and tried to pin-prick the Office; for instance Mr Justice Sellers, who was taking the Commercial List, took papers home by taxi and billed the Clerk of Accounts for the cost. The Lord Chancellor's Office instructed the latter not to pay.[118] On the day of that refusal, the Bill was introduced and Coldstream told Sellers to pay out of his new large salary.[119]

Once again, however, the judges grew nervous as the Bill was put off until after the Recess. Simonds wrote to Churchill about this 'increasing anxiety' and said that 'delay may well create the impression that the Government do not regard this measure as having the constitutional importance which I think we all agree it has'.[120] Churchill tried to humour him: 'The time should soon be opportune.'[121] Meanwhile, Coldstream was warned that many in the House still thought judicial pensions too generous,[122] while Shawcross warned Simonds that the Labour Party was likely to oppose and put the whip on.[123] The brief for the Prime Minister was prepared and 10 Downing Street particularly liked the quote from the US Commission on Judicial and Congressional Salaries that 'our Nation is no stronger than its judiciary.'[124] Simonds drafted the remark that 'a vigilant, strong and fearless Bench is one of the bulwarks of liberty in this country'.[125] Churchill agreed that there was no intention of making the judges

[111] Padmore to Bridges, 7 July 1953, ibid.   [112] Simonds to Butler, 10 July 1953, ibid.
[113] Butler to Simonds, 13 July 1953, ibid.   [114] CP (53) 47, 30 July 1953, LCO 2/5908.
[115] Coldstream to Simonds, 1 Oct. 1953, LCO 2/5907.
[116] Napier to Fiennes (Parliamentary Draftsman), 11 Aug. 1953, ibid.
[117] Memorandum from Oakes (10 Downing Street), 22 Oct. 1953.
[118] Memoranda, 3 and 4 Nov. 1953, ibid. [119] Coldstream to Sellers, 12 Nov. 1953, ibid.
[120] Simonds to Churchill, 11 Dec. 1953, ibid.   [121] Churchill to Simonds, 25 Dec. 1953, ibid.
[122] Arnold Gridley to Coldstream, 19 Dec. 1953, ibid.
[123] Shawcross to Simonds, 12 Nov. 1953, ibid.
[124] Coldstream to Frazer, 9 Mar. 1954, LCO 2/5958.
[125] *Parliamentary Debates* (5th ser.) HC vol. 525, col. 1063: 'The British judiciary, with its traditions and record, is one of the greatest living assets of our race and people, and the independence of the Judiciary is a part of our message to the ever-growing world which is rising so swiftly around us.'

wealthy men, but the Bill attempted to satisfy 'their need to maintain a modest but dignified way of life suited to the gravity, and indeed the majesty, of the duties they discharge'.[126] This time the arguments worked. Labour decided not to oppose the Bill.[127] The Royal Assent was given on 14 April 1954.

Not all the judges were overwhelmed by the parliamentary generosity. Lord Maugham, a former Chancellor, noted, 'The net salary which the High Court Judge was receiving at the date of the Budget of 1953 might well be under £2,500, a sum at which it is impossible to support a wife and children with dignity and to send his sons to a public school.' 'Fortunately,' however, from the judges' point of view, 'Sir Winston Churchill had seen the great importance of preserving the position of the Judges of the Superior Courts of Law.' Lord Maugham still regretted, however, that 'no judge will be able to send two or more boys to public schools, unless he has private means.' When the salaries had been fixed, they had been 'sufficient to enable him to . . . bring up three or more children and send them to public schools'.[128] However élitist the tone of Maugham's observations, they reflected the true change in judicial status. In 1913–14, High Court judges had earned 220 per cent more than the highest decile of barristers' earnings. By 1922/3, this had fallen to 111 per cent of the highest decile at the Bar, and by 1955/6 they earned 107 per cent of the average income of barristers in the highest decile.[129] By 1960, the cost of living had risen 400 per cent since 1913/14;[130] High Court salaries only 60 per cent; and the rates of tax had, of course, grown dramatically.

(c) The Later Years

At last, however, the dyke had been breached. While there was to be criticism of the judges for various reasons over the next decade, in July 1965 the Labour Government kept the pledge made by its predecessors and announced its intention of raising all the salaries of the senior judges by an average of 25 per cent— although the Conservatives by this time had at least some second thoughts on the matter. Moreover, the Act also gave the Government power to handle High Court judges' salaries in the same way as those of County Court judges under the 1957 Act and increase them by delegated legislation.[131]

The rise had first been mooted in 1963 but was then dropped by the

---

[126] By 1955, High Court judges were earning 40% more than they had in 1913. County Court judges had (by 1960) received an increase of 193% since 1913 (to £4,400). In 1913, the average barrister earned £478 and the top decile £1,820. By 1955–6, the figures were £2,032 and £5,003. G. Routh, *Occupation and Pay in Great Britain, 1900–1960* (Cambridge, 1965), 62–70.

[127] Speech of C. R. Attlee, *Parliamentary Debates*, (5th ser.) HC vol 525, col. 1064 (23 Mar. 1954): 'Our people hold egalitarian ideas but we are not living in an egalitarian society, and the State and the Bench have to compete with outside attractions for the services of men of high ability.'

[128] Lord Maugham, *At the End of the Day*, 358–9.

[129] G. Routh, *Occupation and Pay in Great Britain, 1900–1979* (2nd edn. London, 1980), 64, 74.

[130] J. Burnett, *A History of the Cost of Living* (Harmondsworth, 1969), 298.

[131] Judges' Remuneration Act, 1965, sect. 1.

Macmillan Government, probably because of the attacks on the judiciary after the Profumo scandal. After Ministers and MPs, however, had raised their own salaries as a result of the report of the Lawrence Committee, 'legislation to enable similar increases to be paid to the judges was generally expected'.[132] Some felt, however, that it was unfortunate that so large a rise should have been announced at the very moment George Brown was seeking to stabilize wages and prices.[133] The *Observer* felt that 'Eight thousand pounds in 1965 is quite enough to pay even the guardians of our liberties,'[134] while the *Solicitors' Journal* suggested that the judges refuse to draw the increases while the economic crisis continued.[135] In an editorial, the *Guardian* wondered whether all of the fringe benefits for judges—such as the butler, cook, and marshal provided from the central government pool—were still necessary for judges going on circuit.[136] Ultimately a rebel group of Labour MPs kept the House of Commons debating the pay increase until 5.30 a.m.,[137] demanding such reforms as an annual hearing examination for the judges.[138]

The Judges' Remuneration Act provided that the salary of High Court judges should be raised from £8,000 to £10,000, and for the judges of the Court of Appeal from £9,000 to £11,250. In making this change the Government restored some of the financial advantage to the High Court bench. Until the 1930s a High Court salary was four times as large as a County Court salary; but by 1965 a County Court judge was paid almost two-thirds the salary of a High Court judge. The Bill restored the differential by providing that the High Court judge should receive 50 per cent more than the County Court judge. The Bill also meant that, for a short while, High Court judges would be paid more than Permanent Secretaries in government departments, whose relative increases in salaries over the previous hundred years had reflected the increasing importance of the executive and the declining importance of the judiciary.[139]

The establishment of a procedure whereby High Court salaries would be set by delegated legislation rather than by Act of Parliament solved only half the problem. Much of the social history of this period was tied up in the intricacies

---

[132] *The Times*, 2 July 1965.

[133] e.g. Vicky cartoon showing caricature of High Court judge, solemnly asking 'What is an Incomes Policy?' *Evening Standard*, 2 July 1965. See also *The Times*, 15 and 17 July 1965, for details of the revolt of back-bench Labour MPs opposed to the rise.

[134] *Observer*, 18 July 1965.

[135] *Solicitors' Journal*, 109 (9 July 1965), 541.

[136] *Guardian*, 22 July 1965.

[137] *Parliamentary Debates* (5th ser.), HC vol. 716, cols. 1977–2118 (22 July 1965).

[138] *The Times*, 22 July 1965.

[139] While the judges' salaries remained at £5,000 p.a. from 1852 until 1954, and at £8,000 until 1965, senior Civil Service salaries showed the following changes: in 1871, the most senior of the Permanent Secretaries in a government department received a salary of £2,000 p.a. It was not until 1929 that the salary reached £3,000 p.a. By 1950 it had crept up to £3,500 and by 1954 to £4,500. In 1963 the Permanent Secretary of the ordinary department was paid £8,200; while the two most senior received £8,800 p.a. The figures were raised to £8,600 and £9,200 in 1966.

of pay and wage controls[140] and the meaning of relativities.[141] There was still friction between the Civil Service and the High Court bench with respect to salaries. During the 1960s, Permanent Secretaries finally pulled ahead of High Court judges. In 1961, the High Court judges earned £8,000 and the ordinary Permanent Secretary £7,000 (three earned more). Then in 1970, the Heath Administration changed the relativities. Permanent Secretaries were to receive £11,900 and High Court judges £11,500. As *The Times* reported: 'The judges have always argued that as the holders of judicial offices that have a higher standing in the constitution than those of civil servants they should have a commensurably higher salary. In political circles it was well known that they had started a claim to be brought ahead of the new salaries for the top civil servants.'[142] They were soon leap-frogged. By 1971, the High Court judges were still at £11,500; Permanent Secretaries had reached £14,000.

In May of that year, the Conservative Government appointed a permanent body, called the Top Salaries Review Body, 'to advise the Prime Minister on the remuneration of the higher judiciary; senior civil servants . . . '. It included both the recently retired Permanent Secretary in the Lord Chancellor's Office, Sir George Coldstream, and a commercial silk, Anthony Lloyd, QC (now Lord Justice Lloyd). In its *Second Report*, in 1972, it recommended that both High Court judges and Permanent Secretaries be at £15,750.[143] As inflation gathered speed, increases were added on a yearly basis.[144] This process led to another constitutional phenomenon. The 1965 Judicial Remuneration Act had still left overall control of judicial salaries under Parliament. The ministerial order fixing the salary of the judges required an affirmative resolution of both Houses of Parliament. While it was much easier to keep judicial salaries in line with (or even ahead of) the cost of living, Parliament might still hold up the process, which meant that the issue was still a political one and governments were cautious about moving.

In what, in retrospect, was a remarkable move, the Courts Act of 1971 took away any parliamentary control with respect to Circuit judges (as County Court judges became known). Instead, the Lord Chancellor set the salaries (although he was not free to reduce them). The High Court judges were anxious to have the same arrangement. In the Heath administration, Lord Hailsham was sensitive to their wishes and the Administration of Justice Bill of 1973 provided that the High Court judges could have their salaries raised (but not lowered) by the Lord

---

[140] See K. O. Morgan, *The Peoples' Peace: British History, 1945–1989* (Oxford, 1990), 209–15, 411–22. See also G. A. Dorfman, *Wage Politics in Britain, 1945–1967* (London, 1974); S. Brittan and P. Lilley, *The Delusion of Incomes Policy* (London, 1977).

[141] e.g. *Problems of Pay Relativities: Pay Board, Advisory Report, No. 2,* Cmnd. 5535 (1974).

[142] *The Times,* 'Judges to Get Higher Pay', 15 Apr. 1970.

[143] Review Body on Top Salaries, *Report No. 2: Interim Report on Top Salaries,* Cmnd. 5001 (1972).

[144] £300 in 1973; Review Body on Top Salaries, *Report No. 3: Second Interim Report on Top Salaries,* Cmnd. 5372 (1973); £350 in 1974, *Report No. 4: Third Interim Report on Top Salaries,* Cmnd. 5595 (1974).

Chancellor, subject only to the approval of the Minister for the Civil Service (now the Prime Minister). For Scotland, the Secretary of State for Scotland provided a similar function.

The remarkable change was certainly not advertised as such. In the House of Commons, the Attorney-General (Sir Peter Rawlinson) described the Bill as 'technical and perhaps dull'.[145] He explained that 'at present, the salaries of the higher judiciary can be increased by Order in Council subject to a draft of the Order being approved by each House of Parliament. There has been a need, which has been met by successive governments, for more frequent revision of judicial salaries.'[146] He explained that between 1832 and 1965, there had been only two increases, both by Act of Parliament; while the Order in Council Proceeding, introduced in 1965, had been used in 1970 and 1972.

It was left to the former Labour Attorney-General (and future Lord Chancellor) Sir Elwyn Jones to applaud the 'historic importance'[147] of the new plan. He announced that it 'marks a watershed in the relations between Parliament and the judiciary, for it brings to an end all direct control by Parliament over the salaries and pensions of the higher judiciary'. He omitted to note that henceforth the control was in the hands of the executive. He then tried to grab some of the glory of the changes for Labour:

Since the Act of Settlement, salaries of the judges have been determinable only by Parliament, not by the executive. The principle behind that procedure and that doctrine was to preserve the independence of the judiciary, which is an important part of our constitution and of our liberties.

But the requirement that Parliament alone could deal with changes in judicial salaries produced difficulties in practice. It resulted in delays and created the risk of unhappy conflict between Parliament and the Judiciary. Accordingly, under the Judges Remuneration Act of 1965, the Labour Government decided that the salaries of the higher judiciary could be increased by affirmative orders instead of legislation, thereby at any rate reducing the potential of conflict.[148]

The Second Reading was over in two hours. The only concern in the Lords was when, on the behalf of Labour, Lord Gardiner pressed Lord Hailsham for an assurance that the government would automatically accept the advice from the Top Salaries Review Body.[149] The senior judges (for the Act included the Law Lords and the Lords Justice as well as the higher judiciary in Scotland and Northern Ireland) had achieved their financial goals—even if they were in a somewhat odd constitutional position—remarkably easily. The only *quid pro quo* was a curbing of the tax-free status of barristers' fees paid after appointment to the Bench.

So the story went on. The Committee on Top Salaries became the protector

---

[145] *Parliamentary Debates* (5th ser.), HC vol. 851, col. 1715 (1 Mar. 1973).
[146] Ibid., col. 1722.   [147] Ibid., col. 1725.   [148] Ibid., cols 1928–9.
[149] *Parliamentary Debates* (5th ser.), HC vol. 338, col. 401 (29 Jan. 1973).

of judicial salaries—and thus of independence. Until the rejection of its advice by the Major Government in 1992, its recommendations had always been accepted. In many ways, the most fascinating report was the Review Body on Top Salaries, *Report No. 6* in 1974.[150] It admitted that

No formal evaluation of relative responsibilities within the judicial structure seems to have been attempted previously nor can any principle of external comparability be applied.

The (Advisory Group on the judiciary) saw no special merit in principle in the present equivalence between the salaries of a High Court judge and of a Permanent Secretary in the Higher Civil Service; but they considered that it would be wrong in practice for the pay of a High Court judge to fall behind that of the Permanent Secretary and therefore regarded the maintenance of at least the existing parity as a safeguard. They also felt that bar earnings (net of expenses) provided a valuable independent means of checking whether judicial salaries were likely to prove sufficient to maintain satisfactory levels of recruitment.[151]

We have examined the history of judicial salaries since the Eighteenth Century, but we have looked in vain for any well-established principles to guide us in this field, except the need to maintain the status and dignity of the judicial office as an essential element of the constitution.[152]

The Review Body noted that since 1971 the salary for High Court judges had been the same as that for Permanent Secretaries. 'This relationship has evolved without principles, and we have not considered ourselves bound by it. Nevertheless, we consider that a judgment of broad relationships with the judiciary itself and within the public service generally is of greater significance in relation to the Higher Judiciary than direct considerations of earnings.'[153] The Body returned to the issue one last time. 'The group saw no special merit in preserving the present parity between High Court judges and the Permanent Secretary, as the work content is very different. However, because of the importance of maintaining the status of the judiciary itself, the Group concluded that it would be wrong to allow the payment of High Court judges to fall behind that of the Permanent Secretary.'[154] Repetition did not enhance the strength of the argument.

The Advisory Group on the Judiciary also discussed retirement, which had been made mandatory at 75 by the Judicial Pensions Act, 1959. The group felt somewhat defensive about non-contributory judicial pensions, set at 50 per cent of salary (plus a cost of living increase) after fifteen years. 'On retirement, judges are strongly discouraged from entering commerce or industry. No member of the Higher Judiciary has returned to the Bar after retirement for nearly three-hundred years and they may no longer do so.'[155] The assertion was probably not

---

[150] Cmnd. 5846.   [151] Ibid. 6–7.   [152] Ibid. 29.   [153] Ibid. 30.
[154] Ibid. 32.
[155] Ibid. 28. The Group also defended the need for the 12–13 weeks of vacation available to a High Court judge.

good constitutional law,[156] and, even if it were, the arrangement was a particularly attractive one whether the reference group were either private industry or public service.

The Group also took up the relative salary relationship of High Court judges and Circuit judges—the nearest equivalent to County Court judges after the Courts Act, 1971. They decided, after a rather amateur consultation, that the 5 : 3 ratio was 'broadly right'.[157] They did, however, conclude that Lords Justice of Appeal should, for the first time, be paid more than High Court judges.[158] They also determined that because the Lord Chancellor after 1971 was more Minister than judge, there was no problem paying regular judges more than he.[159] Finally, they concluded that it was permissible to pay judges in Scotland less than in England, because the cost of living was lower, as were earnings at the Bar.[160]

By 1979, the Lords Justice earned £27,799; High Court judges £25,886—the same figure as Permanent Secretaries; judges of the Court of Session £24,786; and puisne judges in Northern Ireland £24,717. Circuit judges earned £18,015. The Review Body returned to the issues of Judicial Relativities—for the fourth time—in 1985.[161] The Circuit judges made a strong case to have their salaries come closer to those of the High Court. This claim was ultimately rejected by the Judicial Subcommittee: 'We believe that there should continue to be a substantial difference between these appointments to reflect significant differences, particularly in jurisdictional terms, between the High Court and the Circuit Bench; and in recognition of the calibre of those barristers who are appointed to the High Court Bench.'[162] Nevertheless, the recommendation was that the salary be raised from £33,000 to £40,000 p.a.[163] Meanwhile the High Court

---

[156] This is a largely unexplored issue. It is now not uncommon for appeal judges and some High Court judges to return to their chambers on retirement. While they cannot appear in court or give opinions, they are allowed to give affidavits on English law, and have an active arbitration practice.

What makes everyone nervous is the prospect of salaried employment after the Bench. When, in 1970, Mr Justice Fisher left the Bench after only three years and went to work in the City, the move led to expressions 'of outrage that might be appropriate in the headmistress who hears that one of the most promising of her pupils [has] gone off to be a bunny girl'. *New Law Journal*, 120 (1970), 746–7.

[157] The Group considered an 'analytical survey' of responsibility by management consultants, but decided it would not be appropriate. They therefore instituted an Advisory Group consisting of Lord Beeching (the architect of the Courts Act), Sir George Coldstream, Lord Parker (the former Chief Justice), Mr Justice Talbot, with Lord Guest representing Scotland and Lord MacDermott representing Northern Ireland. Review Body on Top Salaries, *Report No. 6*, Cmnd. 5846 (1974), 30. Some of the visceral feelings about the differences between the two courts came out in the debates in Parliament on the Supreme Court Bill in 1981. Jeffrey Thomas, MP, argued that 'The mere fact one has been a first class Circuit judge is no proper experience for a High Court appointment.' The differences between the Circuit and the High Courts 'is the difference between Woolworths and Harrods'. *Parliamentary Debates* (6th ser.), HC vol. 4, cols. 228–9.

[158] In the 1870s the Lords Justice had given up a differential salary in return for automatic Privy Counsellorships.

[159] *Report No. 6*, 33–4.

[160] Ibid. 34. Although they had already concluded 'we accept also that judicial pay should not attempt to reflect the highest bar earnings.' Ibid. 32.

[161] Review Body on Top Salaries, *Report No. 22: Eighth Report on Top Salaries*, Cmnd. 9525 (1985).

[162] ii. 16.   [163] Senior Circuit judges went from £35,000 to £44,500.

judges argued that 'on recruitment grounds', their salaries should be improved relative to the Circuit Bench. While the Lord Chancellor felt that the differential could in fact be lessened without affecting 'significantly the preparedness of barristers to accept an appointment to the High Court Bench', the Subcommittee worried that 'any shift in the balance could have an adverse effect and there must be a risk that reducing the differential between High Court judges and Circuit judges could diminish the status of the High Court bench in the eyes of the profession and affect recruitment'.[164] The differential was therefore left largely in place, with the High Court judges earning—in future—£60,000.

The arrival of the Top Salaries Committee led the judges to outpace inflation. By 1992, the salary figures were £84,250 for High Court judges, £97,000 for Lords of Appeal, and £93,000 for Lords Justice of Appeal, with £82,780 for Permanent Secretaries. Circuit Court judges were paid £59,900 and—in implementation of the original Gaitskell (or Scottish) plan—Senior Circuit judges £66,500. Virtual parity had appeared in the Celtic fringes. The Northern Ireland Court of Appeal and High Court were paid at the English rate. In Scotland, appeal judges (the Inner House) received £91,400 and trial judges (the Outer House) £82,800. Members of the Cabinet earned £59,914. The Lord Chancellor's Department, by then the publisher of a pamphlet entitled *Judicial Appointments*, noted: 'Judicial salaries are reviewed each year by the Top Salaries Review Body, which makes recommendations to the Government. In consequence, judicial salaries are regularly adjusted and no information is given about them in this booklet because it would rapidly become out of date.'[165]

In fact, since the establishment of the Review Body on Top Salaries, the judges' salaries had kept ahead of inflation. This was chiefly because of the rapid rise in salaries of business executives and members of the Bar. In 1991, the Review Body's Report recorded that the net average earnings in the three years before appointment for those appointed in the High Court were £211,300, and for Circuit judges £75,700. The Body only recommended a 9.5 per cent increase, having recommended a significant increase for Circuit judges the previous year in view of 'persistent recruitment difficulties'.[166] The Report scheduled for January 1992 contained a re-examination of the judiciary salary issue. The publication was postponed by Downing Street until after the April election. In summer 1992 the Government gave a 4 per cent increase rather than the 20 per cent recommended by the Body. The issue of judicial salaries had been re-politicized, but this time the conflict was between judiciary and executive rather than judiciary and legislature.

---

[164] ii. 32–3.   [165] LCO, *Judicial Appointments* (1990), 28–9.
[166] Review Body on Top Salaries, *Report No. 30: Fourteenth Report on Top Salaries*, Cmnd. 1413 (1991), 11–27.

8

The Later Years: Vignettes from the End of Empire

Today, commentators writing about English, Commonwealth, or American cases assume that the personalities and politics of the judges are relevant in analysing their judicial decisions. It was not always so. The English tradition of substantive formalism, for most of the twentieth century, had a pervasive influence, not only on the English legal culture but the legal cultures of Commonwealth and Empire. Staffing of the Judicial Committee of the Privy Council embodied, on the one hand, a rigidly formalistic view of the declaratory theory of law yet, on the other, the vague approach to separation of powers and judicial independence encountered elsewhere.

If the legal systems of some Commonwealth countries still sometimes seem the prisoners of the earlier decisions of the Judicial Committee of the Privy Council, it is perhaps appropriate to ask how that latter court was staffed as life ebbed out of it in the 1940s, 1950s, and 1960s. For a court that was revered by some as a vital link in the imperial chain, the composition of the Committee was surprisingly amateur, even after most Commonwealth countries had rejected the narrow English view of legal formalism. Both Canada and Sri Lanka (Ceylon) provide examples of staffing for formalism—and imperial designs. Behind both was the somewhat naïve notion that only the legal quality of the judge mattered.

(a) Canada Resiles; Sri Lanka Pursues

While the Privy Council decisions on the Bennett 'New Deal' legislation and the O'Connor Report had apparently spelled the end of Canadian appeals to London,[1] Jowitt, who became Lord Chancellor in the Attlee administration in London in 1945, still had a faint hope that Ottawa might retain its appeals to the Judicial Committee. That the Canadian link might be retained was not a totally unrealistic hope. Some of the provinces were reluctant to see the appeal go. In a *Canadian Bar Review* symposium, for instance, it was argued that the Privy Council 'in its anxiety to disclaim imperialistic tendencies offensive to the *zeitgeist*, proved its generosity at the expense of the provinces'. The Dominion, the argument went, could not abolish appeals with respect to provincial powers, despite the Statute of Westminster.[2] Moreover, Mackenzie King, by then Prime

---

[1] See Ch. 4 above.
[2] 'Abolition of Appeals to the Privy Council: A Symposium', 25 *Canadian Bar Review* (1947), 557–72; D. M. Gordon at 558.

Minister, always concerned about 'the British vote', had doubts about whether appeals to London should be abolished.[3]

Jowitt was anxious to save the system of appeals from the 'Old Commonwealth'. As Labour Attorney-General in the 1929–31 administration, he had fought tenaciously to keep the Irish Free State from abolishing appeals. Now, in the post-war period, he visited Canada and then persuaded Attlee, the Prime Minister, to appoint Rinfret,[4] the Canadian Chief Justice, as one of the Commonwealth judges entitled to sit in the Privy Council, hoping this might undermine the Canadian enthusiasm for abolishing appeals to the Privy Council.[5] The ruse did not work, and appeals to London were abolished in 1949.[6] Rinfret, however, remained a member of the British Privy Council, and even after abolition of the Canadian appeal, lobbied to be allowed to sit in the Judicial Committee. Indeed, his relations with the Privy Council Office and the Lord Chancellor's Office provided further evidence that the English approach to the judicial process was, by the standards of final appeal courts in other jurisdictions, casual.

The Rinfret situation became something of a *cause célèbre* which tried Simonds's patience after he became Lord Chancellor in the Churchill administration of 1951. Rinfret regularly invited himself to London. Jowitt—by then out of office—observed of the 1952 visit: 'Rinfret is here and seems to be enjoying himself very much. I meet him at all sorts of dinners. He is sitting on a case from Mauritius, and as this involves French law and practice, it's right up his street.'[7] As late as May 1954, Rinfret wrote to Simonds saying he planned to sit in the Canadian appeals, which were in the pipeline in 1949, and were to be heard in

---

[3] J. G. Snell and F. Vaughan, *The Supreme Court of Canada: History of the Institution* (Toronto and London, 1985), 190.

[4] Rinfret, who was educated both at Laval and McGill, had been appointed to the Supreme Court of Canada in 1924. I.-J. Deslauriers, *La Cour supérieure du Québec et ses juges, 1849–1ᵉʳ janvier 1980* (Quebec 1980), 221. By 1950, he 'tended to show his impatience in court'. Snell and Vaughan, *The Supreme Court*, 197. He did not have a good reputation in civil liberties cases. P. Weiler, *In The Last Resort: A Critical Study of the Supreme Court of Canada* (Toronto, 1974), 187–8.

[5] 'I was myself responsible for suggesting the appointment of Chief Justice Rinfret, and my reason for making the suggestion was that I hoped—rather against hope—that the fact that the Canadian Chief Justice was so appointed might influence the Canadian Government against the abolition of the appeal.' Jowitt to Gordon Walker, 7 Feb. 1951, LCO 2/5227.

[6] The British High Commissioner in Ottawa reported on the dinner to celebrate the confirmation of the Supreme Court of Canada as the final court of appeal: 'From the standpoint of the UK, the proceedings could not have been happier or more gratifying. Every speaker was at pains to make it clear that there was nothing but the highest admiration and respect in Canada for the Judicial Committee of the Privy Council and for the work which it had done for Canada over the years. The change now being made had certainly not come about from any sense of dissatisfaction; on the contrary, there was no Court in the world which had a higher standing than the Judicial Committee and no Court in the world which surpassed it in wisdom, integrity and professional competence; the present change had merely arisen, as it was bound to do in time, in the course of Canada's natural evolution and development.' Sir Alexander Clutterbuck to Dominions Office, 12 Oct. 1950, LCO 2/5227.

[7] Heuston, *Lives of the Lord Chancellors, 1940–1970* (Oxford, 1970), 132.

the Judicial Committee that autumn.[8] Simonds had a constitutional problem. He did not want Rinfret, but with whom did he deal: the Canadian Government via its representative, the High Commissioner, or the representative of the Queen (of the UK and Canada) in Ottawa, the Governor-General? He chose to summon the Canadian High Commissioner in London, Robertson, who reported to Ottawa:

The Lord Chancellor feels it is somewhat inappropriate for a Supreme Court Justice who is retiring by reason of age to return to sit in a Court of Appellate Jurisdiction on cases that might have come before him as Chief Justice of the Supreme Court of Canada. I think it is quite improper, given the abolition of Privy Council appeals, for a Canadian member of the Judicial Committee to volunteer his services to the Judicial Committee. If the initiation and invitation had come from this side, I myself would not have thought it appropriate in the circumstances for a Canadian member of the Committee to accept.[9]

Robertson's letter was too late. The Canadian Government had already agreed to pay Rinfret's way, and it would be 'awkward' for the Canadian Prime Minister to say anything. The Canadian Government's advice—via the Secretary of State—was that Simonds invite Rinfret to a farewell party in London in June, which would mean he could not decently sit in October—and the Canadian Government would pay his way to the party.[10] In fact, Simonds had already written to Rinfret saying there was no need for him in October since there were five law lords available[11]—a not entirely truthful statement. Rinfret, however, ignored the communication and cheerfully replied that he would be arriving to sit in September–October.[12] Simonds tried another tack. After clearing his reply with the Canadian High Commissioner, he reluctantly wrote to Rinfret saying that, while he could not invite him to sit on any Canadian appeals, he might find him a few colonial appeals.[13]

The next news of the retired Chief Justice was a note received by Dallas Waters, Registrar of the Privy Council, on 18 September, from Rinfret's private secretary, asking that the papers in the pending Canadian appeals be sent to the Savoy Hotel where Rinfret was staying.[14] The Secretary of the Judicial Committee replied that the Lord Chancellor did not find it possible for Rinfret to sit in Canadian cases, but offered, by way of consolation, five petitions and a Ceylonese appeal.[15] Behind the scenes, however, Simonds told the Canadian High Commissioner: 'Emphatically I do not want him.'[16]

The following year, 1955, there was an encore. This time, however, the *dramatis personae* were different. Sir George Coldstream had replaced Sir Lewis

---

[8] Rinfret to Simonds, 22 May 1954, LCO 2/5229.
[9] N. A. Robertson to Secretary of State, J. W. Pickersgill, Ottawa, 24 May 1954, ibid.
[10] Secretary of State (Pickersgill) to Robertson, 1 June 1954, ibid.
[11] Simonds to Rinfret, 26 May 1954, ibid.   [12] Rinfret to Simonds, 25 June 1954, ibid.
[13] Simonds to Robertson, 16 June 1954; Simonds to Rinfret, 16 June 1954, ibid.
[14] 18 Sept. 1954, ibid.   [15] Paterson to Rinfret, 21 Sept. 1954, ibid.
[16] Simonds to Robertson, 28 Sept. 1954, ibid.

Napier as Permanent Secretary of the Lord Chancellor's Office, and Viscount Kilmuir had taken over from Simonds as Lord Chancellor. Coldstream warned Kilmuir that Rinfret had written to Paterson at the Privy Council Office, asking to sit.[17] Coldstream further warned that Rinfret 'has already caused much embarrassment to your predecessors'. Simonds had felt his sitting an outrage: 'First because all the Law Lords agree that he is nothing like good enough to sit on the kind of strong Board which you take pains to ensure for Canadian Appeals. Second, because Canadian judicial and other legal opinions are unanimous in the view that he is not good enough.'[18] Kilmuir was more direct with the Canadians, partly because he was much more aware of the political role of the judiciary.[19] He told Rinfret that 'much as I appreciate your offer to sit, I shall not find it possible to accept it.'[20] This time, Rinfret heard. He cancelled his London visit but cheerily warned the Lord Chancellor that 'I am now free to go to London not only in June, but equally for any other of the sittings during the year. I therefore put myself at your entire disposal.'[21] Kilmuir, however, reported to the Canadian High Commissioner that 'it should be easier in the future to deal with the applications which I have no doubt will continue to arrive.'[22]

When the British election of 1951 had brought in the Conservatives, they were faced with another Privy Council problem: what to do about the Privy Council's best customer—Ceylon (Sri Lanka). It was not an issue handled with style. Lord Soulbury (better known as Ramsbottom, wartime President of the Board of Education), the Governor-General, reported that the Prime Minister of Ceylon wanted a semi-permanent judge in London along the lines of the old salaried Indian judges. He had a candidate; he thought he should be paid £4,000 p.a.; and Ceylon was prepared to pay half.[23] Jowitt wanted the arrangement, but knew there was not 'the slightest prospect of our Treasury agreeing to pay half the salary'.[24] Napier noted that Dingle Foot, QC, had 'said Ceylon is a great devotee of the Privy Council and has no intention whatever of stopping appeals. The Treasury might think that they have been paying £4,000 a year for years (for the salaried Indian judges). They might think it worthwhile to pay £2,000.'[25]

The minuet between the future of the Commonwealth on the one hand and the Treasury's parsimony on the other continued. Jowitt's final words to Gordon

---

[17] He had heard there were four cases. 'I must confess I should be anxious to form part of the Boards which will be formed to hear these appeals.' Rinfret to Paterson, 8 Apr. 1955, ibid.

[18] Coldstream to Kilmuir, 19 Apr. 1955, ibid.

[19] Stevens, *Law and Politics*, 421–3.   [20] Kilmuir to Rinfret, 21 Apr. 1955, LCO 2/5229.

[21] Rinfret to Kilmuir, 10 May 1955, ibid.   [22] Kilmuir to Robertson, 14 May 1955, ibid.

[23] Soulbury to Gordon Walker, 7 Sept. 1951, ibid.

[24] Jowitt also observed, however, that 'I feel it essential that we should not let down the reputation and standing of the Court and he obviously could not sit on appeals from Dominions other than Ceylon.' Jowitt to Waters, 13 Oct. 1951, ibid. This was apparently before Jowitt knew Ceylon had a Roman–Dutch system. Ibid.

[25] Pencil memorandum in file from Napier, n.d., ibid.

Walker before he left office were: 'On political grounds it may well be very desirable to fortify that attitude (loyalty to the Privy Council) by adopting Soulbury's proposal . . . the judicial and political arguments together might be strong enough to warrant the payment of £2,000 . . . The proposal, however, would have a much greater chance of success if Ceylon were prepared to pay the whole of the salary.'[26]

Viscount Simonds, the new Lord Chancellor, was more judge than politician. He confided to the new Commonwealth Relations Secretary, Ismay, 'some doubts' about the proposed arrangement. Will we get a judge 'who makes the grade?' Would he be useful in Colonial appeals as East and West Africa developed? '[T]here may be some objection.' His appointment might lead to 'demands' from other new Commonwealth nations, but the objections 'are outweighed by the importance of any strengthening of the link between this country and Ceylon'.[27] Ismay hastened to assure Soulbury that he thought 'it' was a good idea, but Britain by then ran its Empire on the cheap. He suggested that Ceylon pick up the whole tab, although 'the selection would be made by the Lord Chancellor, who would naturally take into consideration any recommendation which you and your Prime Minister might make'.[28] The good news reached London in December 1951: 'The gentleman that the Prime Minister has in mind to recommend possesses very considerable private means and might therefore be inclined to accept a moderate salary provided by the Ceylon government.'[29] The appointee turned out to be Mr L. M. D. de Silva, a former Acting Supreme Court Justice, and the rumour the following month was that he would be prepared to serve without salary.[30]

All seemed to be settled. Yet, at this very moment, all kinds of crises broke out. Mr de Silva unwisely asked what his tax status would be, while the Clerk to the Privy Council asked under what statutory authority Mr de Silva was being appointed.[31] Both questions were to cause embarrassment. Lord Salisbury, by then at the Commonwealth Relations Office, sent a dispatch to Lord Soulbury, which, in addition to warning the Governor-General that 'we see no prospect of the passage of legislation providing for a contribution from U.K. funds,' also enclosed a note from Sir Eric Bamford of the Inland Revenue warning that de Silva would be taxed on his remittances from Ceylon.[32] Meanwhile, Salisbury protested to R. A. Butler, the Chancellor of the Exchequer:

If the position as to taxation is as stated in Sir Eric Bamford's letter . . . [it] would be deplorable from a Commonwealth point of view. We all want to maintain the Privy Council as a Commonwealth link and we ought therefore to do all in our power [and] . . . we ought not to do anything which might lead her [Ceylon] to take such a step [abolish appeals].[33]

[26] Jowitt to Gordon Walker, 22 Oct. 1951, ibid.
[27] Simonds to Ismay, 29 Nov. 1951, ibid.
[28] Ismay to Soulbury, 4 Dec. 1951, ibid.
[29] Soulbury to Ismay, 15 Dec. 1951, ibid.
[30] Soulbury to Ismay, 4 Jan. 1952, ibid.
[31] Waters to Napier, 8 Apr. 1952, ibid.
[32] Salisbury to Soulbury, 25 Apr. 1952, ibid.
[33] Salisbury to Butler, 16 May 1952, ibid.

Meanwhile, Coldstream, at the Lord Chancellor's Office, was trying to persuade Willis of the Inland Revenue that, in the next Finance Act, there ought to be an exception from tax for Ceylonese members of the Judicial Committee.[34] Willis eventually agreed that the matter could be settled outside a statute. If the Ceylon government would create de Silva a judge in Ceylon, he could then take advantage of the double taxation treaty as a civil servant.[35] Coldstream thought the 'Revenue proposal has a somewhat hole-in-the-corner flavour to it',[36] but the Inland Revenue refused to change its position.[37] De Silva was thus appointed a Supreme Court judge on 1 October 1952.[38] The idea was that he would sit until Christmas and then move to London.

At this point, Simonds got cold feet, remembering the 'Colliery Explosion' in 1871–2. The 1871 Judicial Committee Act had allowed the appointment of paid judges of the Privy Council, with one of the qualifications being that of having been a Superior Court judge in England. Collier was made a judge of the Court of Common Pleas for two days and then appointed as a salaried member of the Privy Council.[39] There were violent attacks on Gladstone, none more vigorous than that from Lord Salisbury's grandfather. The Commonwealth Relations Secretary was defensive; his grandfather had attacked 'jobs for the boys' and, in any event, de Silva would have sat for three months.[40] When 'Bobbity' Salisbury was beset with guilt, however, it was always a problem.[41]

Simonds was also beset with guilt. It was true that it was not a case of jobs for the boys, but it was a violation of the spirit of the Act—and very close to the Collier situation. 'I should eternally blame myself if, through my default, you were the target for any attack.' He consoled himself with the thought that 'the Bing boys are unlikely to have heard of the Collier Case.'[42] His final thought

---

[34] Coldstream to files, 27 May 1952, ibid.

[35] Willis to Sir Charles Dixon (Commonwealth Relations Office), 4 June 1952, ibid.

[36] Coldstream to Napier and Simonds, 10 June 1952, ibid. Napier agreed the whole thing was silly. Napier to Simonds, 10 June 1952, ibid.

[37] Willis to Dixon, 25 June 1952, ibid.   [38] CRO incoming cable, 29 Sept. 1952, ibid.

[39] Stevens, *Law and Politics*, 50.   [40] Salisbury to Simonds, 8 Oct. 1950, LCO 2/5227.

[41] For Harold Macmillan's view of Salisbury's style, see A. Horne, *Macmillan*, ii. *1957–1986* (London, 1989), 37–9.

[42] Geoffrey Bing, QC, was a left-wing Labour MP, associated with the Tribune Group. He later served as Attorney-General of Ghana. J. Platts-Mills, 'Geoffrey Henry Cecil Bing', *Dictionary of National Biography, 1971–1980* (Oxford, 1986), 57.

Interestingly enough, when Bing was Attorney-General of Ghana, he lobbied to have two Ghanaian judges put on the Privy Council. Under the mistaken impression that de Silva was paid by the UK Government, he wanted them treated in the same way. Kilmuir wrote to Lord Home at the Commonwealth Office, 'I am a protagonist of the view that we should maintain the commonwealth link by every means in our power and that the Judicial Committee is an apt instrument for this purpose if it can be fitted to suit the new Commonwealth arrangements.' 2 Apr. 1957, LCO 2/5243.

Eventually, the British Government agreed to one Ghanaian member (Sir Henley Coussey). Home wrote to Kilmuir (18 Apr. 1957), 'In order to avoid any question of discrimination (racial or other) against Ghana, it might be well to make the point to him [President Nkrumah of Ghana] that all the overseas members of the Commonwealth who use the Privy Council object to appeals from their

was to urge Salisbury to read Atlay's *Lives of the Lord Chancellors*: 'very good reading'.[43] Salisbury apparently read it, and it led to a cable to the Governor-General explaining that things must not be rushed and that de Silva would not be made a Privy Councillor until 1953.[44] The shortage of judicial manpower continued to disrupt both the Privy Council and the English courts.[45]

Finally, in January 1953, the hapless Mr de Silva arrived in London.[46] Dallas Waters at the Privy Council Office reported that de Silva was upset that he was allowed to sit only in Ceylonese appeals, 'through the sordid reason that the U.K. Government refuses to pay any part of Mr de Silva's salary'.[47] Indeed, he was under-employed; but the real reason he did not sit in the non-Ceylonese cases was not the parsimony of the UK government but because the Inland Revenue continued to threaten to tax him on remittances if he sat in non-Ceylonese cases.[48] Mr de Silva, in turn, reported that D. S. Senanayake, the outgoing Ceylonese Prime Minister, had said he would suffer 'political embarrassment' if de Silva's salary had to be paid wholly by the Ceylonese government, especially if he heard non-Ceylonese cases. De Silva, however, planned to ask the new Prime Minister if he might sit as a 'volunteer' in such cases.[49] Once again, the ugly spectre of the Inland Revenue appeared,[50] but in April 1953 they agreed to allow such volunteer work and still treat his remittances as tax-free.[51] As Coldstream observed in the best tradition of Civil Service understatement: 'There has been a certain maladroitness in this business.'[52]

The de Silva 'problem', however, would not go away. He became vital to the functioning of the Judicial Committee.[53] Although he did not sit in Canadian, Australian, or New Zealand cases,[54] Coldstream thought him 'a cautious and patient judge, and with a good mind . . . up to the standards of the Judicial

courts being heard by judges from any other member of the Commonwealth except the United Kingdom.' Home to Kilmuir. 18 Apr. 1957, ibid.

In the end, Nkrumah withdrew Coussey's name. The reasons were not clear. Officially it was said to be because Coussey refused to serve as Speaker of the Assembly. Nkrumah to High Commissioner, 3 Jan. 1958. Unofficially, the British Government believed it was because Nkrumah was not prepared to have any other Ghanaian made a Privy Councillor before he was. Ibid. Nkrumah was in due course made a Privy Counsellor in time to be one of the three Privy Counsellors to sign the deportation orders of Archbishop Makarios from Cyprus to exile in the Seychelles.

[43] Simonds to Salisbury, 9 Nov. 1952, LCO 2/5227.
[44] Cable, CRO to Governor-General, 13 Oct. 1952, ibid.
[45] When Gerald Gardiner, QC, protested to Coldstream that his clients suffered extra losses and expenses because Sir Lionel Leach, the Official Referee, took off to the Privy Council, Coldstream explained that it was for an important murder appeal from Ceylon with the possibility of re-instituting the conviction, and there was a danger of the Committee being deadlocked 2 : 2. Gardiner to Coldstream, 21 Nov. 1952; Coldstream to Gardiner, 21 Nov. 1952, LCO 2/5950.
[46] Sir Alan Rose (Chief Justice of Ceylon) to Simonds, 13 Jan. 1953, LCO 2/5227.
[47] Waters to Napier, 30 Jan. 1953, ibid.   [48] Napier to Coldstream, 9 Feb. 1953, ibid.
[49] De Silva to Simonds, 23 Mar. 1953, ibid.   [50] Napier Minute, 23 Mar. 1953, ibid.
[51] E. R. Brooks (IR) to Privy Council Office, 23 Apr. 1953, ibid.
[52] Coldstream to Napier, 9 Feb. 1953, ibid.
[53] By 1955, he had sat in 65 appeals (14 from Ceylon) and 86 petitions (9 from Ceylon). He had written 14 opinions. Paterson to Coldstream, 29 Sept. 1955, LCO 2/5228.
[54] Coldstream to Kilmuir, 1 Dec. 1955, ibid.

Committee . . . his understanding of the Oriental mind might be valuable for other appeals as well.'[55] De Silva, however, still wanted to be paid.[56] The Lord Chancellor's Office thought he should be, but the Treasury could find nothing 'unfair' in the situation.[57] Eventually he was paid £5 a day for 'expenses'.

The Rinfret and de Silva cases show either the English genius for compromise or an ability to find *ad hoc* solutions which defied all principle. The only clear principles that may be drawn from the episodes is that in the English legal culture of the time, the notion that the judicial process was a mechanical one—and thus the personage of the judges relevant only as to the 'quality' needed for legal reasoning—was a profound one. The very reason that made the Judicial Committee a less than ideal court for the purposes of constitutional adjudication made it possible for both Labour and Conservative administrations to engage in imperial politics which have about them some of the flavour of Gilbert and Sullivan.

(b) And Who, Pray, shall Sit?

The politics of the Rinfret and de Silva experiences, however, also raised an important constitutional point. Since 1895, so-called Colonial judges could be appointed as members of the Privy Council; but the question was which ones should be chosen? The assumption was that if the judges were 'good', their political or social background mattered not at all, let alone their nationality. Politics, however, inevitably intruded. During the Second World War, Watermeyer, the newly appointed South African Chief Justice, was made a member of the Privy Council. Since South African appeals were in the process of ending,[58] the appointment may be thought to have been made more in the cause of the war, than the jurisprudential, effort.

The civil servants were somewhat sceptical about these developments. Rinfret had been an idea of Jowitt's when he had been visiting Canada, and his appointment had been cleared by both Attlee and the Governor-General.[59] Yet when the Dominions Office started pressing for the appointment of the New Zealand Chief Justice, Sir Humphrey O'Leary, in 1947, Napier was cool. He wrote to Lord Justice du Parcq and Dallas Waters in the Privy Council Office to see whether O'Leary was 'up' to the Privy Council standard. Eventually, Dominions Office pressure won out, and O'Leary was appointed.[60]

---

[55] Coldstream to files, 6 Oct. 1955, ibid.

[56] He went to see Simonds with his demands on 28 Sept. 1955. He wanted to be given a permanent appointment to the Privy Council. He was currently having a dispute with Sir John Kotelawala, the Prime Minister of Ceylon, who had denied de Silva a knighthood and was said to be interested in replacing him on the Privy Council. Minute, Sir Cecil Syers, High Commissioner to Ceylon. 29 Nov. 1955, ibid.

[57] Dixon called on Coldstream. Coldstream to files, 24 Nov. 1955, ibid.

[58] Finally abolished in 1950. Swinfen, *Imperial Appeal*, 157–61.

[59] LCO 2/3453.   [60] 17 Sept. 1947, ibid.

At home, meanwhile, there was a shortage of law lords. By 1946, the clerks of the Privy Council were complaining. It was not so much that there were more cases, but that they were taking much longer. With only one ex-Lord Chancellor available, the Judicial Committee had been borrowing from the Court of Appeal, and for six weeks in 1945 the House of Lords had to suspend sittings. The only area where the clerks felt comfortable was in Indian appeals where there were still two salaried ex-Indian Judges available.[61] The hearing of Indian appeals with only three judges, however—the two 'Indian' judges and one other—was anathema to the India Office, because it strengthened the hostility to appeals to London. If respect for appeals was to be maintained, the India Office demanded that 'real' law lords had to outnumber the salaried judges.[62]

The Prime Minister agreed to two additional Law Lords with surprisingly little fuss, although the Treasury insisted on a certificate of need before anyone was actually named.[63] Filling the positions proved to be treacherous, since Thankerton had resigned, and du Parcq was openly upset about weakening the Court of Appeal by raiding it for Law Lords,[64] but in March 1947 Oaksey, Morton, and MacDermott were appointed. The Commonwealth problem, however, would not go away.

In August 1949, Jowitt was writing to Attlee, complaining that he was having trouble staffing both the Privy Council and the House of Lords:

Maugham, Roche, and I regret to add, Wright, have become too old, too deaf or too garrulous. The other judges are now objecting to sit with the latter. Simon still helps from time to time but is getting very slow and whenever he presides the case takes far longer than it should if properly handled.[65]

Jowitt was anxious that Canadian and Indian cases be well heard; and, as we have seen, he still harboured the hope that both would retain appeals to the Privy Council.[66] One of the problems with Indian appeals was that Sir Madharam Nair, one of the two paid Indian judges, was 'rather a broken reed'.[67] It had become clear, moreover, that once India proclaimed itself a republic, appeals from that quarter would end.[68] By January 1950, the era was all over and

---

[61] Memorandum from Clerks of the Privy Council and House of Lords, 26 Nov. 1946, LCO 2/3461.

[62] Kemp to Napier, 30 Nov. 1946, ibid.   [63] Ibid.

[64] Waters (Privy Council) to Jowitt, 16 Jan. 1947, ibid.

[65] Jowitt to Attlee, 5 Aug. 1949, LCO 2/4506.

[66] The Canadian Bar was arguing that the date of abolition be delayed. Memorandum, 8 Sept. 1949, ibid.

[67] Jowitt to Attlee, 5 Aug. 1949, LCO 2/4506.

[68] How to staff Indian appeals was a problem all year. Napier was concerned to know what would happen when Beaumont, one of the two paid Indian judges, retired. Could they use Sir Lionel Leach, a former Chief Justice of Madras, by then an Official Referee. Leach refused to give up the Official Referee's job unless he was paid for his work on the Privy Council. Napier to Waters (Clerk of Privy Council), 26 May 1949. Waters thought an 'iron curtain' on the appeals would come down on Republic Day, but suggested that India be asked to pay the £2,000—part of a judicial salary—to see whether it was 'serious'. Independence (Republic) Day was postponed from 15 Aug. 1949 to 26

the Republic declared. The High Commissioner in New Delhi reported that 'nothing has impressed the people of India more than the high sense of detachment, independence and impartiality which have invariably governed the deliberations and decisions of the Privy Council.'[69]

As the Labour administration drew to a close in 1951, Patrick Gordon Walker, the Commonwealth Relations Secretary, wrote to Jowitt about membership of the Judicial Committee of the Privy Council. He thought that although Canada had abolished appeals, the tradition of appointing its Chief Justice should be continued.[70] He also thought it important that the Chief Justice of Ceylon, a country which had continued appeals, should be appointed. Although South Africa had abolished appeals and Prime Minister Malan had turned down a Privy Counsellorship for himself, perhaps he would let his Chief Justice take one. India and Pakistan presented a special problem. By this time, both had abolished appeals, and India, as has been seen, had become a Republic. Prime Minister Nehru of India was not offered a Privy Counsellorship; and Liaquat Ali Khan of Pakistan had turned his down. 'Nevertheless, you may think it desirable (if India and Pakistan agree) to make an effort to have their Chief Justices available for the Judicial Committee. This might serve, apart from anything else, as a valuable Commonwealth link with the two countries.'[71]

Napier drafted Jowitt's response. It might be a 'good Commonwealth policy' to appoint the Chief Justice of Canada to the Privy Council, but it would be of little help in the work. It was possible that Australia and New Zealand might allow the Chief Justice of Canada to sit in its appeals, but 'neither would tolerate the presence on the Board of the Chief Justice of any other Dominion'. To this, Jowitt added: 'It has always been interesting to me to observe how insistent they all are, as was Canada herself in the old days, that appeals should not be heard before a Board comprising judges from other Dominions.' Napier and Jowitt, however, were unimpressed with the arguments in favour of keeping the Indian and Pakistan Chief Justices: 'Many Colonies might resent the presence of either of them on the Board.' In addition to race, there was always the problem of the oath of allegiance as India became a Republic and Pakistan contemplated such a move.[72]

Jan. 1950. All appeals were to cease then. F. F. Turnbull (CRO) to Napier, 28 June 1949. Jowitt advised Attlee in the 'interests of economy' that Leach be appointed in the interim. Jowitt to Attlee, 5 Aug. 1949. Herbert Morrison, Lord President of the Council, agreed, '. . . although it seems a pity to make a man a Privy Councillor only when a limited period of judicial work is required'. Ibid. Leach was appointed and sat for a number of years in the Privy Council, as needed, sometimes undermining his work as Official Referee. Originally, it looked as if India wanted all cases in the list as of October heard, but the Privy Council argued that it had 'constitutional grounds' for not hearing cases after 26 Jan. It therefore 'ordered out' all Indian appeals. LCO 2/4506.

[69] High Commissioner to Noel Baker, 25 Jan. 1950, LCO 2/4507.

[70] The UK High Commissioner in Ottawa was also lobbying for the Canadian Chief Justices to be allowed to sit. Clutterbuck to Liesching, 12 Oct. 1950, LCO 2/5227.

[71] Gordon Walker to Jowitt, 15 Jan. 1951, ibid.

[72] Jowitt to Gordon Walker, 7 Feb. 1951, ibid.

Australia and New Zealand presented rather different problems. In 1950, in the *Bank Nationalization Case* from Australia, the Privy Council conceded that 'the problem to be solved is not so much legal as political, social and economic'.[73] During 1951, Jowitt toured the Antipodes and frightened many lawyers there by his narrow mechanistic approach to the judicial process ('It is our duty to expound what we believe the law to be . . . do not get yourself into the frame of mind of entrusting to the judges the working out of a whole new set of principles which does accord with the requirements of modern conditions. Leave that to the legislature, and leave us to confine ourselves to trying to find out what the law is').[74] What Jowitt noticed, however, was that the Bars in these two countries were upset that English appeal courts did not refer to Australian and New Zealand precedents, and they were apparently unimpressed by Jowitt's explanation that they could not be referred to by the judges unless they had been referred to by counsel. Jowitt's solution was to encourage the Chief Justices of Australia and New Zealand to sit in the Privy Council, especially in Colonial cases.

The problem was that everyone wanted to use the Judicial Committee of the Privy Council to help keep the Commonwealth together—but it would cost money. Jowitt was horrified at the cost of bringing the judges over. Prime Minister Robert Menzies thought some Australian money would be available, and the New Zealand judges had sabbaticals.[75] It was agreed that Jowitt would talk to Prime Minister Attlee after the Election.[76] The Election of course produced a different Prime Minister and a different Lord Chancellor, but the deed of appointing an Australian judge as a member of the Privy Council was soon done. The UK High Commissioner in Canberra, E. J. Williams, talked to Menzies, who reported that Sir John Latham was 'getting a little past his prime . . . and had become exceedingly garrulous'. Sir Owen Dixon was appointed.[77]

Even with such possibility of help—and Australian judges were reluctant to sit until dissents were allowed—there was a shortage of law lords. While both the House of Lords and the Judicial Committee were hearing fewer cases, they were taking far longer. Indeed, by 1954, it took, on average, twice as long to hear an appeal as it had in 1939.[78] More care was being taken with appeals. Lord Reid urged on Kilmuir the importance of having especially good panels in Australian appeals, as criticism of the Judicial Committee increased in Australia.[79] Reid thought, as Simonds had, that five Lords of Appeal in Ordinary should always sit

[73] *Commonwealth of Australia* v *Bank of New South Wales* [1950] AC 235, 310 (PC). On the sensitivity of the law lords to the political aspects of Privy Council work, see A. A. Paterson, *The Law Lords* (London, 1982), 88.

[74] Stevens, *Law and Politics*, 338–9.

[75] Jowitt to Gordon Walker, 28 Sept. 1951, LCO 2/5227.

[76] Gordon Walker to Jowitt, 12 Oct. 1951, ibid.

[77] Williams to Liesching, 16 Jan. 1952, ibid. Ismay, the new Secretary for Commonwealth Relations confirmed that Simonds did not want New Zealand judges sitting in rotation—the wish of their government. Ismay to Simonds, 18 Dec. 1951; Simonds to Ismay, 20 Dec. 1951, ibid.

[78] Stevens, *Law and Politics*, 324.   [79] Coldstream to Kilmuir, 31 Oct. 1955, LCO 2/5234.

in Australian appeals: 'Their Lordships are all exceedingly anxious to meet Australian opinion in connection with appeals to the Judicial Committee.' Indeed he thought that, if necessary, hearings in the Lords should be aborted to meet personnel needs in Australian cases.[80]

As with the experiments with Rowlatt and Warrington in the 1930s, the Office began to search around for persons who might be appointed either to the Judicial Committee or as law lords outside the regular Lords of Appeal in order to staff other appeals. There were those who had questioned under what authority de Silva could be appointed. Coldstream became fascinated with how Lord Parmoor (and there were others such as Lord Hobhouse) had come to be appointed in Edwardian times although they were not Lords of Appeal. In December 1955, Coldstream had consulted Schuster, the former—and omnipotent—Permanent Secretary in the Lord Chancellor's Office. Schuster reported that Parmoor's right to sit was a combination of his peerage and the 1833 Judicial Committee Act which allowed the Crown to appoint two judges who had not held 'high judicial office'.[81] At least that was what Schuster thought: 'You will bear in mind that (Sir Kenneth Muir) Mackenzie (the then Permanent Secretary) was completely unscrupulous in interpreting a statute, and disregarded its provisions if they did not suit him.' Schuster reported that Parmoor's appointment, in any event, was 'disastrous'.[82] 'The other holder under the 1833 Act was that old rogue, Ameer Ali, who was well qualified to hold judicial office because his tender conscience would not allow him to give judgment against a Moslem, when engaged in litigation with an opponent of any other faith.'[83]

(c) A Commonwealth Court?

It is a monument to the English belief in a mechanistic view of the judiciary and to the declaratory theory of law—often, it is true, mixed with a dated view of

[80] Memorandum, 5 Nov. 1955. Kilmuir minuted: 'Thank you for drawing to my attention the real difficulty. Nonetheless I think the reasons advanced by Lord Reid and accepted by Lord Simonds should prevail and we must do our best to minimize the resultant troubles.' Ibid.

[81] Schuster to Coldstream, 7 Dec. 1955, LCO 2/5233: 'Whatever was the Statutory situation at the time of Parmoor's appointment, it has been completely changed by subsequent legislation, under which substantial salaries have been provided for men appointed ad hoc, not holding or having held high judicial office, or any of the judicial offices in the Dominions or colonies specified in the original Act. Those new offices were invented to meet the case of India, and were intended to be held by one Hindu and one Moslem. I do not know how this has worked out since the scuttle.'

[82] 'To add the human touch of interest, this appointment was disastrous. Parmoor was for years a thorn in the flesh of successive Chancellors and of their unfortunate Permanent Secretaries. He wouldn't sit when he was asked to do so. He would sit when he was asked not to, and his colleagues, who anyhow disliked him, objected to sitting in a mob. He was, by this time, a disappointed and embittered man. He had expected to hold a Law Officership under the Conservatives; he had formed eccentric opinions on the merits of the War; and he hated Haldane, whom he regarded as the author of the War, in alliance with Grey. Hence he was always mauvais coucheur, and the unfortunate secretary (who had to deal also with Loreburn), bitterly pro-German, and bitterly hating Haldane, was in a difficult and dangerous position.' Ibid.

[83] Ibid.

Empire—that English politicians remained so deaf to the oft-repeated views and advice of the old Dominions. From the turn of the century, the older Dominions had made it clear that while at some time the final appeal to the Judicial Committee might go, in the meantime, they would rather have their appeals heard by English law lords than by judges from other colonies or Dominions. English politicians had to be reminded of this with some regularity, as they also had to be reminded that unless England, Scotland, and Ireland (later Northern Ireland) were prepared to have their appeals go to the Privy Council rather than the House of Lords, the final appeal would look increasingly as if it were discriminatory.

In the middle of the Second World War, in 1943, Sir Wilfrid Greene, MR, in many ways the high priest of the formalistic approach to law,[84] turned his attention to the Judicial Committee of the Privy Council. He concluded that 'unless steps are taken to place the Judicial Committee in a position of authority which will be accepted by the Dominions, the disappearance of its jurisdiction in Appeals from the Dominions in a comparatively short time is inevitable.'[85] He saw the Judicial Committee 'as a most valuable Imperial link' and 'as a means of ensuring uniformity of legal principle throughout the Empire'. Greene's solution involved turning the Judicial Committee into a peripatetic court. It was not a new idea. Simon and Hanworth had discussed it in the early 1930s.[86] It was also on the agenda of Conservative reformers in 1945.[87]

While Viscount Simon, the wartime Lord Chancellor, did not feel in a position to run with the idea, he certainly saw that, unless something were done, the Privy Council 'will peter out in a generation or less'. Simon also saw that nothing would work unless English appeals, instead of going to the House of Lords, went to the Judicial Committee. 'I can quite see that such a change might draw many protests from those who cling to the existing order, and I do not at all believe that the decisions of what is now called the House of Lords would as a matter of law be necessarily improved by introducing a new element. But neither do I think they would be rendered any worse.'[88]

With respect to the peripatetic aspect of the court, the biggest issue turned out

---

[84] e.g. the remarks in his Haldane lecture: '. . . the function of the judiciary is to interpret and enforce the law. The judiciary is not concerned with policy. It is not for the judiciary to decide what is in the public interest. Those are the tasks of the legislature, which is put there for the purpose . . .'. W. A. Greene, 'Law and Progress', 94 *Law Journal* (1944), 349, 351.

[85] 23 Nov. 1943, LCO 2/7233.   [86] Hanworth Papers, *passim*.

[87] See meeting between Viscount Simon and Conservative Committee on Law Reform, 8 Mar. 1945, LCO 2/3827.

[88] Memorandum, 11 Dec. 1943, LCO 2/7233. Simon had received some support for a peripatetic court from Vincent Massey, then serving as High Commissioner for Canada in London: 'The more I thought about this imaginative idea, the more I liked it . . . [it] would remove most of the serious objections [in Canada].' Massey to Simon, 11 Dec. 1943, ibid. The problem was that anglophilia was Massey's Achilles' heel. C. Bissell, *The Imperial Canadian: Vincent Massey in Office* (Toronto, 1986), ch. 1. Simon also noted 'is it not probable that after Australia and New Zealand have helped defeat Japan by driving the Japanese out of our Colonial Empire, they will expect to have more to say in respect of those areas than at present?' Memorandum, 11 Dec. 1943, LCO 2/7233.

to be the racial one. Sir David Monteith wrote to Simon from the India Office explaining the danger of embarrassment:

It is almost certain that South Africa and quite likely that Canada and Australia would decline to allow an Indian judge to be eligible to hear appeals in South Africa, Canada and Australia. (It is equally likely that for some time to come India would object to allowing South African Judges to sit on the Board in India.) But if Indian judges are to be ineligible to sit elsewhere than in India, would it not be embarrassing to prescribe that a Dominion judge should be eligible to sit else-where than in his own Dominion.[89]

Embarrassment was in fact spared by Churchill's decision. He told Simon that, 'Though the idea, as you expound it, is an attractive one, I do not myself think that the present time is a suitable one in which to raise a question of this kind.'[90]

The issue was rapidly revived in 1945 when Jowitt became Lord Chancellor after the Labour election landslide. Jowitt, like some other Lord Chancellors with a liberal reputation, in fact had a surprisingly traditional view of Empire. As MacDonald's Attorney-General he had not shared Sankey's enthusiasm for the Statute of Westminster, and his efforts to keep the Canadian connection have already been described. Indeed, this episode was part of his effort to keep the Commonwealth together by resuscitating the Judicial Committee of the Privy Council. In November 1945, he was writing to Lord Addison, the Commonwealth Secretary:

I always like to think that one of the ties which binds Canada to us is the Privy Council Appeal. Of course, there are those in Canada who may think it is rather derogatory . . . . Supposing we were to send a really strong Court to Canada to sit in Ottawa, might it not appeal to the Canadian imagination . . . I am doubtful of the wisdom of bringing any of the other Dominions in to sit. I think Canada might not like this, but I wish there were more distinguished Commonwealth judges who could sit with us if we do go to Ottawa.[91]

Addison in fact preferred a wider orbit, arguing that all the Dominions should be brought in, and that English and Scottish appeals should go to the Privy Council. Once again, however, Addison warned about 'the problem of India'.[92] Goddard, a Conservative whom Jowitt had appointed as Lord Chief Justice, egged the Lord Chancellor on, reporting that when he was in Canada 'Opinion [was] by no means unanimously in favour of abolition'. Indeed, 'several people' had said that if the Privy Council were to sit in Ottawa, 'abolition would be dead'.[93]

[89] Monteith to Simon, 12 Jan. 1944, LCO 2/7233. [90] Churchill to Simon, 2 Feb. 1944, ibid.
[91] Jowitt to Addison, 2 Nov. 1945, ibid. [92] Addison to Jowitt, 22 Nov. 1945, ibid.
[93] Goddard to Jowitt, 2 Nov. 1945, ibid. This approach ignored the many signs indicating a contrary view: e.g. on 5 Dec. 1945, Mr Justice Barlow (Ontario) wrote to Goddard: 'psychologically it would lose its appeal if the Throne came to the litigants. The tradition, the ceremonial, the distance, the fact that the court sits in the centre of the Empire would all be lost. The august, learned, elevated Judicial Committee would lose all its mystery if it came to sit in the Dominions.' Reported, Goddard to Jowitt, 7 Dec. 1945, ibid.

Jowitt was captivated by the scheme; his civil servants were not. George Coldstream, then Deputy Permanent Secretary, wrote to Lord Schuster—the former Permanent Secretary—noting that 'the Lord Chancellor has become enamoured of the old scheme to send the Judicial Committee on circuit,' and reporting that he was preparing a memorandum for Cabinet. 'There is, as I believe, no reason to suppose that a peripatetic body would be particularly welcome in the Dominions.'[94]

The Cabinet memorandum was, however, drafted with a bullish tone. Most of the earlier objections in Imperial Conferences were ignored or played down. India again loomed large in the thinking: 'it is doubtful whether an Indian judge would be welcomed as a member of this court (say) in Australia or Canada. If, on the other hand, Indian judges are not to be eligible to sit in a court outside India, an embarrassing situation would arise. Moreover, there may be difficulties in finding Indian judges of sufficient eminence to become members of the panel.'[95] Rather lukewarmly, the memorandum suggested that English and Scottish appeals should go to the new body.[96] As a fall-back position, the Cabinet was urged to consider a limited scheme with just Canada.[97] It was, however, Canada that administered the *coup de grâce*. The following month, January 1946, Jowitt reported to Addison that Louis St Laurent, the Canadian Minister of Justice, had been 'most interested and most helpful, but expressed the very clear view that as a matter of timing now was not the time to raise the question'.[98] Addison urged Jowitt, in the light of St Laurent's views, not to send the memorandum to Cabinet.[99]

[94] The most Coldstream thought might fly was a Canadian Privy Council with one or two law lords added. Coldstream to Schuster, 21 Dec. 1945, ibid.

[95] Judicial Committee of the Privy Council: Proposals for an Itinerant Board: Memorandum by the Lord Chancellor, Dec. 1945, p. 9 (another draft is dated Jan. 1946), ibid.

[96] 'Whatever the reaction to this proposal may be from English and Scottish critics, I cannot but think that the proposal for reciprocal action as regards English and Scottish appeals might have a considerable effect in assuring the Dominions that the scheme for an itinerant Board was a good one'. Ibid.

[97] 'If it proved impracticable to secure general Dominion agreement to the idea of an itinerant Board, I think it would be well worth considering inviting Canada to participate in some modified scheme. The English and Scottish members of the Board might be made members of the Canadian Privy Council, and would sit in Canada as members of the Dominion Privy Council, together with Canadian Judges who are Privy Counsellors of that Dominion. This would not be an itinerant Board in the sense of a single corpus of Judges (though of varying membership) travelling from Dominion to Dominion. The relative ease of travel between this country and Canada, and the particularly strong ties formed during the war between that Dominion and this country make the scheme, prima facie, really practicable in the case of Canada. Although the Canadian Bill to abolish the right of appeal to the Privy Council received a very fair measure of support in the Canadian Parliament in 1938, it is doubtful whether the situation is not now rather different. In any event, it is questionable whether all the Provinces of the Dominion are really in favour of abolition. If this view of the probable Canadian reaction is right it would surely be worth making soundings in Canada, whatever may be the outcome of the appeal to the Privy Council which will probably not be heard before the late summer of 1946.' Ibid.

[98] Jowitt to Addison, 9 Jan. 1946, ibid. See also Coldstream to Sir Arthur Dawe at the Colonial Office: 'Perhaps I should tell you in confidence that in taking this course, Lord Jowitt and Lord Addison were much influenced by the informal expression of opinion which had been given to Lord

Another decade passed. Canadian appeals were abolished in 1949; Indian, Pakistani, and South African in 1950.[100] In 1954, Churchill replaced Simonds with Kilmuir as Lord Chancellor and by the end of the year the new Chancellor was making noises about a peripatetic Privy Council. Alex Lennox Boyd, the Colonial Secretary, who was by then wrestling with a rather different problem— vigorous, political independence movements in most of Britain's colonies—liked what he heard.[101] Sir Charles Dix, the Commonwealth Office Constitutional Adviser, reminded the Lord Chancellor that no scheme would work unless English and Scottish appeals went to the new court—and even then, that there was little enthusiasm in the Commonwealth for any such scheme.[102] Sir George Coldstream, by then the Permanent Secretary in the Lord Chancellor's Office, produced a tired response to the Lord Chancellor, worthy of *Yes, Minister*: '[you] still think there is something to be said for the simple solution of sitting in places other than London.'[103]

In December, Coldstream produced a memorandum for Kilmuir warning that the peripatetic court was an 'old issue'. The history of the early decades of this century was rehearsed, and then the 1920s and 1930s:

The question was raised, somewhat half-heartedly, from time to time in the 1920s and 1930s, but never got anywhere. Lord Schuster (who understood so well the art of the practicably possible) told me in 1945 that he had become convinced that the proposals for an itinerant Board would be unlikely to find favour with the Dominions and were very likely to raise dissensions that were then at rest.

He then retraced the Simon resuscitation and the Jowitt resuscitation; and pointed out that whereas 'the accent at that time was upon the maintenance of this link between the Mother Country and what I may term the old Dominions', the problem had changed. What Coldstream did endorse was the suggestion that 'the project of an Itinerant Board is well worth considering in relation to Colonial Appeals and probably to appeals from the Supreme Courts of Federations within the Commonwealth which have not achieved Dominion status, and even those which may not achieve independent status for many years to come. It is for those members that the maintenance of an effective right of appeal to the Privy Council is likely to prove such a valuable constitutional link.'[104]

Jowitt by Mr. St. Laurent, the Canadian Minister of Justice, who is at present in this country. St. Laurent suggests that the Canadian appeal to the Privy Council which will be heard this summer might well result in a decision that Canada is perfectly free to abolish the right of appeal to the Privy Council by Canadian legislation. That being so, a proposal along the lines suggested, would, if made to the Dominion now, give the impression that it was a last minute effort by the UK to retain some sort of superior right.' Ibid.

[99] Addison to Jowitt, 21 Jan. 1946, ibid.

[100] Swinfen, *Imperial Appeal*, ch. 6. The last Canadian appeal was not heard until 1959. *Ponoka-Calmar Oils Ltd*. v *Earl F. Wakefield Co*. [1960] AC 18. See W. G. Morrow, 'The Last Case', 16 *Alberta Law Review* (1978), 1–19.

[101] Lennox-Boyd to Kilmuir, 7 Dec. 1945, LCO 2/7233.

[102] Memorandum, Dix, 20 Dec. 1954, ibid.   [103] 19 Jan. 1955, ibid.

[104] Memorandum, Coldstream to Kilmuir, 16 Dec. 1954, LCO 2/7237.

Africa was an obvious candidate within the Coldstream guidelines. Sir Barclay Nihill, President of the Court of Appeal for Eastern Africa, lobbied hard for a member of his court to be appointed on terms similar to those which Mr de Silva, the Ceylonese (Sri Lankan) judge, had been given.[105] Kilmuir, however, still hankered for a peripatetic court. He called a ministerial meeting in March 1955 to assess the situation. In addition to the civil servants, the Lord Chancellor, the Lord President, the Dominion Secretary; and the Colonial Secretary were there. Kilmuir opened the discussions, arguing that Simon and Jowitt had failed but that 'he considered that the importance of this proposal lay not in the relationship to the old Dominions so much as the new territories which would shortly be achieving independence—the Central African Federation, Nigeria, and the Gold Coast (Ghana)'.

The discussion was, in its own way, fascinating. The Commonwealth Secretary, for instance, noted that 'the members of the Judicial Committee were not young and it would be a strain for them to travel long distances by air to countries where the climate was bad'. Delay, the quality of counsel, the quality of colonial judges, the absence of good libraries were all noted. The Colonial Secretary was the strongest supporter, arguing that 'there are some African Judges who are good enough to be members of the Privy Council'. The Lord President was doubtful: 'He thought that any advantage that might be conferred upon Colonial territories would not be worth while if the prestige of the court was lowered in the eyes of the older Commonwealth countries.'

To today's observer, the discussion emphasized the unreality both of the Commonwealth and of the attempt to apply the simplistic mechanistic English approach to judicial decision-making to societies with very different political environments. One of those at the meeting noted that 'some Commonwealth countries could be relied upon to propose good men, but others could not'. Another noted, 'The standard of the local Bar would present a great difficulty: the standard varied in different Colonial territories, and in West Africa it was so low that there was not one single competent advocate.' Another emphasized the racial problem. If 'colonials' were appointed to the Privy Council, 'this would not be liked by the older Commonwealth countries'.[106]

After the somewhat abortive discussion, C. W. B. Rankin, Private Secretary to the Lord Chancellor, was instructed to produce a paper. This was a more realistic assessment than the politicians and lawyers were capable of:

---

[105] 'I have hesitated to put forward this matter before for a personal reason. I am approaching the age of retirement and as the senior Appellate Judge in East Africa, I should naturally be disappointed if my name were not considered for appointment.' Nihill memorandum, Nairobi, 7 Jan. 1955, LCO 2/7233. Nihill suggested that following the Ceylon model the East African governments should pay £2,500 per annum to support such a judge. Nihill had actually been recommended for such an appointment by Jowitt in a letter to Napier, 25 Mar. 1954, LCO 2/5788. The Attorney-General of Kenya, Sir John Wyatt, preferred a peripatetic Privy Council. He wrote a highly articulate letter to the Governor of Kenya—for transmission to London—dated 21 Feb. 1955, LCO 2/7233.

[106] The Peripatetic Privy Council, 25 Mar. 1955, ibid.

Modern Colonial policy, as I understand it, is not to meet nationalism head on, but to try to deflect it into productive channels useful to us. This means that we must avoid appearing in any way to derogate from the grant of self-government within the Commonwealth; and I think that this proposal if put into effect would have that appearance. . . . however welcome to the judiciary and the legal profession the extension of the jurisdiction of the Judicial Committee might be, it would be regarded by politicians and administrators in the new countries with impatience. . . . It seems to me that an itinerant Board, instead of increasing the influence of the Judicial Committee, might just as easily provoke premature demands for the abolition of the right of appeal altogether.[107]

While Coldstream purported to add a more balanced comment before the paper went to Kilmuir, he did not believe the peripatetic scheme would help with 'links' to the older Commonwealth. Indeed, 'short of some whole-hearted expression of desire from Australia, the practical effect might be to cause resentment rather than gratitude.' On the other hand, and perhaps coming as a surprise to those who have questioned the English judiciary's competence in matters of constitutional law,[108] Coldstream argued for

the value of a great, authoritative Supreme Judiciary in the formative years of a new constitution. . . . It should be represented as a contribution which the British Government would be ready and willing to make towards the younger but nevertheless independent, members of the Commonwealth fellowship. It would be a real and significant contribution, because no one doubts that the quality of British justice is the best in the world, and young nations are doubtless as anxious as young persons to have the best of anything.[109]

Kilmuir, it seems, got the message from Rankin rather than Coldstream. He commented on the paper: 'I am grateful—if slightly depressed—for this very clear statement of the arguments . . . It may be that we have missed the bus.' Indeed, the reactions were to be expected. The fear of the insertion of colonial judges into the Privy Council was enough for Australia to insist later in that year that its appeals should always be heard by five English law lords. Kilmuir made that commitment.[110] Indeed, when the following year a Conservative MP was planning to revive the issue of a Commonwealth Court in the House of Commons, he was warned behind the scenes that Australia and New Zealand 'would not be amused' to have their cases heard by colonial judges.[111] Even the Duke of Edinburgh, who enquired about a Commonwealth Court that same

---

[107] Proposal for an Itinerant Board of the Judicial Committee, Rankin to Coldstream, 5 Apr. 1955, ibid.

[108] Some, for instance, would argue that the Privy Council decision in *Adegbenro* v *Akintola* [1963] AC 614 (PC, Nigeria) helped precipitate the Biafran War. It certainly precipitated the abolition of appeals to the Privy Council from Nigeria. For other comments on the Board's later constitutional work, see Stevens, *Law and Politics*, 608 n.

[109] LCO 2/7233.

[110] The decision was the result of discussions between Kilmuir and Lord Reid. Simonds was also involved. Coldstream to Kilmuir, 31 Oct. 1955, LCO 2/5234. See also Coldstream to file, 31 Oct. 1955, ibid. Sir Owen Dixon had made it clear that Australia would not allow an African to sit on Australian appeals. Memorandum from Lord Kilmuir, 21 Nov. 1958, LCO 2/7236.

[111] Coldstream to Theisiger, 28 June 1956, LCO 2/5237.

year got a bland response. The Duke was warned that it was 'a controversial issue'; the best judges were not easy to get; and in some colonies, the standards of Bench and Bar were not high.[112]

Some of the absurdity and amateurism of the situation was reflected in the rules for who might appear before the Judicial Committee of the Privy Council. Lord Atkin, despite his reputation as a liberal, was conservative on the Commonwealth. He opposed the Statute of Westminster and also held that Commonwealth QC's—with the exception of members of a Bar in the United Kingdom—might not appear in appeals from another jurisdiction. Thus in 1955, Sir Garfield Barwick, the Australian QC, was retained in a New Zealand appeal. He wrote to the Clerk of the Privy Council asking permission to appear.[113] A few weeks later he was writing to the Lord Chancellor ('Dear David . . . Yours Gar') questioning the retaining of appeals to the Privy Council, but at least urging the merger of the Privy Council and the House of Lords and urging Kilmuir to 'resist American influence'.[114] With respect to the particular request, Kilmuir railed that Atkin was 'insular', while he (Kilmuir) was under the impression that the Privy Council was an Imperial Court so that any QC from any of Her Majesty's Dominions might appear.

Coldstream met with Simonds and Oaksey, both of whom felt any QC should be free to appear; after all, the Privy Council was free to hear whomever it wished. Apparently the Bar Council had concluded this as early as 1900. Nevertheless, the law lords argued that New Zealand should be consulted. Meanwhile, Coldstream worried—why it is not clear—that a 'coloured counsel' from West Africa might appear in an East African case.[115] In the meantime, Kilmuir warned the Attorney-General that Barwick was thinking of becoming an English junior in order to appear, although the New Zealand Government had no objection to his appearing.[116] In the meantime, the Lord Chancellor's Office decided that the English Bar 'should or would' not object;[117] so Barwick was given the go-ahead.[118] The following year Barwick was back, asking to appear in a Fijian case.[119] The Colonial Office was consulted;[120] they consulted the Fijian Government and once again Barwick was able to appear.[121] The matter, however, was never settled as one of principle.

Even then, however, Kilmuir could not let the idea of a peripatetic Privy Council drop. In late 1958, the Lord Chancellor once again floated the idea, sending a memorandum to all the law lords about his dream—apparently resuscitated by a discussion with Sir Owen Dixon, the Chief Justice of Australia, although the latter was not in fact in favour of such a system. The idea floated was for one Division of the Privy Council to sit in London, while the other

[112] Kilmuir to Commander Parker, 13 July 1956, LCO 2/5238.
[113] Barwick to Paterson. 31 Mar. 1955, LCO 2/5231.   [114] 21 Apr. 1955, ibid.
[115] Coldstream to file, 3 May 1955, ibid.
[116] Lord Chancellor to Attorney-General, 10 May 1955, ibid.   [117] 12 May 1955, ibid.
[118] Kilmuir to Barwick, 16 May 1955, ibid.   [119] Barwick to Kilmuir, 13 Feb. 1956, ibid.
[120] Coldstream minute, 24 Feb. 1956, ibid.   [121] Memorandum, 2 Mar. 1956, ibid.

went on circuit, although, Kilmuir insisted, the 'touring side' would have to be as good as the 'home team'. For instance, the Lord Chancellor thought that in Year 1, the touring side might go to the Federations of Rhodesia and Nyasaland, East Africa, West Africa, and Ghana. In Year 2 it might be the Caribbean Federation and British Honduras; and in Year 3, Australia, New Zealand, and Hong Kong. The rhetoric was familiar:

The common law constitutes a bond between the countries of the Commonwealth which should be strengthened to bring them together . . . (and to ensure the) uniform development of law throughout the Commonwealth . . . As new Commonwealth countries achieve independence, political control over them is lost; but the Judicial Committee provides an opportunity to exercise control of a different kind and to guide development indirectly by the exercise of a jurisdiction which commands universal respect . . . everything must be done to keep the jurisdiction alive and appeals should be encouraged . . . the inhabitants of the territories visited by the Committee would get to know and respect its members personally and would be able to observe themselves the virtues of the Court . . . the reproach would be removed that the decisions of the Judicial Committee taken in the remote calm of Downing Street are based upon no direct experience or knowledge of the conditions existing in distant territories . . . The ease and comfort of air travel now make it possible for the first time in history for the Court to go on circuit, and such discomforts as there may be are nothing compared to what the Judges of Assize had to put up with until comparatively recent times.

Kilmuir also saw the arguments against such a circuit system:

The arguments for an itinerant Court do not take sufficient account of the nature and vigour of nationalism in the Commonwealth . . . In all cases where the right of appeal has been abandoned, it has not been because of complaints about the working of the court . . . but for purely nationalistic reasons . . . there is a feeling, so long as it exists, that the 'colonial' country has not really achieved independence . . . Far from being a link, it is argued, the jurisdiction of the Judicial Committee in these circumstances is a chain which, if past experience is a guide, is likely to chafe against nationalist sentiment and irritate it. . . . the political problem in Canada was not lessened by the fact that Canadian Privy Counsellors sat to hear appeals in London . . . We may well be thankful for example that the relations of the United Kingdom with South Africa and Pakistan have not been put to what might have been a fatal strain if an appeal had been brought to the Judicial Committee on the question of the entrenched clauses in the South Africa Act or the constitutional validity of the recent actions of the Governor-General in Pakistan . . . Remoteness is not necessarily a weakness, and it is debatable whether the physical presence of the members of the Judicial Committee in Commonwealth countries would increase the attraction of the Court. Their aloofness from local politics would certainly be less, if only through unavoidable social contacts.

For Kilmuir, however, the advantages outweighed the disadvantages: 'I consider that from the standpoint of the Commonwealth policy at large, the arguments in favour of the Judicial Committee sitting in certain Commonwealth countries outweighs the objections . . . Lawyers everywhere regard London as the Centre of the Legal World.'[122]

Only Lord Denning among the law lords was enthusiastic about the scheme: 'The only hope of restoring the Judicial Committee to something like its former glory is to turn it into the Supreme Court of the Commonwealth . . . Just as Henry II revolutionized the administration of justice in England by sending his judges round the country on circuit, so I think the administration of justice in the Commonwealth can be revolutionized by sending the Privy Council round the countries which acknowledge its jurisdiction.' Indeed, Denning was in favour of including South Africa, Canada, and India—and he thought it important to have the Law Lords wear robes. Yet only Lord Reid offered Denning any support: 'unless we go forward we may slip back and more Commonwealth countries may stop appeals to London. While certainly Australia would not want its constitutional cases adjudicated, other countries might want this,' and that 'might lessen fears of minorities'.

The basic case against was argued by Kilmuir's predecessor—Viscount Simonds.[123] The proposal, while having 'superficial attraction', has been 'so often made and been so often dropped upon examination . . . its advantages are speculative and uncertain, its disadvantages certain, patent and overwhelming.' Simonds did not take the common law argument seriously, since most new Commonwealth countries did not have 'real' common law but basically customary law and ordinances. Moreover, he was aware that the Privy Council was not at its best on constitutional issues. 'I have often been painfully aware how inadequate has been my own training in the very special field of legal problems which arise out of a federal constitution.'

On Simonds went: 'Some will remember the row there was when the late Sir John Rowlatt (Rowlatt of all people!) sat to hear some Australian appeals.'[124] 'A Chief Justice of Nigeria or the Caribbean would not be more favourably received.' The notion of a peripatetic Privy Council was a 'wholly disadvantageous idea with respect to Australia and New Zealand'. Moreover, some law lords would never have accepted the job if they had known they were required to go on circuit. 'A Board sitting in Downing Street at a distance of some thousands of miles is more likely to inspire and retain the respect of the natives of Ghana than is a body of old gentlemen visiting the territory . . . it is, in my opinion, a matter not for reproach but for congratulation that the decisions of the Committee are taken "in the remote calm of Downing Street".' Simonds finished with three final thoughts: what about wives? What about expense? Finally: 'The quality of the native counsel may not be such as to give the Bench the assistance which they surely need.'

---

[122] Kilmuir, memorandum, n.d., LCO 2/7236.

[123] Memorandum, 2 Nov. 1958, ibid.

[124] He probably meant Canadian appeals, particularly Rowlatt's role in striking down the Canadian 'New Deal'.

The other law lords concurred with Simonds. Lord Morton noted,

I have grave doubts that the scheme would achieve the good results mentioned . . .
Eleven-and-a-half years of sitting in the Judicial Committee lead me to the belief that it is
not well suited to go on circuit . . . I think that the Africans, who love pomp and circum-
stance and are (or used to be) inclined to judge a man's importance from appearance,
might feel rather 'let down' when five old men in ordinary clothes appeared.

Lord Tucker announced:

This is a political and not strictly a judicial question and is therefore one upon which my
opinion is not of much value, but I feel bound to say I am sceptical with regard to the
anticipated results and am inclined to the view that the consequences would be more
likely to be detrimental than beneficial.

Tucker had been reluctant to come to the Lords because 'Law Lords are so often
expected to take on jobs of a non-judicial nature, a practice of which I disap-
prove and for which I do not consider myself qualified.' Going on the
Commonwealth circuit would be worse.

Lord Somervell did not approve of second appeals; he thought local appeal
courts 'not bad'; thought a peripatetic Privy Council would not strengthen the
Commonwealth and would just send up costs. Lord Keith did not think the proposal 'expedient'. Lord Cohen admitted he used to be in favour and had once
thought that a peripatetic court would have discouraged Canada from abolishing
appeals. He no longer thought that. Lord Radcliffe opposed the scheme because
it would expose the Committee's ignorance of local conditions, although he
shared the view that a Commonwealth Constitutional Court might be of some
value.[125] When the meeting of law lords was finally held on 1 December 1958,
six of the nine said bluntly they would not go on circuit. Many felt with Lord
Cohen it would do more harm than good. Kilmuir accepted that 'clearly the
proposal could go no further at present'.[126]

Although we now know that Harold Macmillan thought Kilmuir a light-
weight,[127] he has on balance been treated generously by commentators and historians.[128] Certainly Kilmuir's encounter with a peripatetic Privy Council or a
Commonwealth Court might well be assumed to have been the end of the story.
Strangely enough, it was not. The mechanistic approach to law was so heavily
ingrained in English legal thinking, especially on the so-called political Left, and
political reality was so elusive to the legal mind, that there was to be one last
canter through the process. It was a strange tale.

During the late 1950s and early 1960s, it looked as if the Commonwealth
might break up over South Africa. What the Commonwealth represented was

---

[125] Coldstream memorandum of Radcliffe visit, 15 Oct. 1958, LCO 2/7236.
[126] Minutes of 1 Dec. 1958 meeting, ibid.
[127] Macmillan wrote, 'He was always a "beta minus"; the stupidest Lord Chancellor . . . hopeless
in Cabinet—that's why I got rid of him . . .'. Horne, *Macmillan*, ii. 316.
[128] Stevens, *Law and Politics*, 420–5; Heuston, *Lives of the Lord Chancellors, 1940–1970*, 181–204.

less and less clear. Even the Conservatives finally thought Britain's future lay with the European Community. In 1964, however, the Labour Party was returned and Harold Wilson chose Gerald Gardiner as his Lord Chancellor. Gardiner thought of himself as a radical of the Left; yet he was remarkably conservative on so many issues. Few Chancellors have been so conservative with respect to the profession (indeed it was the current Conservative Chancellor Lord Mackay, who proved to be the radical). Gardiner, however, saw the Commonwealth through the eyes of a lawyer's lawyer, tinged with the bourgeois hue of the Society of Labour Lawyers and the élitist Marxism of the Haldane Society.[129]

Gardiner's rather strange position was that the judicial role of the House of Lords should be abolished to save litigants' money, but a peripatetic Commonwealth Court should be established (which would substitute for the House of Lords and be the only appeal court for the Court of Appeal, the Court of Criminal Appeal, the Court of Session, and the Court of Appeal for Northern Ireland) to save the Commonwealth.[130] Moreover, he saw all members of the Commonwealth participating. In May 1965, Gardiner proceeded to float the idea in Parliament and received support primarily from a group of Conservative MPs who had been toying with the idea for the previous couple of years.[131] The next month—June 1965—the Commonwealth Conference turned a largely deaf ear to the idea. The older Dominions took their traditional position of severe scepticism, while the new African countries had adopted a form of African Socialism that owed little to Gardiner's intellectual concerns. Only Malaysia, which had worked out a special relationship with the Privy Council, was supportive.[132] There was, however, to be one last public appearance of the idea—at the Commonwealth and Empire Law Conference in Sydney in September. While the English Attorney-General felt 'confident' that the Conference would endorse the idea of a Commonwealth Court, and while Gardiner thought he had the support of the Indian Chief Justice, it proved an embarrassing non-starter.[133] The Commonwealth Court was dead; the Judicial Committee of the Privy Council was on the way to extinction.[134]

Such an ignominious end was in so many ways predictable. A mechanistic jurisprudence is pretence. A declaratory theory of law cannot be intelligently applied in supra-national situations. Whatever the pressures that sustain it in a single jurisdiction, they are inconsistent with the politics of reality that inevitably

---

[129] Heuston, *Lives of the Lord Chancellors, 1940–1970*, 207–43; Stevens, *Law and Politics*, 431–6.

[130] G. Gardiner and A. Martin, eds., *Law Reform NOW* (London, 1963), 16.

[131] The support in Parliament was based on a group of Tory MPs, Graham Page, Derek Walker-Smith, and Edward Gardner. Swinfen, *Imperial Appeal*, 185. Ch. 7 of Swinfen's book ('The Commonwealth Court Revisited') is based on interviews with members of the Lord Chancellor's Office about this last foray into a Commonwealth Court.

[132] Stevens, *Law and Politics*, 415–16.   [133] For details, see Swinfen, *Imperial Appeal*, 211–16.

[134] Australian appeals were abolished by the Australia Act, 1986, and the last case was heard in 1987: *Austin v Keele*, 61 *Australian Law Journal*, (1987), 585.

impinge in a broader context. For the older Dominions, abolition was closely related to political maturity. Some Third World countries abolished appeals because they feared the Privy Council might undermine their economic goals and their increasingly repressive regimes. The Canadian Courts have wrestled far more effectively with constitutional issues since the abolition of appeals to London in 1949 and the patriation of the Constitution in 1982. Some of the former colonies have thrived legally; others have not. In the intervening twenty-five years the English too have veered away somewhat from the mystical view of judicial formalism, the irrelevance of the judge—both politically and person-ally—and the primacy of logic.[135] The collapse of the Privy Council jurisdiction strangely enough coincided with the apparent demise of substantive formalism and the declaratory theory of law in the English legal process.

[135] See e.g. Lord Mackay, 'Can Judges Change the Law?' 73 *Proceedings of the British Academy* (1988), 285–308. Mackay appears to adopt the Dworkian approach that judges are concerned with the development of principles, not policies. Lord Scarman was the chief proponent of this approach on the Bench.

Epilogue

The vicissitudes of the Commonwealth Court provide a fitting place to end the overall discussion of judicial independence. The history of the Judicial Committee of the Privy Council exemplifies the English judges' social and intellectual attitudes to their work. For much of the twentieth century the judges in applying—or interpreting—the law have been regarded as performing a primarily mechanical function: the application of pre-existing rules to new facts. Since this has been regarded virtually as a declaratory role, it has been thought, even in a appeal court, that it is irrelevant which judges sit provided they are sufficiently well trained in a technical sense. If technical competence, however, is the only criterion for appointment, it suggests that the ambit of judicial independence is narrow. As will be seen, in the years since 1960, one of the apparently most pressing issues in the debate about judicial independence has been whether, since technical competence is such a significant matter, the appointment of judges should be controlled by the profession. Ironically it has also been in the years since 1960 that the judges—or at least some of them—have moved away from judicial passivity and in some areas have become exponents of judicial activism.

From 1830 to 1880, the English legal system had received the powerful imprint of Benthamite Reform. For much of the life of the Lord Chancellor's Office after 1880, there was but tinkering with reform. Corners were rounded; edges smoothed; but structures remained. The judges continued at the centre of the system. As their power and financial status eroded, their prestige flourished. While the general concept of judicial independence was vague, the independence of individual judges was protected. The judges' reputation for personal and professional integrity justifiably rose. Nevertheless, as their public political role lessened, a form of social political conformity emerged. The highly formalized and elegant Bar and the highly formalized and elegant Bench were the reverse sides of the same coin. A mystique embraced both. Moreover, the profession and judiciary were insulated from effective management by their own version of the Civil Service—the Lord Chancellor's Office.

(a) The Last Decades

This playing-out of roles lasted until about 1960. It was based on a series of assumptions which had begun to wear thin. By 1960, the notion of consensus politics and government on the Inner Circle appeared to destine Britain for second- or even third-class status. It was becoming obvious that the

Commonwealth was an elegant way of abandoning imperialism, but no basis for an economic future.[1] Prime Minister Macmillan's unsuccessful attempt to take Britain into the EEC was as important for a basic change in political attitudes as was the 'Winds of Change' speech. The dismal politics of the 1960s and 1970s led ultimately to the period of confrontational politics associated with Thatcherism.

In the thirty years since 1960, both the structure and style of profession and judiciary have changed far more rapidly than they had changed in the previous eighty years. The success of the profession is apparent—at least superficially. The number of barristers rose from 1,919 in 1960 to 5,367 in 1985. By 1992 it had reached 7,271. Solicitors went from 19,069 to 46,490 in that same period.[2] By 1992 there were 59,566. The Bar was aided in its rapid growth by criminal legal aid, which was put on a market basis in the mid-1960s, and by the wider use of courts. A segment of the solicitors' branch of the profession also flourished through criminal legal aid. The amount of public money going to the legal profession rose from £479 million in 1988 to £857 million in 1992. Solicitors also, at least in the larger centres, were caught up in the commercial revolution, which was manifested most obviously in the 'Big Bang' in the City. Especially in the latter part of the 1980s many parts of the profession waxed wealthy.

Outwardly, too, the judiciary flourished. Gone were the days when the judges had to beg for salary increases; they came automatically.[3] Some, although by no means all,[4] of the reluctance to appoint as many judges as necessary had gone. Between 1970 and 1990 the number of professional judges quadrupled. Today, there are ten Lords of Appeal authorized in the House of Lords, twenty-nine Lords Justice in the Court of Appeal, eighty-five High Court judges, and 420 circuit judges. What has been lacking is a willingness to analyse the relationship of the work allocated to different levels of the judiciary. The Children's Act,

---

[1] By 1992, the idea of Commonwealth—at least in the old sense—was effectively dead. The Labour Party in Australia appeared ready to commit itself to Republicanism and even the *Globe and Mail*, the pillar of the Canadian British Establishment, saw it as logical to end Canada's link with the Crown when Elizabeth's reign ended. Editorial, 26 Oct. 1991.

The Hilary 1992 sittings for the Judicial Committee of the Privy Council revealed four appeals from Mauritius, four from Hong Kong, two from Jamaica, and one each from the Bahamas, the Gambia, the Cayman Islands, and Trinidad and Tobago. Judgment was waiting to be given in one appeal from Barbados and one from Trinidad and Tobago. Of the 'colonial' judges entitled to sit, six were from New Zealand and one from the Bahamas.

Not all the cases were unimportant. The future of 200 prisoners on Jamaica's 'Death Row' could ultimately be decided by the Judicial Committee of the Privy Council.

[2] R. L. Abel, *The Legal Profession in England and Wales* (Oxford, 1988), 342.

[3] Although in autumn 1991, Prime Minister Major announced that he intended delaying the most recent recommendations of the Top Salaries Committee.

[4] Judicial manpower in the High Court is supplemented by Deputy Judges, part of the '20 days of National Service' expected of all leading counsel. In 1990, High Court judges sat for 13,955 judge days, deputies for 2,539. *Judicial Statistics, 1991*, tables 9.1 and 9.2. At the lower levels, Recorders sat for 17,144 judge days, an average of 23 per person p.a., and Assistant Recorders for 890 judge days, an average of 21 per Assistant Recorder.

1989, may, however, be the first stage in changing that, at least with respect to family matters.

Whatever the numbers say, important—indeed crucial—changes in Bench, profession, and Civil Service have occurred in the years since 1960. For much of the period, the profession just seemed to prosper. In retrospect, the Benson Commission in 1979 was remarkably bland in its suggestions about the legal profession and legal services.[5] By 1990, however, change was in the air. While outwardly the Government lost the dispute with the Bar over legal aid funding in 1986 and 1987, in fact the Civil Service and the Conservative Government had clearly resolved not to be outmanœuvred in that way again. The intervening years have seen a clear intention of making the Lord Chancellor's Department operate like any other government department.

The Legal Services Act of 1988 and the Courts and Legal Services Act 1990 caused a minor earthquake of restructuring. Moreover—no doubt spurred on by Margaret Thatcher—Lord Mackay, who became Lord Chancellor in 1987, made it clear that the legal profession had to change. As Green Paper gave way to White Paper and ultimately to the Courts and Legal Services Act of 1990, while there was a weakening of the original plan to have a total restructuring of the legal profession, vital changes were made. Even with the departure of Mrs Thatcher, the momentum for radical reform may well still be there. It should be noted, however, that, as of this date, the Bar managed to hold off the efforts to broaden the right of advocacy.

Controversial as she became, there is no doubt that Mrs Thatcher changed the vision of virtually all institutions in Britain. She assaulted the Civil Service with demands for privatization and an emphasis on management, and a willingness to appoint as Permanent Secretaries those who were seen as 'one of us'. It was a great change in philosophy; and the mandarins in Whitehall were less than happy.[6] While less direct in her assault on the institution of the judiciary, there is no doubt it has been under fire—partly from its own troops.

Certainly over the last thirty years the judges have become increasingly cautious about what they have seen as assaults on their privileges and positions. The dangers were explained by Lord Denning in discussing the Courts Act of 1971:

The Lord Chancellor's Department is bound to be, whatever it is in name, a Ministry of Justice. Great powers are given to the Lord Chancellor and his Department. Take, for instance the Circuit Judges who would be appointed by him . . . the salaries . . . are to be fixed by him . . . the power of removal of Circuit Judges is in the Lord Chancellor's hands. In having the Ministry of Justice, so long as we have Lord Chancellors such as the Lord Chancellor . . . we need have no fear that the independence of the judges will be assailed. I only hope this will always be so, because the independence of our judges is perhaps the most important feature of our whole constitution. If salaries can be altered, if

---

[5] *The Royal Commission on Legal Services: Final Report*, Cmnd. 7648 (1979).
[6] Paxman, *Friends in High Places*, 134–42.

dismissals can be made, by a Ministry of Justice . . . independence might be assailed. Fortunately it is still maintained in regard to High Court judges.[7]

Certainly Circuit judges disappeared rapidly, as the Lord Chancellor exercised his right to dismiss for misbehaviour. When Judge Bruce Campbell attempted to evade customs duties on significant amounts of whisky and cigarettes his departure from the Bench was rapid. When High Court judges appeared to come close to the line the process was much more obviously one of 'ear stroking'.[8] The conviction of Lord Justice Russell for drunken driving did not prevent his promotion to the House of Lords as Lord Russell. *The Times* reported that Mr Justice Melford Stevenson had been reprimanded by the Lord Chancellor for referring to the Sexual Offences Act as a 'Bugger's Charter'.[9] The response was more public when Judge Argyle, a judge at the Old Bailey, made anti-immigrant remarks.[10] Judge Pickles, who refused to abide by the Kilmuir Rules which effectively gagged all judges, was publicly rebuked in 1983 by the Lord Chancellor's Permanent Secretary (Sir Derek Oulton) for writing to the *Daily Telegraph* about penal policy. Judge Pickles dared Mrs Thatcher's first Lord Chancellor, Lord Hailsham (1979–87), to act: 'I realise you may well try to dismiss me. You are certainly ruthless enough and you may be shortsighted enough.'[11] Pickles in fact survived and Lord Mackay, Hailsham's successor, rapidly abolished the Kilmuir Rules,[12] which had been defended by Hailsham on the ground that they protected impartiality.[13] There was, however, certainly something to be said for Hailsham's caution. When Lord Denning in 1982 expressed his views on the peremptory challenge of jurors where blacks were involved, it became clear it was time even for him to retire.[14]

During the 1960s, whether on their own, or through parliamentary action, the judges moved from behind their cloud of anonymity. The Restrictive Practices Court and the Industrial Relations Court are obvious examples. The willingness of the judges over these years to develop administrative law is also well known; and the judges took a more instrumental approach to tax law.[15] The attitudes of the Lord Chancellors were also important. In the 1950s, Lord Kilmuir called for

---

[7] Shetreet, *Judges on Trial*, 401.

[8] R. Light, 'Judges over the Limit', 39 *New Law Journal* (9 June 1989), 783–4.

[9] *The Times*, 9 July 1978.

[10] M. Zander, *A Matter of Justice: The Legal System in Ferment* (Oxford, 1989), 130–1.

[11] Ibid. 136.

[12] J. Rozenberg, 'The Kilmuir Rules KO'd', *Guardian*, 21 July 1989.

[13] Zander, *A Matter of Justice*, 134. Lord Hailsham refused to allow judges to appear on the BBC.

[14] E. Heward, *Lord Denning* (London, 1990), ch. 17. On racial discrimination, he upset the Sikh community in *Mandla* v. *Dowell Lea* [1982] 3 WLR 932 (CA). It was his speech at the 1981 Lord Mayor's Dinner and a chapter in *What Next in the Law* (London, 1982) which were the final nails in the coffin. With respect to references in the latter, Lord Denning faced libel writs from jury members in the case discussed. The matter was settled out of court.

[15] Stevens, *Law and Politics*, ch. 12. It is arguable that in these fields, in the 1980s, the judges retreated to a more formalistic stance. D. Feldman, 'Public Law Values in the House of Lords', 106 *Law Quarterly Review* (1990), 246–76; D. McBarnet and C. Whelan, 'The Elusive Spirit of the Law: Formalism and the Struggle for Legal Control', 54 *Modern Law Review* (1991), 848–73.

the law to be more relevant. In the 1960s, Lord Gardiner allowed the House of Lords to overrule its own earlier decisions,[16] and members of the Privy Council to dissent,[17] changes which in turn were supported by Gardiner's system of reform of 'lawyer's law' through the Law Commission. It was once more politically acceptable to argue that the judges should 'function as a distinct force in government'.[18]

The year 1959 was significant for the judges. Under the Judicial Pensions Act there was finally a retiring age for all judges appointed after that year. The change meant a younger cohort of judges, and there was evidence that they were more in touch with reality than earlier generations of judges. The embarrassing statements tended to come from the Dennings and Melford Stevensons who had been appointed before the mandatory retirement age. The arrival of 'no fault' divorce meant that judges were deprived of the opportunity of pontificating on sexual morality while hearing divorce petitions, pontifications which, until the 1960s, helped fill the columns of the *Evening Standard*. Incidentally the Bar on divorced persons on the Bench appeared to have evaporated.

Critics, however, felt that judgeships were an attractive form of public partial retirement for a private profession, normally involving less work, a large and assured salary, a significant pension (inflation-adjusted) after fifteen years (scheduled to be raised to twenty),[15] a knighthood, and a considerable amount of deference. Lord Hailsham put it more delicately. He described judicial work as 'the real crown of a legal career for the absence of which money alone cannot compensate. Judicial work is a privilege, a pleasure and a duty. It is one of the highest forms of public service.' In 1985 Lord Hailsham reported: 'It is rare indeed for a High Court judgeship to be declined; and not many refuse the circuit bench.'[20] In 1988, Lord Mackay said that, with respect to the High Court, difficulties of recruitment were 'tolerable at present', but that recruitment for the Circuit Court was 'proving an immediate problem'.

The Top Salaries Review Body meant that judges' salaries kept pace with inflation, and *de facto* were on a par with those of Permanent Secretaries. In real terms their salary was worth only one-half of the salary of High Court judges in 1931. It should be noted, however, that in 1992 law lords were paid appreciably more than Justices of the Supreme Court of the United States. Occasionally there would be a call for a return to the really old days. In 1988, Neil Gow, a Scottish QC, argued that the real analogy should be with company chairmen, implying that an appropriate salary for High Court judges would be £250,000.[21]

---

[16] Practice Direction (Judicial Precedent) [1966] 1 WLR 1234 (HL). Paterson, *The Law Lords*, ch. 7.
[17] Judicial Committee (Dissenting Opinions) Order in Council, 1966.
[18] A. W. B. Simpson, 'The Judges and the Vigilant State', (1989) *Denning Law Journal*, 145, 146.
[19] *The Times*, 15 Dec. 1990.   [20] *New Law Journal*, 26 July 1985, p. 741.
[21] While the reasoning is not clear, the argument is related to the survey by the Office of Manpower Economics showing that legal earnings were going up 10–15 per cent p.a. and that the gross salary for QC's was £121,000. N. Gow, 'Are We Paying Our Judges Enough?', 138 *New Law*

In the run-up to the 1992 Election, the Top Persons' Salary Review Board re-commended a dramatically increased award (19 per cent), well ahead of inflation, for the judges, but it was kept under wraps until after the Election. Then, for the first time since the system had been established in early 1970s, the Government rejected the award, requiring the judges to be satisfied with 4 per cent. Politics had not entirely been drained from the issue of judicial salaries.

It was understandable why this should have been so. The notion of compar-ability of salaries is an art, not a science, and it is arguable that the Review Body on Top Salaries has been forced to rely on intuition rather than principle. It has simply assumed that judicial salaries should bear some comparison with those of leaders in industry and leaders at the Bar. To take only the latter, however, the Thatcher years, with the growth in commercial work and the rapid growth in legal aid, meant that the practising Bar experienced a financial bonanza.

In 1984, of those appointed to the High Court Bench, during the preceding three years (at 1984 prices) the average net income was £86,000 and the median £69,000. The lowest quartile earned £51,582; and since High Court salaries were £51,250—revised to £60,000 the following year—one may assume a quar-ter of barristers increased their salaries or suffered no serious diminution by going on the High Court Bench.[22] The Report of the Top Salaries Review Board also revealed that between 1980 and 1982 the average person increased his salary on going on the Circuit Bench. The Report also showed that the average English QC earned, net, £67,508.

Five years later, in 1989, while inflation had risen 29.2 per cent between 1984 and 1989, the average English QC was earning £146,900—a 120 per cent increase in income in four years. When one considers that the top tax rate also fell from 60 per cent to 40 per cent during these years, the figures are remark-able. By 1991, the average English QC earned, net, £183,500—a 200 per cent increase in eight years. Whereas the average earnings of QCs appointed to the Circuit Bench in 1981–2 had been £27,450, for the period 1984–9 it was £90,600. For the period 1990–1 it was £113,900. With respect to the High Court the 1981–4 average, in 1984 pounds, was £86,000; for the period to 1991, in 1991 pounds, it was £227,300—an increase of close to 300 per cent in eight years.[23]

(b) The Perplexing Problems of Judicial Independence

While recruitment was probably no more of a problem than it had ever been, while the salary situation was stabilized, and while the new generation of judges

Journal (18 Nov. 1988), 842–3. For a list of QCs and solicitors alleged to be earning over £1 million a year, see the *Observer*, 15 Dec. 1991.

[22] Review Body on Top Salaries, *Report No. 22: Eighth Report on Top Salaries*, Cmnd. 9525, i (1985), 46; see also ii. 95–6.
[23] See generally, Review Body on Top Salaries, *Report No. 29: Thirteenth Report on Top Salaries*, Cm 928 (1990), and *Report No. 33: Fifteenth Report on Top Salaries*, Cm 2015 (1992).

had given the Bench a more relevant image, all was not easy after 1960. The issue of extra-judicial statements has already been discussed. There were, however, much wider issues with respect both to the executive and legislature. This, in turn, raised again the issue of how judges should be appointed.

There were, moreover, increasingly complex nuances about subtle government pressures. In addition to statute, judicial independence had always been thought to imply freedom from government pressure, and among other things, this was thought to imply a full-time judiciary, which was not a career judiciary and therefore did not have to look for promotion. While this may have been true at the top (although the use of deputy judges belied this), it was far less true at the periphery after the Courts Act, 1971. Increasingly, criminal work was done by part-time judges—Recorders and Assistant Recorders. The bulk of serious criminal work was thus done either by part-time judges or by Circuit judges who had no effective constitutional protection of their positions.

The myth that there was no career judiciary in England was also weakening. In the 'lower' judiciary, District judges might be promoted to Circuit judges, at a much higher salary. Circuit judges might look for promotion to the High Court with its obvious status and perks. Whatever was said, many High Court judges looked for promotion to the Court of Appeal, which involved less travel, provided a more intellectual fare, offered yet more status (a Privy Counsellorship) and, by the end of the period, was better paid. Among Lords Justice, too, interest in promotion to the House of Lords was clear in many cases.

If the prospect of promotion sullied the purity of the relationship between the judiciary and the executive, there were other factors at work. The change reflected in the 1956 Restrictive Trade Practices Act set the pace for other experiments. In the mid-1960s the use of Lord Radcliffe in the Vassall Inquiry[24] and Lord Denning in the Profumo Inquiry[25] had led Harold Wilson to talk of a 'blithe disregard for our constitutional distinction between the executive and the judiciary',[26] and the *Financial Times* to talk of 'Government by judge or Q.C.'. In relative terms, however, the 1960s were an era of consensus politics. The mood of the nation was, however, changing. The Industrial Relations Act of 1971 introduced the short-lived Industrial Relations Court. Which way causation flows is never easy to determine; but at the very time that consensus politics was beginning to disintegrate, these experiments in extending the use of courts were paralleled by the increasing use of judges for non-judicial work. Moreover, the secondment of High Court judges, which had appeared revolutionary in 1956, became accepted in the following decades as judges left their regular duties to chair the Law Commission, serve as President of the Employment Appeals Tribunal, to work in Luxemburg, and, in the case of one Circuit judge, to serve as Inspector of Prisons.

[24] *Report of the Tribunal appointed to Inquire into the Vassall Case and Related Matters*, Cmnd. 2009 (1962).
[25] *Lord Denning's Report. [Profumo Affair]*, Cmnd. 2152 (1963).   [26] *The Times*, 16 Sept. 1963.

While judges—and indeed the Judicial Office—may be admirably suited to factual investigations, such as accidents, when judges are assigned tasks as commission or committee chairs, which require them to articulate policies and to choose between these policies, the separation of powers is inevitably blurred. However one defines it, judicial independence is threatened. This becomes especially important when the Cabinet rejects reports that it has commissioned from judges. This has happened at least twice within relatively recent memory.

In 1959, Harold Macmillan asked Lord Chancellor Kilmuir to produce a judge to investigate the Riots in Nyasaland. He nominated Mr Justice Devlin, who produced a highly critical report. Macmillan described it as 'dynamite', which 'may well blow this Government out of office'. Sir Roy Welensky described it as 'one of the most controversial State Papers of modern times'. The government rejected the report and commissioned a rival report from the much-criticized Governor, Sir Robert Armitage. Even so, the Devlin Report was important in the collapse of the Central African Federation.[27] The same treatment was meted out by Harold Wilson to Lord Radcliffe's *Report on 'D' Notices*. It was rejected.[28]

The borderline of the judicial, executive, and legislative is approached in a number of other areas. There have been various judicial inquiries into mismanagement in the public service, including Mr Justice James's *Tribunal of Inquiry into the Collapse of the Vehicle and General Insurance Company*[29] and Mr Justice Croom-Johnson's *Tribunal of Inquiry into the Crown Agents*.[30] There is a Standing Committee, called the Security Commission, headed by a judge. Mr Justice Scarman was called in to investigate the riots at Red Lion Square[31] and Brixton.[32] In the turbulent 1970s the judges were much used to investigate industrial unrest.[33]

Perhaps the most dramatic 'misuse' of the judges, as the critics would say, occurred in Northern Ireland. There were at least seven such inquiries in the period between 1969 and Mrs Thatcher's coming to power in 1979. Mr Justice Scarman undertook the first, entitled *Violence and Civil Disturbances in Northern Ireland, 1969*.[34] That report was much criticized because it did not appear until 1972. By that time the Cameron Report had appeared (Lord Cameron was a

---

[27] Horne, *Macmillan*, ii. 180-1. 'Why Devlin,' Macmillan asked in his diaries. His answer was: 'The poor Lord Chancellor [Lord Kilmuir]—the sweetest and most naive of men—chose him. He was able; a Conservative; runner up or nearly so for Lord Chief Justice. I have since discovered that he is (a) *Irish*—no doubt with that Fenian blood that makes Irishmen anti-government on principle, (b) a *lapsed* Roman Catholic. His brother is a priest; his sister a nun, . . . he was bitterly *disappointed* at my not having made him Lord Chief Justice.' Ibid. 181.

[28] See *White Paper on 'D' Notice System*, Cmnd. 3312 (1967).   [29] 1971-2 HC 133.

[30] 1981-2 HC 364.   [31] Cmd. 5919 (1975).

[32] Cmnd. 8427 (1981) (under the Police Act, 1964).

[33] See various Reports of Courts of Inquiry under the Industrial Courts Act: *Electricity Supply*, Cmnd. 4594 (1971) (Wilberforce); *Miners*, Cmnd. 4903 (1972) (Wilberforce); *Grunwick*, Cmnd. 6922 (1977) (Scarman).

[34] Cmnd. 566 (NI).

Scottish judge).[35] The Widgery Report on 'Bloody Sunday'[36] was dismissed as a 'whitewash' because Widgery, later to be Lord Chief Justice of England, was alleged to have interviewed only British army witnesses.[37] The *Independent* later commented that the inquiry was 'so blatantly biased in its findings that it brought British justice into contempt in many parts of the world'.[38] Then Lord Parker, the Lord Chief Justice, chaired a Committee of Privy Counsellors to look at *Interrogation Methods*.[39]

Perhaps the most significant report was that by Lord Diplock: *Legal Procedures for Dealing with Terrorists*.[40] This Departmental Committee was alleged to have abrogated the rule of law because it instituted arrest without warrant. It also made confessions easier to admit and detention simpler, while changing the burden of proof when firearms were found.[41] The report was seen as illogical for, on the one hand, maintaining the courts, but on the other instituting detention. It was alleged that the Northern Irish judges and Bar were not consulted.[42] Although this was regarded as an arrogant report, 'Diplock courts' became an integral part of the security forces' apparatus.

Lord Gardiner, as Lord Chancellor, was sent by Harold Wilson to write one more report,[43] and Judge Bennett had a further look at *Police Interrogation Procedures*.[44] The process was increasingly seen as the shuffling-off of responsibility by the politicians. To different segments in Ulster all the reports were unacceptable. There was public rejection of the vaunted impartiality and independence of the English judges.

Meanwhile, the return of Labour in 1974 was followed by a dismantling of the Industrial Relations Court and the purported development of the 'Social Contract'. By the time this had happened, however, the attacks on Sir John Donaldson, President of the Industrial Relations Court, had reached a level of enthusiasm not seen in England with respect to the judiciary since the nineteenth, or possibly the seventeenth, century. Indeed, the Industrial Relations Court interlude was a natural prelude to the demise of consensus government.[45] Lord Devlin argued that the courts were inappropriate institutions to enforce non-consensual law. 'The prestige of the judiciary, their reputation for stark

[35] On Cameron and Scarman, see R. Rose, *Governing without Consensus: An Irish Perspective* (London, 1971), ch. 4.

[36] *Report of the Tribunal Appointed to Enquire into the Events on Sunday, 30 January, 1972 which Led to a Loss of Life in Connection with the Processions in Londonderry on that Day*, 1971–2 HL 101/HC 220.

[37] C. K. Boyle, T. Hadden, and P. Hillyard, *Law and the State: The Case of Northern Ireland* (London, 1975), 127.

[38] 'In Cold Blood', *Independent*, 18 Jan. 1992, Magazine, p. 20.   [39] Cmnd. 4901 (1972).

[40] Cmnd. 5185 (1972).   [41] Boyle, Hadden, and Hillyard, *Law and State, passim*.

[42] Ibid. 95.

[43] *Report of a Committee to Consider, in the Context of Civil Liberties, and Human Rights, Measures to Deal with Terrorism in Northern Ireland*, Cmnd 5847 (1975).

[44] Cmnd. 7497 (1979).

[45] On the legal implication of that, see J. Jowell and D. Oliver, eds., *The Changing Constitution* (Oxford, 1985), esp. chs. 8 (T. Daintith, 'The Executive Power Today') and 12 (A. Lester, 'The Constitution').

impartiality to be kept up in appearance as well as in fact, is not at the disposal of any government: it is an asset that belongs to the whole nation.'[46] Lord Diplock put it in a more judicial context. In discussing the Trade Disputes and Labour Relations Act of 1974, which pushed the frontiers of tortious liability for unions back towards the pre-1906 solution, he said: 'at a time when many more cases involve the application of legislation which gives effect to policies that are the subject of bitter public and parliamentary controversy, it cannot be too strongly emphasised that the British Constitution, though largely unwritten, is firmly based upon the separation of powers; Parliament makes the laws, the judiciary interprets them.'[47]

We should perhaps recall, however, that Mr Justice Donaldson announced when the Industrial Relations Court began: 'The Industrial Court is a court of law. As such, it is independent of the government and is in no way concerned with its policies. Equally it is independent of the parties to the dispute . . . .'[48] The statement did not stop Donaldson being the subject of vigorous criticism. In December 1973, 187 Labour MPs moved an address to remove the President of the Industrial Relations Court for 'political prejudice and partiality'.[49] While the motion was not debated, Lord Hailsham asked voters 'to strike a blow for the integrity and independence of the judges of this country' by voting Conservative in the then forthcoming election.[50] This the voters declined to do, and Prime Ministers Wilson and Callaghan refused to promote Donaldson to the Mastership of the Rolls while there was a Labour Government. Lord Justice Donaldson achieved that position under Mrs Thatcher. It is believed that the Lord Chancellor, Lord Hailsham, reported to Mrs Thatcher that 'a number of judges expressed the strong opinion that John Donaldson was the wrong man for the job.' Mrs Thatcher replied: 'Fortunately Lord Chancellor, your judges do not appoint the Master of the Rolls, I do.'[51] And she did.

If the Thatcher administration used the judges virtually not at all for policy-oriented Royal Commissions and related functions, it was primarily out of a feeling that government belonged in the Cabinet, and especially to the Prime Minister. Judicial inquiries were limited primarily to factual inquiries about soccer riots and sinking ferries. The change was not made out of an interest primarily in protecting the reputation and independence of the judiciary. When Mrs Thatcher became Prime Minister in 1979 the judiciary was treated much as any other Quango. 'Shuffling off' political responsibilities to judges became as out-of-date as the search for consensus.[52] The country had, perhaps, reached a new stage in the evolution of judicial independence and/or impartiality.

---

[46] *Sunday Times*, 6 Aug. 1972.   [47] *Duport Steels* v. *Sir* [1980] 1 All ER 529, 541 (HL).
[48] *Secretary of State for Employment* v. *ASLEF* [1972] ICR 7, 14.
[49] Shetreet, *Judges on Trial*, 405; *Parliamentary Debates* (5th ser.), HC vol. 865, cols. 1092, 1142, 1200 (4 Dec. 1973).
[50] Zander, *A Matter of Justice*, 127.
[51] A. Samuels, 'Appointing the Judges', 27 *New Law Journal* (Jan. 1984).
[52] The pendulum may of course be swinging back as the Thatcher star has faded. 1991 saw the

Many, however, felt the judges, in their judicial work, were not impartial during the Miners Strike of 1984–5. A Gallup Poll conducted in February 1985 found that, since June 1969, the number of persons who thought the judges were influenced by the government in power had risen from 19 per cent to 43 per cent, while those who thought the judges to be independent had dropped from 67 per cent to 46 per cent. Part of the drop was attributed to the strong party political attitude of Lord Hailsham, but other remarks that had been influential included Mrs Thatcher's expressed hope that, in the *Ponting* case, 'an appropriately severe member of the judiciary would be on hand to hear the case'.[53] Whether it was *Spycatcher*[54] or the *Thalidomide* case,[55] it seemed it was Commonwealth or European courts, rather than the English courts, that were protecting English freedoms.

(c) Criticizing the Judiciary

The related issue of criticizing the judges was to provide one of the rich ironies in judicial history. As the judges were increasingly criticized in the late 1970s Lords Donaldson and Hailsham issued a call to moderate 'the intemperate criticism' to which the judges were being subjected.[56] In fact, however, Lord Hailsham, as Quintin Hogg, QC, had been instrumental in dramatically weakening the old law of contempt of court for criticizing the judges. In 1968 he had published an article in *Punch*, vigorous in tone and inaccurate in fact, criticizing a Court of Appeal decision. That court held that the article had not amounted to a contempt of court.[57] Such a conclusion may have influenced Hailsham in his decision to keep in place the so-called Kilmuir rules which prevented the judges from speaking publicly about policy issues.

The late 1980s were to produce an unfortunate series of public relations setbacks for the judiciary. In 1988 the Lord Chancellor's Office published a series of Green Papers suggesting far-reaching modifications in the restrictive practices in the legal profession.[58] The recommendations, while extensive, were nevertheless

May Committee looking at the various suspect convictions (perhaps justifiable in narrow terms) and the Runciman Commission looking at criminal procedure. Moreover, the House of Commons Committees, somewhat rejuvenated, began looking into issues (e.g. the BCCI scandal) where a judicial inquiry (in that case under Lord Justice Bingham) was already underway. The possibility of a constitutional clash clearly existed.

[53] D. Oliver, 'Independence of the Judiciary', *1986 Current Legal Problems* (London, 1986), 237–43.
   It has been suggested that during the Heath administration, Lord Chancellor Hailsham lobbied Lord Denning, the Master of the Rolls, about decisions on industrial relations. H. Young, 'Muttering Judges', *Guardian*, 30 Apr. 1992, p. 18.   [54] M. Fysh, ed., *The Spycatcher Cases* (London, 1989).
[55] A.G. v *The Times Newspapers* [1973] 3 All ER 54 (HL); *Sunday Times* v *United Kingdom*, 2 EHRR 245 (1979).
[56] Zander, *A Matter of Justice*, 131–2.
[57] *R v Commission of Police for the Metropolis ex parte Blackburn (No. 2)* [1968] 2 QB 150 (CA).
[58] Lord Chancellor, *The Work and Organisation of the Legal Profession*, Cm 570 (1989); *Contingency Fees*, Cm 571 (1989); *Conveyancing by Authorised Practitioners*, Cm 572 (1989).

in line with the pro-competitive market orientation of the Thatcher administration; and their provenance was probably more the Department of Trade and Industry than the Lord Chancellor's Department. The legal profession was irate, but their response was measured.

The Bar Council took the position that 'the Government's proposals would be an important step on the road to government interference with the independence of the judges and the legal profession'.[59] In particular they felt that 'a judiciary drawn from lawyers in the government Legal Service or the Crown Prosecution Service would not have the constant training in independence of mind necessary for an independent judiciary, and would not be seen by the public as independent.'[60] The Bar Council also felt independence would be compromised by the Lord Chancellor choosing areas of specialization, by the majority of lay persons on the Advisory Committee, by the Lord Chancellor controlling professional codes, rights of audience, discipline, and education. 'These matters have always . . . been a essential element in the independence of the judiciary and of the legal profession from which the judiciary has been drawn.'[61]

The Supreme Court judges collectively were reported as believing that the Advisory Committee on Advocacy, recommended by Lord Mackay, was a 'grave breach of the doctrine of separation of powers'. As a result of the proposals as a whole 'in due course the quality of judges would be reduced'. Their resistance to discussing the Green Papers during normal court hours was characterized by the tabloids as 'a judges' strike'.[62] Mr Justice Brown, President of the Family Division, saw the Green Papers as threatening 'the administration of the law on which our civilization depends'.[63]

It was the judges in the House of Lords who put a somewhat unfortunate slant on the events. Law lords, appeal judges who are also members of the Upper House, have always presented a serious problem to those attempting to analyse the separation of powers and judicial independence. The conventional thing to say has been that they do not speak on controversial topics, but that has been frequently broken. In the 1920s Lord Dunedin defended General Dyer for his actions at Amritsar, while Lord Carson opposed the Irish Treaties. More recently, and closer to the line, has been some law lords' opposition to divorce reform or the abolition of capital punishment. Lord Goddard, and his successor Lord Parker, at least in his early years as Lord Chief Justice, were enthusiastic about hanging and flogging, and there are other delicate issues which posed political problems.[64]

---

[59] General Council of the Bar, *Quality of Justice: The Bar's Response* (London, 1989), 16.
[60] Ibid. 163.   [61] Ibid. 166.
[62] J. Rozenberg, 'Packaging the Judges', *Guardian*, 14 Nov. 1990.
[63] Robin C. A. White, *A Guide to the Courts and Legal Services Act, 1990* (London, 1991), 44.
[64] Lord Goddard's views were so extreme that, at the Lord Mayor's Dinner in 1952, Lord Simonds, the Lord Chancellor, publicly disagreed with him. Abel-Smith and Stevens, *Lawyers and the Courts*, 302. In the 1980s various books and plays suggested that Lord Goddard had derived sexual

Clearly the law lords thought of the Green Papers, which were followed by a watered-down White Paper, and ultimately by a weaker Bill (the Courts and Legal Services Bill), as a non-controversial matter, or a legal Bill on which they might speak. Unfortunately, as reported in the press, some of the Law Lords' speeches gave a hint of having been written in the offices of *Private Eye*. Lord Hailsham, the former Lord Chancellor, accused the Government of 'thinking with its bottom and sitting on its head'.[65] With shades of the 1930s the Lord Chief Justice, Lord Lane, announced that the Lord Chancellor's Office had produced 'one of the most sinister documents ever to emanate from government'.[66]

The debate had been joined by Lord Chancellor Mackay, who saw the Green Papers as 'a comprehensive programme for securing a better and more cost-effective service to the public from lawyers and the courts'.[67] Following the Civil Justice Review he looked for a *de facto* merging of the court structure, under which 'the High Court will be reserved for public law and other specialist cases including judicial review; and for general cases of unusual importance, substance and complexity'.[68] The Lord Chancellor looked for a profession based on merit: 'Is there any difference between the independence of barristers who practise from chambers and the independence of those barristers who may be employed?'[69]

The relatively modest approach satisfied few peers. For Lord Elwyn-Jones, the former Labour Lord Chancellor, market solutions were anathema. He found that the Benson Commission had produced an admirable report. It was indeed he who began a hare about Nazism: 'I well remember that in Nazi Europe and the Fascist countries before the War, the authoritarian regimes' first victims were the independence of the judiciary and the independence of the legal profession.' Elwyn-Jones poured scorn on market solutions, a scorn shared by Lord Hooson for the Liberal Democrats. He deplored the 'determination to go on the American route with all its limitations and deficiencies'. For him, the 'proposed powers of the Lord Chancellor [were] totally excessive', and threatened the independence of the profession, as it had been threatened in South Africa, Malaysia, and Singapore.[70] Judges must be 'felt to be completely independent of the State', and there was a danger of 'going down the American path'.[71]

Lord Lane took on the mantle of Lord Hewart. He was offended by the genesis of the Green Papers: 'It would therefore perhaps have been courteous, or even helpful, if those responsible for drafting the papers on the organization of the legal profession had seen fit to consult the judges upon the draft.' In a further re-run of the 1930s, apparently Lord Lane had been asked by the Lord

---

pleasure from ordering such punishments. Whether the allegation was true or not, it became part of the chorus about the failings of the senior judiciary.

[65] *The Times*, 15 Apr. 1989.   [66] *Guardian*, 17 Feb. 1989.
[67] *Parliamentary Debates* (5th ser.), HL vol. 505, col. 1307 (7 Apr. 1989).
[68] Ibid. col. 1308.   [69] Ibid. col. 1311.   [70] Ibid. col. 1313.   [71] Ibid. col. 1319.

Chancellor if the judges were interested in consulting about the Green Papers and he had rejected the offer. Forgetting this, he could only feel the future was bleak: 'as Parliament is increasingly liable to do what the government of the day [may] wish it to do . . . it is . . . becoming more and more necessary to preserve intact the courts' power of judicial review . . . the one thing that will stop a bullying government in its tracks.'[72] If, however, there were an Advisory Committee with a majority of laymen, staffed by the Lord Chancellor's Department, 'with all these powers in the hands of the executive, if these proposals become law, the one thing which at all costs must be avoided is likely to come about; and that is control by the executive of the principal means available for the ordinary citizen of controlling that same executive'. With this he moved into his stride: 'loss of freedom seldom happens overnight . . . oppression does not stand on the doorstep with a toothbrush moustache and a swastika armband.[73] It creeps up step by step; and all of a sudden the unfortunate citizen realises it has gone.' He was forced to ask 'whether we are not seeing tools being fashioned which some future, perhaps less scrupulous, government may use to weaken the independent administration of justice and so undermine the rule of law'.[74]

Lord Hailsham, who had been 'appalled' by the Green Papers, which were 'an outrage', rushed to the defence of 'the most upright and the most independent legal profession known to man . . . the judiciary remains the guardian of the liberties of the people . . . The independence of the judiciary depends more upon the independence and integrity of the legal profession than upon any other single factor.' Finally, with a dig at Mrs Thatcher, whose Lord Chancellor he had been, Hailsham noted that professions 'are not like the grocer's shop at the corner of a street in a town like Grantham'.[75]

Lord Donaldson insisted that 'to maintain the independence of the judiciary is not enough. We must maintain the independence of the entire judicial process. This involves providing protection and independence for the legal profession from governmental (as distinct from parliamentary) pressures and interferences . . . one does not have to look far from our shores to see what happens when this is not achieved.' The idea that the government should control professional conduct was 'an affront to the constitutional doctrine of the separation of powers'. (All this was somewhat odd, since the judges had lobbied hard to have their salaries removed from parliamentary control and given to the government.) Donaldson then quoted Hewart in the *New Despotism* with approval. Hewart had 'rightly described it as using the sovereignty of Parliament to frustrate the rule of law'. It was at this point that Donaldson adopted the phrase, 'get your tanks off my lawn'.[76]

---

[72] Ibid. col. 1330.
[73] A remark enshrined in D. Hare, *Murmuring Judges* (London, 1991), 7.
[74] *Parliamentary Debates* (5th ser.), HL vol. 505, col. 1331 (7 Apr. 1989).
[75] Ibid. cols. 1332–4.   [76] Ibid. cols. 1367–9.

The late 1980s were particularly unfortunate for Lord Chief Justice Lane, who announced his premature retirement early in 1992. It was reported that he had vetoed Lord Hailsham's idea for a Judicial Complaints Board.[77] The public estimation of the judiciary, however, was probably less affected by these debates on reforming the profession than by the highly publicized miscarriages of justice growing out of trials of the alleged IRA members. The release of the 'Guildford Four' and the Birmingham bombers was made the more embarrassing by the earlier quotes from Lord Denning and the apparent behaviour of the Chief Justice.[78] Lord Lane had also been involved in the Tottenham Riot case, where a later Court of Appeal took the unprecedented step of apologizing to the accused. Nevertheless, on the occasion of Lord Lane's retirement, the Master of the Rolls (Donaldson) and the Chairman of the Bar Council apparently insisted it was the Lord Chancellor and the civil servants in his department who were responsible for the perceived failings of the Lord Chief Justice.[79] For a period in 1990 and 1991, however, it looked as if the English judiciary could do nothing right in terms of public relations.[80]

(d) The Judiciary Reformed?

It was in this atmosphere that apparently serious suggestions were made for reforming the judiciary. Some of the suggestions were for the traditional kind of English reforms—within the current structure. There was only one woman in the Court of Appeal, three in the High Court, eighteen out of 422 Circuit judges, and twenty-five out of 450 QCs.[81] Racial minorities fared even worse. There was one minority member of the High Court Bench, one in the Circuit Court, and five out of 703 Recorders. Many, however, felt that the structures had to be changed if there was to be greater diversity on the Bench.

Geoffrey Bindman, a radical solicitor, argued that the paucity of minorities on the Bench violated the spirit if not the letter of the Race Relations legislation. The Lord Chancellor was sufficiently concerned to take counsel's opinion

---

[77] Zander, *A Matter of Justice*, 129–30.

[78] 'The Birmingham Six were convicted in 1974. In 1976 they appealed. Their appeal was refused. In 1987, the Home Secretary referred their cases to the Court of Appeal because of new evidence. The Court of Appeal, through Lord Lane, announced that "The longer the hearing has gone on the more convinced this Court has become that the verdict of the jury was correct. We have no doubt that these convictions were both safe and satisfactory." In 1990, the Home Secretary referred the case back to the Court of Appeal for the second time. In March 1991, the Court of Appeal set these men free.' Griffith, *The Politics of the Judiciary*, 196.

[79] 'Legal World Rallies to Defence of Lord Lane', *Independent*, 16 Apr. 1992; 'Judges Attack Lane's Critics', *The Times*, 16 Apr. 1992.

[80] Paxman, *Friends in High Places*, 110. There was some evidence, however, that the judiciary was prepared to strike back. When *The Times* and the *Sunday Telegraph* suggested that Mr Justice Tudor Evans had summed up improperly in a murder case, there was a threat of libel actions, public apologies, and payments to charities. J. Rozenberg, 'Press Gets a Wigging', *Guardian*, 20 Feb. 1991.

[81] 6.5% of Recorders are women. Some 11% of the Assistant Recorders are women, and 18% of barristers are women. Law Society, *Judicial Appointments* (London, 1991).

(counsel—David Pannick—concluded that it was not).[82] Lord Mackay then went on the offensive. While insisting on his commitment to a diverse Bench, he made it clear that 'it is not a function of the judiciary to be representative of the population as a whole'. Indeed, 'nothing would be worse for the reputation of the judiciary than for me to lower the standards for appointments to the judiciary simply to ensure a different racial or sexual mix.'[83] The Bar, however, committed itself to a quota of two representatives of racial minorities in each set of Chambers, and Mr Justice Brooke, Chair of the Bar Committee on Race Relations, produced a report on how to recruit more black judges.[84]

In the House of Commons the criticism was put at its most blunt and extreme by Brian Sedgemore, the Labour MP for Hackney. He wanted to know, 'How can black people trust the system of justice when all they ever see before them are the cloistered, geriatric, white men?'[85] He did not hesitate to link this background to the various judicial embarrassments in the late 1980s: 'The character of these cloistered, geriatric, white men can explain some of the tragic mistakes that the Court of Appeal made in the cases of the Guildford Four and the Birmingham Six. Perhaps the character of these geriatric, cloistered, white men can also help to explain the reaction of judges to the Lord Chancellor's proposals to get rid of the restrictive practices of barristers and solicitors.'[86]

In many ways, however, the Bench reflected elegantly the best traditions of English law. While the bulk of the work was private law and while the English trial was heavily oral and adversarial, the English had the Bench they needed. What, however, if the assumptions of Evershed were undone, and Britain was to buy in more to the Continental method of litigation or even to the trendier attractions of mediation? As some pointed out, the many apparent failings of judges to do justice in major criminal cases were in fact failings of the police with respect to doctored evidence and uncorroborated confessions. A judiciary which saw itself as having a more inquisitorial role, rather than serving as umpires in an adversarial joust, might have better protected the innocent. Some of the same criticisms were applied to civil cases.

It was in this context that it was argued that the *cursus honorum* from junior to silk to judge might need to change dramatically. Similarly, what if the diet of the courts changed? What if Britain were to have a written Constitution protected by its judiciary? Such was the suggestion of the Institute for Public Policy Research, and its draft Constitution called for judicial review of legislation.[87] It was not attractive either to civil servants or to the Conservative administration;

---

[82] 'Appointing Judges without Discrimination', *New Law Journal*, 9 Nov. 1991.

[83] *New Law Journal*, 9 Nov. 1991.

[84] 'Move to Recruit Black Judges for United Kingdom', *Observer*, 13 Oct. 1991; 'Barristers Set Ethnic Quotas and Urge Same for Judges', *Guardian*, 14 Oct. 1991.

[85] *Parliamentary Debates*, HC vol. 164, col. 666 (21 Dec. 1989; Weekly Hansard).

[86] Ibid. col. 664.

[87] Institute for Public Policy Research, *The Constitution of the United Kingdom* (London, 1991), ch. 9.

but in 1992 a Bill of Rights was endorsed both by the new Chief Justice, Lord Taylor, and the new Master of the Rolls, Sir Thomas Bingham.[88] It also found favour with John Smith and the 'new' Labour Party. It may well be the wave of the 1990s.[89] A new vision of judicial independence and a further rewriting of the separation of powers may be on the way. The idea of the judiciary as a co-equal branch of government is clearly the goal of some.

Certainly the focus of political debate moved to the appointment of judges.[90] Since the Courts Act of 1971 it had been possible for solicitors to be promoted to the Circuit Court. The 1990 legislation indirectly made it possible for solicitors to be appointed directly to the High Court Bench if they held the appropriate advocacy qualifications. The Law Society was lobbying for direct appointment to the High Court irrespective of the advocacy qualification. The President of the Law Society saw this as one way of breaking with 'monochrome male middle-aged judges'.[91] The Law Society also set about undermining the mystique of the judiciary: 'Our approach is that judicial appointments are, in principle, simply a category of senior appointments in the public service.'[92] It was all a very far cry from 1825.

Most importantly, the broader questioning raised the issue of how judges were chosen and how they should be chosen. The Left in England has traditionally taken the view that since law is essentially a mechanical process, if judges really behaved as highly technical lawyers, they could exclude all personal values, and give good decisions. If the judges behaved 'properly', therefore, their views ought to be immaterial, and they should be chosen from the technically most competent. The argument was an extreme form of judicial restraint. Views were changing. Thus in the 1970s Professor J. A. G. Griffith made these assumptions[93] and even went further, arguing that in order to avoid political influence, the judges should not be chosen by a political Lord Chancellor, but by the legal profession itself:

A better system would be to create a judicial service commission, . . . which would decide on new appointments. The members of such a body might include representatives of the judiciary, the Bar and the Law Society; they should themselves have security of tenure and steps could be taken to ensure this impartiality.[94]

---

[88] It had not been supported by their predecessors. See e.g. Lord Donaldson, quoted, *Guardian*, 12 Oct. 1991.

[89] *The Constitution of the United Kingdom* defined the 'three essential features of judicial independence' as '(1) freedom from political influences in the appointment of judges; (2) the protection of judges from undue political pressure while serving on the bench; and (3) protection from improper removal from office' (p. 19).

[90] On appointments, see A. Paterson, 'Becoming a Judge', in *The Sociology of the Professions: Lawyers, Doctors and Others*, ed. R. Dingwall and P. Lewis (London, 1983), ch. 12.

[91] J. A. Holland, *The Times*, 19 Oct. 1990. [92] Law Society, *Judicial Appointments* (1991).

[93] J. A. G. Griffith, *The Politics of the Judiciary* (1st edn. Manchester, 1977), *passim*. For a more sophisticated jurisprudential defence of this position, see R. M. Dworkin, *Law's Empire* (Cambridge, Mass., 1986). For a polemical critique of these views see S. Lee, *Judging Judges* (London, 1988) chs. 3 ('Dworkin's Noble Dream') and 5 ('That Man Griffith and his Nightmare').

[94] T. C. Hartley and J. A. G. Griffith, *Government and Law* (2nd edn. London, 1981), 180.

Griffith (and his co-author) were also attracted by the 'fact that [what] promotes the independence of the superior judiciary is that they are all drawn from the Bar after successful careers as barristers, a profession which tends to foster self-confidence and independence of mind'.[95]

After eleven years of Mrs Thatcher, the views had changed dramatically. In 1991, Griffith concluded: 'These judges have by their education and training and the pursuit of their profession as barristers, acquired a strikingly homogeneous collection of attitudes, beliefs and principles, which to them represent the public interest.'[96] Thus, instead of concluding that all would be well with the judges, if only they would mechanically apply neutral principles of law, Griffith had apparently concluded that God was dead, and that where the public interest was involved, the judges had no place:

My thesis is that judges in the United Kingdom cannot be politically neutral because they are placed in positions where they are required to make political choices which are sometimes presented to them, and often presented by them, as determinations of where the public interest lies; and that their interpretation of what is the public interest and therefore politically desirable is determined by the kind of people they are and the position they hold in our society; that this position is a part of established authority and so is necessarily conservative and illiberal.[97]

Most critics did not share this view—or at least its implication that judges should not be used for public law or cases where policy was involved. The spotlight had, however, focused on how judges were chosen. In the 1960s some critics had called for judges to be chosen in a more public way, through a Judicial Commission.[98] The issue became more public in 1972, when Justice, an organization of the moderate legal establishment, refused to endorse a report by its subcommittee on the judiciary, partly because it suggested the Lord Chancellor should be aided in judicial selection by an advisory committee. The report also suggested that solicitors be eligible for appointment directly to the Circuit Bench and that judges receive training.[99] Lord Hailsham at once attacked the suggestions.[100]

The suggestions reappeared, however, during the later part of the 1980s. In an effort to make the process of judicial appointment appear less intimidating, the Lord Chancellor's Office in 1990 produced a pamphlet entitled *Judicial Appointments*. Although it failed to deal directly with how the actual choices were made, it did reveal indirectly that, *de facto*, the rationalized system of choos-

---

[95] Hartley and Griffith, *Government and Law*, 181.
[96] Griffith, *The Politics of the Judiciary* (1991), 275.   [97] Ibid. 319.
[98] Abel-Smith and Stevens, *In Search of Justice*, 192–6.
[99] The report was published without the imprimatur of the Council of Justice. Justice, *The Judiciary* (London, 1972).
[100] 'I am pretty sure the system the Lord Chancellor's Office has worked out for consultation is infinitely more sophisticated and flexible, and far more efficient in selecting the right personnel, with the Lord Chancellor at the top responsible to Parliament, than any system run by an outside body is ever likely to be,' Lord Hailsham, *The Listener*, 13 July 1972.

ing the judges, developed by Sir Derek Oulton after the passage of the Courts Act, 1971, gave the four senior judges (the Master of the Rolls, Lord Chief Justice, Vice-Chancellor, and President of the Family Division) a controlling voice in choosing High Court judges, while effectively delegating to the Civil Service the basic task of choosing Circuit Judges, Recorders, and Assistant Recorders.

Publicly, the Solicitor-General, Sir Nicholas Lyell, was, however, more willing than his predecessors to discuss what really went on as the Lord Chancellor made his decisions about who should be judges. The decisions were made

on the basis of the widest and fullest possible consultation with the senior judiciary and leaders of the Bar. The purpose is to obtain the verdict of the professional community on each candidate, in so far as there is one. The main method of consultation is by organised rounds of regular consultation with all Supreme Court judges and Law Lords and annual meetings with a broad cross-section of the circuit bench, including all the resident and designated judges, and with the leaders of the circuits and the Bar as a whole. Particular efforts are now made to seek out views on solicitor candidates for appointment.[101]

Meanwhile the Bar had come round to the position that judicial appointments should be taken away from the Lord Chancellor and given to the profession— ideally to a Committee of Judges.[102] The Law Society favoured a Commission which contained judges, practising and academic lawyers, and 'a strong lay element', in what would be an advisory capacity to the Lord Chancellor.[103] The senior judiciary was apparently unsympathetic, and Lord Donaldson attacked the suggestion that any change should be made in the system.[104]

(e) The Lord Chancellor's Department and the Future

The crucial bell-wether for these suggested changes will be the Lord Chancellor's Department. The Courts Act of 1971 brought the fiscal side of the courts within the ambit of the Department, and in so doing, emphasized that in the English system the judges control neither the administration of the courts nor their finances. At the same time, the increasing sense of fiscal stringency for the public services in the 1970s and 1980s underlined the importance of the ultimate control of the Legal Aid Scheme—today a significant part of the Department's work—by the Lord Chancellor's Department. As the 'fairness concept' of criminal fees had been extended in the mid-1960s, at the very time Beeching left vague the question of how to handle Class Four crimes, the Department became the paymaster of a scheme which led to a trebling of the size of the Bar, as well as becoming a source of considerable profit for solicitors. When the Thatcher

[101] *Parliamentary Debates*, HC 21 Dec. 1989, col. 670 (Weekly Hansard).
[102] General Council of the Bar, *Quality of Justice: The Bar's Response* (1989), 187. The Bar appeared to be subrogating itself to the judiciary's rights under the Act of Settlement of 1700.
[103] Law Society, *Judicial Appointments* (1991), para. 5.01.
[104] 'Donaldson Attacks Open Judge Choice', *Guardian*, 12 Oct. 1991.

administration ultimately decided that the apparently open-ended scheme had to have limits, the Bar, a long time bastion of free enterprise, appeared to become the advocate of socialized law.

The 1986 litigation by the Bar Council and Law Society underlined the change from Office to Department. No longer was the Lord Chancellor's Department the sole preserve of the legal (and judicial) profession, nor were they and the judges quite in the same special position. The irony of the litigation was that the Department was opened to further political scrutiny which, in the long run, may lead to administrative restructuring, a result which is unlikely to be in the long-term professional interests of judges or lawyers. In 1990 legislation further integrated the Lord Chancellor's Department into the regular Civil Service, for instance, by introducing a retirement age of 62 for future Permanent Secretaries. The Department was also, in line with other Departments, made subject to a House of Commons Select Committee. In 1991, it was announced that a Minister would be appointed to answer questions about the Department in the House of Commons.

Political control through budgetary constraints was most clearly recognized by the Vice-Chancellor, Sir Nicholas Browne-Wilkinson, in his Mann Lecture, 'The Independence of the Judiciary in the 1980s'.[105] In addition to the usual concerns about freedom from government pressure secured by payment out of the Consolidated Fund, there was 'a subtler threat' through the 'executive's control of finance and administration'. The theme was that 'the control of finances and administration of the legal system is capable of preventing the performance of those very functions which the independence of the judiciary is intended to preserve'.[106] In particular, the Vice-Chancellor saw the fact that, unlike the Federal courts in the United States, having court administrators reporting to the Civil Service rather than to the judges threatened the independence of the judiciary.

Equally threatening was the allocation of funds for legal aid. The judges had not been consulted about the capping of available funds. Browne-Wilkinson alleged the application of the Thatcher doctrine of FMI ('Value for Money') undercut judicial independence. While the British Medical establishment was debating whether rationing should be explicit (as in Oregon) or implicit (as recommended by Sir Raymond Hoffenburg in his Harvean lecture),[107] the judiciary apparently felt it could not engage in the same debate. The courts were not the National Health Service: 'The requirements of judicial independence make the Lord Chancellor's Department wholly different from any other department of state,'[108] said Browne-Wilkinson. This led even Lord Chancellor Hailsham to scoff at the idea that his judges should be free 'to run a sort of legal Arcadia'.[109]

---

[105] *1989 Public Law*, 44.

[106] Ibid. 47, 52. See also J. Deschênes, *Masters in their own House* (Toronto, 1979); F. Mount, *The British Constitution Now* (London, 1992), ch. 4.

[107] 'Rationing: The Search for Sunlight', *British Medical Journal*, 303 (1991), 1561.

[108] Browne-Wilkinson, 'The Independence of the Judiciary in the 1980s', 48.

[109] *Civil Justice Quarterly*, 8 (1989), 308.

Yet judges were obviously upset that they had not been consulted when the Lord Chancellor's Department had produced their 'yardsticks' for the Treasury's analysis: 'A number of judges think that there is some form of civil service conspiracy designed to erode the independence of the judiciary and their powers.'[110] The paranoia was further increased when some judges chose to read a consultative paper in the Civil Justice Review, conducted by the Department in 1988, as implying that judges were indolent. Of the Civil Justice Review, Lord Ackner, one of the law lords, claimed that 'an ill-disguised attempt was made seriously to weaken in the long term the strength of the High Court bench by proposals which would have resulted in the abolition of the Circuit system as we now know it and the transfer to the County Courts of virtually all High Court work.'[111] It was in this context that there was further discussion of the possibility of a Ministry of Justice; and one could detect a level of friction between Civil Service and judiciary which had resonances of the relations between Schuster and Hewart, and Hewart and Sankey.

As to whether there will be a Ministry of Justice, one can look at that as much ado about nothing.[112] In the past, many have viewed even the lean Muir Mackenzie-esque Office as a Ministry of Justice. Haldane would have made the Home Office the Ministry of Justice—the Irish model. The Liberal Democrats would have a version of the US Department of Justice, by incorporating the Law Officers, the Director of Public Prosecutions, and the Treasury Solicitor. This would in some ways push the Office back to being the sole preserve of lawyers, and would have all its ministers be lawyers. Sam Silkin, on behalf of the Labour Party, has argued that, if the Law Officers were kept independent, there would be no reason why the ministers should be lawyers.[113] Whatever the future holds—whether it is a more formalized Ministry of Justice or a less professional department—the Department is now effectively integrated into the Civil Service. This suggests that it will increasingly treat the courts as part of the welfare state and judges and lawyers as providers of services within such a social service. That in itself is scarcely a radical vision; yet it may well underline still further the need for fiscal constraint. It will surely demand a serious analysis—finally—of the independence of the judiciary. Does England want an independent judiciary or does it want to protect the independence of individual judges? What is the relationship of this independence to the public services which the courts and the judges provide?

The role of the Lord Chancellor's Office and Department has been consistently underrated. It remains the mirror image of the status of judges. In England, without any clear separation of powers, the status of the judges has become the core of the discussion of the independence of the judiciary. Analysis

---

[110] Browne-Wilkinson, 'The Independence of the Judiciary in the 1980s', 51.

[111] *Parliamentary Debates*, HL vol. 505, col. 1415 (9 Apr. 1989).

[112] G. Drewry, 'Ministers, Parliament and the Courts', 142 *New Law Journal* (17 Jan. 1992), 56.

[113] S. C. Silkin, 'The Legal Machinery of Government', (Summer 1984) *Public Law*, 179–86.

of that concept is essential if judges are to play an appropriate role in the future both of the Constitution and of the public service. How much of its national income is Britain prepared to dedicate to funding the legal system, including the courts? How far beyond the independence of individual judges does England wish to go? How far is it prepared to restructure its government to give further powers to the judges? How far is it prepared to provide support for a concept of the separation of powers, and within that a concept of judicial independence which would allow the English judges to be thought of as a co-ordinate branch of government? Britain in the 1990s will have to face these questions. In such analysis, comprehending the interactions of the three branches of government over the last one hundred years will be vital.

Table of Offices

	Prime Minister	Lord Chancellor	Permanent Secretary to the Lord Chancellor
1880	W. E. Gladstone (1880–5)	Lord Selborne (1880–5)	
1881			
1882			
1883			
1884			
1885	Lord Salisbury (1885–6)	Lord Halsbury (1885–6)	Sir K. Muir Mackenzie (1880–1915)
1886	W. E. Gladstone (Feb.–Aug.)	Lord Herschell (Feb.–Aug.)	
	Lord Salisbury (1886–92)	Lord Halsbury (1886–92)	
1887			
1888			
1889			
1890			
1891			
1892	W. E. Gladstone (1892–4)	Lord Herschell (1892–5)	
1893			
1894	Lord Rosebery (1894–5)		
1895	Lord Salisbury (1895–1902)	Lord Halsbury (1895–1905)	
1896			
1897			
1898			
1899			
1900			
1901			
1902	A. Balfour (1902–5)		
1903			
1904			
1905	Sir H. Campbell-Bannerman (1905–8)	Lord Loreburn (1905–12)	
1906			
1907			
1908	H. H. Asquith (1908–16)		
1909			
1910			
1911			
1912		Lord Haldane (1912–15)	
1913			
1914			
1915		Lord Buckmaster (1915–16)	Sir C. Schuster (1915–44)

Chancellor of the Exchequer	Permanent Secretary to the Treasury	Home Secretary
W. E. Gladstone (1880–2)	Sir R. R. W. Lingen (1880–6)	Sir W. V. Harcourt (1880–5)
H. C. E. Childers (1882–5)		
Sir M. Hicks-Beach (1885–6) Sir W. V. Harcourt (Feb.–Aug.) Lord R. Churchill (1886–7) G. J. Gooschen (1887–92)	Sir R. E. Welby (1886–94)	Sir R. Cross (1885–6) H. C. E. Childers (until Aug.) Henry Matthews (1886–92)
Sir W. V. Harcourt (1892–5)		H. H. Asquith (1892–5)
	Sir F. Mowatt (1894–1902)	
Sir M. Hicks-Beach (1895–1902)		Sir M. W. Ridley (1895–1900)
		C. T. Ritchie (1900–2)
C. T. Ritchie (1902–3)	Sir F. Mowatt Sir E. Hamilton } (1902–3)	A. Akers-Douglas (1902–5)
A. Chamberlain (1903–5)	Sir E. Hamilton Sir G. Murray } (1903–8)	
H. H. Asquith (1905–8)		H. Gladstone (1905–10)
D. Lloyd George (1908–15)	Sir G. Murray (1908–11)	
	Sir R. Chalmers (1911–13)	W. S. Churchill (1910–11) R. McKenna (1911–15)
	Sir T. Heath Sir J. Bradbury } (1913–16)	
R. McKenna (1915–16)		Sir J. Simon (1915–16)

Cont./

1880–1915 Continued from page 187

	Permanent Secretary to the Home Office	Lord Chief Justice	Master of the Rolls
1880		Lord Coleridge (1880–94)	Sir G. Jessel (1880–3)
1881			
1882			
1883			Lord Esher (1883–97)
1884			
1885	G. Lushington (1885–95)		
1886			
1887			
1888			
1889			
1890			
1891			
1892			
1893			
1894		Lord Russell of Killowen (1894–1900)	
1895	Sir K. Digby (1895–1903)		Sir N. Lindley (1897–1900)
1896			
1897			
1898			
1899			
1900		Lord Alverstone (1900–13)	Sir R. Webster (1900)
			Sir A. Smith (1900–1)
1901			Sir R. Collins (1901–7)
1902			
1903	Sir M. Chalmers (1903–8)		
1904			
1905			
1906			
1907			Sir H. Cozens-Hardy (1907–1
1908	Sir E. Troup (1908–22)		
1909			
1910			
1911			
1912			
1913		Lord Reading (1913–21)	
1914			
1915			

President of Probate, Divorce, and Admiralty, (Modern) Family Division	Attorney-General
Sir J. Hannen (1875–91)	Sir Henry James (1880–6)
	Sir R. Webster (1885–6) Sir C. Russell (1886–7) Sir R. Webster (1886–92)
Sir C. Parker Butt (1891–2) Sir F. H. Jeune (1892–1905)	Sir C. Russell (1892–4)
	Sir J. Rigby (1894) Sir R. Reid (1894–5) Sir R. Webster (1895–1900)
	Sir R. Finlay (1900–5)
Sir G. Barnes (1905–9)	Sir J. Walton (1905–8)
	Sir W. Robson (1908–10)
Sir J. Bigham (1909–10)	
Sir S. Evans (1910–18)	Sir R. Isaacs (1910–13)
	Sir J. Simon (1913–15)
	Sir E. Carson (May–Oct.) Sir F. E. Smith (1915–19)

1916–1953 Continued on page 190

1916–1953 Continued from page 189

	Prime Minister	Lord Chancellor	Permanent Secretary to the Lord Chancellor
1916	D. Lloyd George (1916–22)	Lord Finlay (1916–19)	
1917			
1918			
1919		Lord Birkenhead (1919–22)	
1920			
1921			
1922	A. Bonar Law (1922–3)	Lord Cave (1922–4)	
1923	S. Baldwin (1923–4)		
1924	J. R. MacDonald (Jan.–Nov.)	Lord Haldane (Feb. to Nov.)	
	S. Baldwin (1924–9)	Lord Cave (Nov. 1924–8)	
1925			
1926			
1927			
1928		Lord Hailsham (1928–9)	
1929	J. R. Macdonald (1929–35)	Lord Sankey (1929–35)	
1930			
1931			
1932			
1933			
1934			
1935	S. Baldwin (1935–7)	Lord Hailsham (1935–8)	
1936			
1937	N. Chamberlain (1937–40)		
1938		Lord Maugham (1938–9)	
1939		Lord Caldecote (1939–40)	
1940	W. S. Churchill (1940–5)	Lord Simon (1940–5)	
1941			
1942			
1943			
1944			Sir A. Napier (1944–54)
1945	C. R. Attlee (1945–51)	Lord Jowitt (1945–51)	
1946			
1947			
1948			
1949			
1950			
1951	Sir W. S. Churchill (1951–5)	Lord Simonds (1951–4)	
1952			
1953			

Chancellor of the Exchequer	Permanent Secretary to the Treasury	Home Secretary
A. Bonar Law (1916–19)	Sir T. Heath Sir J. Bradbury ⎱ (1916–19) Sir R. Chalmers ⎰	Sir H. Samuel (until Dec.) Sir G. Cave (1916–19)
A. Chamberlain (1919–21)	Sir W. Fisher (1919–39)	E. Shortt (1919–22)
Sir R. Horne (1921–2) S. Baldwin (1922–3)		W. Bridgeman (1922–4)
N. Chamberlain (1923–4) P. Snowden (Jan.–Nov.) W. S. Churchill (1924–9)		A. Henderson (Jan.–Nov.) Sir W. Joynson-Hicks (1924–9)
P. Snowden (1929–31)		J. R. Clynes (1929–31)
N. Chamberlain (1931–7)		Sir H. Samuel (1931–2) Sir J. Gilmour (1932–5)
Sir J. Simon (1937–40)		Sir J. Simon (1935–7) Sir S. Hoare (1937–9)
	Sir H. Wilson (1939–42)	Sir J. Anderson (1939–40)
Sir K. Wood (1940–3)		H. Morrison (1940–5)
Sir J. Anderson (1943–5)	Sir R. Hopkins (1942–5)	
H. Dalton (1945–7)	Sir E. Bridges (1945–56)	Sir D. Somervell (May–Aug.) C. Ede (1945–51)
Sir S. Cripps (1947–50)		
H. Gaitskell (1950–1) R. A. Butler (1951–5)		Sir D. Maxwell-Fyfe (1951–4)

Cont./

1916–1953 Continued from page 191

	Permanent Secretary to the Home Office	Lord Chief Justice	Master of the Rolls
1916			
1917			Sir C. Eady (1918–19)
1918			Lord Sterndale (1919–23)
1919			
1920		Lord Trevethin (1921–2)	
1921		Lord Hewart (1922–40)	
1922	Sir J. Anderson (1922–32)		
1923			Sir E. Pollock (Lord Hanworth) (192
1924			
1925			
1926			
1927			
1928			
1929			
1930			
1931			
1932	Sir R. Scott (1932–8)		
1933			
1934			Lord Wright (1935–7)
1935			
1936			Sir W. Greene (1937–49)
1937			
1938	Sir A. Maxwell (1938–48)		
1939			
1940		Lord Caldecote (1940–6)	
1941			
1942			
1943			
1944			
1945			
1946		Lord Goddard (1946–58)	
1947	Sir F. Newsam (1947–57)		
1948			Sir R. Evershed (1949–62)
1949			
1950			
1951			
1952			
1953			

President of Probate, Divorce, and Admiralty, (Modern) Family Division	Attorney-General
Lord Sterndale (1918–19) Sir H. Duke (Lord Merrivale) (1919–33)	Sir G. Hewart (1919–22)
	Sir E. Pollock (Mar.–Oct.) Sir D. Hogg (1922–4)
	Sir P. Hastings (Jan.–Nov.) Sir D. Hogg (1924–8)
	Sir T. Inskip (1928–9) Sir W. Jowitt (1929–32)
Lord Merriman (1933–62)	Sir T. Inskip (1932–6)
	Sir D. Somervell (1936–45)
	Sir D. Maxwell-Fyfe (May–Aug.) Sir H. Shawcross (1945–51)
	Sir L. Heald (1951–4)

1954–1992 Continued on page 194

1954–1992 Continued from page 193

	Prime Minister	Lord Chancellor	Permanent Secretary to the Lord Chancellor
1954		Lord Kilmuir (1954–62)	Sir G. Goldstream (1954–68)
1955	Sir A. Eden (1955–7)		
1956			
1957	H. Macmillan (1957–63)		
1958			
1959			
1960			
1961			
1962		Lord Dilhorne (1962–4)	
1963	Sir A. Douglas-Home (1963–4)		
1964	H. Wilson (1964–70)	Lord Gardiner (1964–70)	
1965			
1966			
1967			
1968			Sir D. Dobson (1968–77)
1969			
1970	E. Heath (1970–4)	Lord Hailsham (1970–4)	
1971			
1972			
1973			
1974	H. Wilson (1974–6)	Lord Elwyn-Jones (1974–9)	
1975			
1976	J. Callaghan (1976–9)		
1977			Sir W. Bourne (1977–82)
1978			
1979	M. Thatcher (1979–90)	Lord Hailsham (1979–87)	
1980			
1981			
1982			Sir D. Oulton (1982–9)
1983			
1984			
1985			
1986			
1987		Lord Mackay (1987–)	
1988			
1989			Sir T. Legg (1989–)
1990	J. Major (1990–)		
1991			
1992			

Chancellor of the Exchequer	Permanent Secretary to the Treasury	Home Secretary
H. Macmillan (1955–7)		G. Lloyd George (1954–7)
	Sir N. Brook ⎫ (1956–60) Sir R. Makins ⎭	
P. Thorneycroft (1957–8) D. Heathcoat Amory (1958–60)		R. A. Butler (1957–62)
S. Lloyd (1960–2)	Sir N. Brook ⎫ (1960–2) Sir F. Lee ⎭	
R. Maudling (1962–4)	Sir N. Brook ⎫ (1962–3) W. Armstrong ⎭ Sir L. Helsby ⎫ (1963–8) Sir W. Armstrong ⎭	H. Brooke (1962–4)
J. Callaghan (1964–7)		Sir F. Soskice (1964–5) R. Jenkins (1965–7)
R. Jenkins (1967–70)	Sir W. Armstrong Sir D. Allen (1968–74)	J. Callaghan (1967–70)
I. Macleod (June–July) A. Barber (1970–4)		R. Maudling (1970–2)
		R. Carr (1972–4)
D. Healey (1974–9)	Sir D. Wass (1974–83)	R. Jenkins (1974–6)
		M. Rees (1976–9)
G. Howe (1979–83)		W. Whitelaw (1979–83)
N. Lawson (1983–9)	Sir P. Middleton (1983–91)	L. Brittan (1983–5)
		D. Hurd (1985–9)
J. Major (1989–90)		D. Waddington (1989–90)
N. Lamont (1990–)		K. Baker (1990–2)
	Sir T. Burns (1991–)	
		K. Clarke (1992–)

Cont./

1954–1992 Continued from page 195

	Permanent Secretary to the Home Office	Lord Chief Justice	Master of the Rolls
1954			
1955			
1956			
1957	Sir C. Cunningham (1947–66)		
1958		Lord Parker of Waddington (1958–71)	
1959			
1960			
1961			
1962			Lord Denning (1962–82)
1963			
1964			
1965			
1966	Sir P. Allen (1966–73)		
1967			
1968			
1969			
1970			
1971		Lord Widgery (1971–80)	
1972			
1973	Sir A. Peterson (1973–7)		
1974			
1975			
1976			
1977	Sir R. Armstrong (1977–9)		
1978			
1979	Sir B. Cubbon (1979–88)		
1980		Lord Lane (1980–92)	
1981			
1982			Sir J. Donaldson (1982–92)
1983			
1984			
1985			
1986			
1987			
1988			
1989	Sir C. Whitmore (1989–)		
1990			
1991			
1992		Lord Taylor (1992–)	Sir T. Bingham (1992–)

President of Probate, Divorce, and Admiralty, (Modern) Family Division	Attorney-General
	Sir R. Manningham-Buller (1954–62)
Sir J. Simon (1962–71)	Sir J. Hobson (1962–4)
	Sir E. Jones (1964–70)
	Sir P. Rawlinson (1970–4)
Sir G. Baker (1971–9)	
	Sir S. Silkin (1974–9)
Sir J. Arnold (1979–88)	Sir M. Havers (1979–88)
Sir S. Brown (1988–)	Sir P. Mayhew (1988–91)
	Sir M. Lyall (1991–)

Bibliography

A. REPORTS

The Brixton Disorders, 10–12 April 1981, Report of Inquiry, Cmnd. 8427 (1981).

Civil Judicial Statistics, 1900.

Civil Judicial Statistics, 1910.

Coal Industry Commission, Reports and Minutes of Evidence on the First Stage of the Inquiry, Cmnd. 359 (1919).

Colonial Conference Papers, Cmnd. 3524 (1907).

Commission to Consider Legal Procedures to Deal with Terrorist Activities in Northern Ireland: Report, Cmnd. 5185 (1972).

Committee of Privy Counsellors to Consider Authorised Procedures for the Interrogation of Persons Suspected of Terrorism, Cmnd. 4901 (1972).

Committee on Procedure in Matrimonial Causes: Interim Report, Cmnd. 6945 (1945).

Committee on Procedure in Matrimonial Causes: Final Report, Cmnd. 7024 (1946).

Contingency Fees, Cmnd 571 (1989).

Conveyancing by Authorised Practitioners, Cmnd 572 (1989).

Correspondence Relating to the Proposed Establishment of a Final Court of Colonial Appeal (HMSO, 1901).

Final Report of the Committee on Supreme Court Practice and Procedure, Cmnd. 8878 (1953).

General Council of the Bar, *Quality of Justice: The Bar's Response* (London, 1989).

Institute for Public Policy Research, *The Constitution of the United Kingdom* (London, 1991).

Justice, *The Judiciary* (London, 1972).

Law Society, *Judicial Appointments* (London, 1991).

Lord Chancellor's Department, *Judicial Appointments* (London, 1990).

Lord Denning's Report. [Profumo Affair], Cmnd. 2152 (1963).

The Monopolies and Restrictive Practices Commission, *Report on Collective Discrimination*, Cmnd. 9504 (1955).

O'Connor, W. F., *Report Pursuant to Resolution of the Senate to the Honourable the Speaker by the Parliamentary Counsel Relating to the Enactment of the British North America Act, 1867, Any Lack of Consonance between its Terms and Judicial Construction of them and Cognate Matters* (Ottawa, 1939).

Problems of Pay Relativities: Pay Board, Advisory Report, No. 2, Cmnd. 5535 (1974).

Proceedings of the Imperial Conference, Cmnd. 5745 (1911).

The Red Lion Square Disorders of 15 June 1974, Report of Inquiry, Cmnd. 5919 (1975).

Report of a Committee to Consider, in the Context of Civil Liberties, and Human Rights, Measures to Deal with Terrorism in Northern Ireland, Cmnd. 5847 (1975).

Report of the Committee on Alterations in Criminal Procedure (Indictable Offences), 1921, Cmnd. 1813 (1923).

Report of the Committee to Consider what Rearrangements of the Circuits can be Effected so as to Promote Economy and the Greater Dispatch of the Business of the High Court, Cmnd. 1831 (1923).

Report of the Committee on Higher Civil Service Remuneration, Cmnd. 7635 (1948).

Report of the Committee of Inquiry into Interrogation Procedures in Northern Ireland, Cmnd. 7497 (1979).

Report of the Committee on Ministers' Powers, Cmnd. 4060 (1932).

Report of a Court of Inquiry into a Dispute between Grunwick Processing Laboratories Limited and Members of the Association of Professional, Executive, Clerical and Computer Staff, Cmnd. 6922 (1977).

Report of a Court of Inquiry into a Dispute between the National Coal Board and the National Union of Mineworkers, Cmnd. 4903 (1972).

Report of a Court of Inquiry into a Dispute between the Parties Represented on the National Joint Industrial Council for the Electricity Supply Industry Report, Cmnd. 4594 (1971).

Report of the Machinery of Government Committee, Cmnd. 9230 (1918).

Report of the Royal Commission Appointed to Enquire into the Causes of Accidents, Fatal and Non-Fatal, to the Servants of Railway Companies and of Truck Owners, Cmnd. 41 (1900).

Report of the Royal Commission on the Despatch of Business at Common Law, 1934–6, Cmnd. 5065 (1936).

Report of the Royal Commission on the Selection of Justices of the Peace, Cmnd. 5250 (1910).

Report of the Tribunal Appointed to Inquire into Certain Issues Arising out of the Operations of the Crown Agents as Financiers on own Accounts in the Years 1967–74, 1981–2 HC 364.

Report of the Tribunal Appointed to Inquire into the Events on Sunday, 30 January, 1972 which Led to a Loss of Life in Connection with the Processions in Londonderry on that Day, 1971–2 HL 101/HC 220.

Report of the Tribunal Appointed to Inquire into the Vassall Case and Related Matters, Cmnd. 2009 (1963).

Report of the Tribunal of Inquiry into the Collapse of the Vehicle and General Insurance Company, 1971–2 HC 133.

Reports by the Royal Commission on Registration of Title in Scotland, Cmnd. 5316 (1910).

Review Body on Top Salaries, *Report No. 2: Interim Report on Top Salaries*, Cmnd. 5001 (1972).

—— *Report No. 3: Second Interim Report on Top Salaries*, Cmnd. 5372 (1973).

—— *Report No. 4: Third Interim Report on Top Salaries*, Cmnd. 5595 (1974).

—— *Report No. 6, Report on Top Salaries*, Cmnd. 5846 (1974).

—— *Report No. 22: Eighth Report on Top Salaries*, Cmnd. 9525 (1985).

—— *Report No. 29: Thirteenth Report on Top Salaries*, Cmnd 928 (1990).

—— *Report No. 30: Fourteenth Report on Top Salaries*, Cmnd. 1413 (1991).

—— *Report No. 33: Fifteenth Report on Top Salaries*, Cmnd 2015 (1992).

Royal Commission on Legal Services: Final Report, Cmnd. 7648 (1979).

Royal Commission on the Press, 1961–1962: Report, Cmnd. 1811 (1962).

Violence and Civil Disturbances in Northern Ireland, 1969: Report of the Tribunal Inquiry, Cmnd. 566 (NI) (1972).

White Paper on 'D' Notice System, Cmnd. 3312 (1967).

The Work and Organisation of the Legal Profession, Cmnd 570 (1989).

B. UNPUBLISHED PAPERS

Bodleian Library, Oxford
  Asquith Papers
  Hanworth Papers
Fulham Palace Library
  Selborne Papers, Letters, vol. xii
Lord Chancellor's Office Papers
  LCO 1/ to 32/

C. NEWSPAPERS AND JOURNALS

British Medical Journal
Civil Justice Quarterly
Daily Telegraph
The Economist
Evening Standard
Guardian
Law Journal
Law Times
Listener
Montreal Gazette
Montreal Star
Morning Post
New Yorker
Northern Echo
Observer
Private Eye
Solicitors' Journal
Sunday Times
The Times
Winnipeg Free Press

D. ARTICLES

'Abolition of Appeals to the Privy Council: A Symposium', 25 *Canadian Bar Review* (1947), 557–72.

ALLEN, C. K., 'Some Aspects of Administrative Law', (1929) *Journal of the Society of the Public Teachers of Law*, 10.

BARTRIP, P. W. J., 'Beveridge, Workmen's Compensation and the Alternative Remedy', 14: 4 *Journal of Social Policy* (1985), 491–511.

BELL, J., 'The Judge as Bureaucrat', in *Oxford Essays in Jurisprudence*, 3rd ser., ed. J. Eekelaar and J. Bell (Oxford, 1987).

BROWNE-WILKINSON, SIR N., 'The Independence of the Judiciary in the 1980s' (Mann Lecture), (Spring 1988) *Public Law*, 44–57.

CAIRNS, A. C., 'The Judicial Committee and its Critics', 4 *Canadian Journal of Political Science* (1971), 301–45.

DREWRY, G., 'Ministers, Parliament and the Court', 142 *New Law Journal* (17 Jan. 1992), 50 and 57.

FELDMAN, D., 'Public Law Values in the House of Lords', 106 *Law Quarterly Review* (1990), 246–76.

FITZPATRICK, SIR CHARLES, 'The Constitution of Canada', 34 *Canadian Law Times* (1914), 1016–32.

GOW, N., 'Are We Paying our Judges Enough?', 138 *New Law Journal* (18 Nov. 1988), 842–3.

GREENE, W. A., 'Law and Progress', 94 *Law Journal* (1944), 349–67.

GREENWOOD, F. MURRAY, 'Lord Watson, Institutional Self-Interest, and the Decentralization of Canadian Federalism in the 1890s', 9 *University of British Columbia Law Review* (1974), 244–70.

HANBURY, H. G., 'Lord Hewart', *Dictionary of National Biography, 1941–1950* (London, 1959).

HIGGINS, J., 'Partition in India', in M. Sissons and P. French, eds., *Age of Austerity* (London, 1963), 200.

HOLDSWORTH, W. S., 'The Constitutional Position of the Judges', 48 *Law Quarterly Review* (Jan. 1932), 25–34.

HYDE, H. MONTGOMERY, 'Diary of a Judge', *Sunday Times*, 7 Apr. 1963.

JENNINGS, W. I., 'The Statute of Westminster and Appeals to the Privy Council', 52 *Law Quarterly Review* (1936), 173.

—— 'Constitutional Interpretation: The Experience of Canada', 51 *Harvard Law Review* (Nov. 1937), 1–39.

LESTER, A., 'Fundamental Rights: The United Kingdom Isolated?' (Spring 1984) *Public Law*, 46–72.

LIGHT, R., 'Judges over the Limit', 39 *New Law Journal* (9 June 1989), 783–4.

LOWE, A. V., and YOUNG, J. R., 'Executive Attempt to Rewrite a Judgment', 94 *Law Quarterly Review* (1978), 255–75.

MCBARNET, D., and WHELAN, C., 'The Elusive Spirit of the Law: Formalism and the Struggle for Legal Control', 54 *Modern Law Review* (1991), 848–73.

MCEVOY, J., 'Separation of Powers and the Reference Power: Is there a Right to Refuse?', 10 *Supreme Court Law Review* (1988), 429–68.

MACKAY, LORD, 'Can Judges Change the Law?', 73 *Proceedings of the British Academy* (1987), 285–308.

MORROW, W. G., 'The Last Case', 16 *Alberta Law Review* (1978), 1–19.

OFFER, A., 'The Origins of the Law of Property Acts, 1910–25', 40 *Modern Law Review* (1977), 505–22.

OLIVER, D., 'The Independence of the Judiciary', *1986 Current Legal Problems* (London, 1986), 237–43.

PATERSON, A. A., 'Becoming a Judge', in R. Dingwall and P. Lewis, eds., *The Sociology of the Professions: Lawyers, Doctors and Others* (London, 1983), ch. 12.

—— 'Judges: A Political Elite?', 1 *British Journal of Law and Society* (Winter 1974), 118–35.

—— 'Scottish Lords of Appeal, 1878–1888', *Juridical Review* (1988).

PLATTS-MILLS, J., 'Geoffrey Henry Cecil Bing', *Dictionary of National Biography, 1971–1980* (Oxford, 1986), 57.

RICHLER, M., 'A Reporter at Large (Quebec)', *New Yorker*, 25 Sept. 1991, pp. 40–52, 65–72, and 79–92.

ROZENBERG, J., 'Packaging the Judges', *Guardian*, 14 Nov. 1990.

—— 'Press Gets a Wigging', *Guardian*, 20 Feb. 1991.

—— 'The Kilmuir Rules KO'd', *Guardian*, 21 July 1989.

SAMUELS, A., 'Appointing the Judges', 27 *New Law Journal* (Jan. 1984).

SCRUTTON, T. E., 'Work of the Commercial Courts', 1 *Cambridge Law Journal* (1921), 6.

SILKIN, S. C., 'The Legal Machinery of Government' (Summer 1984) *Public Law*, 179–86.

SIMPSON, A. W. B., 'The Judges and the Vigilant State' (1989) *Denning Law Journal*, 145–67.

STEVENS, R. B., 'The Final Appeal: Reform of the House of Lords and Privy Council, 1867–1876', 80 *Law Quarterly Review* (1964), 343–69.

—— 'The Independence of the Judiciary', 8 *Oxford Journal of Legal Studies* (1988), 222.

—— 'Judicial Salaries: Financial Independence in the Age of Equality', 13 *Journal of Legal History* (Aug. 1992), 155–77.

—— 'The Role of the Judiciary: Lessons from the End of Empire', in *Essays for Patrick Atiyah*, ed. P. Cane and J. Stapleton (Oxford, 1991), 151–78.

—— 'The View from the Lord Chancellor's Office', *1987 Current Legal Problems* (1987), 181–205.

—— 'Vignettes from the End of Empire', 40 *University of New Brunswick Law Journal* (1991), 145–57.

WEXLER, S., 'The Urge to Idealize: Viscount Haldane and the Constitution of Canada', 29 *McGill Law Journal* (1984), 608–50.

YOUNG, H., 'Muttering Judges', *Guardian*, 30 Apr. 1992.

E. BOOKS

ABEL, R. L., *The Legal Profession in England and Wales* (Oxford, 1988).

ABEL-SMITH, B., and STEVENS, R., *In Search of Justice: Society and the Legal System* (London and New York, 1968).

—— *Lawyers and the Courts: A Sociological Study of the English Legal System, 1750–1965* (London, 1967; Cambridge, Mass., 1968).

ADAMSON, I., *A Man of Quality* (London, 1964).

—— *The Old Fox* (London, 1963).

ALLEN, C. K., *Law and Orders* (London, 1945).

BARTRIP, P. W. J., *Workmen's Compensation in Twentieth Century Britain* (Aldershot, 1987).

BISSELL, C., *The Imperial Canadian: Vincent Massey in Office* (Toronto, 1986).

BLACKSTONE, SIR WILLIAM, *Commentaries on the Laws of England* (4 vols., Oxford, 1765).

BLOM-COOPER, L., and DREWRY, G., *Final Appeal* (Oxford, 1972).

BOYLE, C. K., HADDEN, T., and HILLYARD, P., *Law and the State: The Case of Northern Ireland* (London, 1975).

BRESLER, F., *Lord Goddard* (London, 1977).

BRITTAN, S., and LILLEY, P., *The Delusion of Incomes Policy* (London, 1977).

BROWNE, G. P., *The Judicial Committee and the British North America Act* (Toronto, 1967).

BURNETT, J., *A History of the Cost of Living* (Harmondsworth, 1969).

CARTWRIGHT, T. J., *Royal Commissions and Departmental Committees in Britain* (London, 1975).

COLERIDGE, E. H., *Life and Correspondence of John Duke, Lord Coleridge, Lord Chief Justice of England* (2 vols., London, 1904).

CREIGHTON, D. C., *Canada's First Century, 1867–1967* (Toronto, 1970).

DANGERFIELD, G., *The Strange Death of Liberal England* (New York, 1935).

DESCHÊNES, J., *Masters in their own House* (Montreal, 1981).

DENNING, LORD, *The Due Process of Law* (London, 1980).

—— *What Next in the Law* (London, 1982).

DESLAURIERS, I.-J., *La Cour supérieure du Québec et ses juges, 1948–1er janvier 1980* (Quebec, 1980).

DORFMAN, G. A., *Wage Politics in Britain, 1945–1967* (London, 1974).

DWORKIN, R. M., *Law's Empire* (Cambridge, Mass., 1986).

EDDY, J., and SCHREUDER, D., eds., *The Rise of Colonial Nationalism: Australia, New Zealand, Canada and South Africa First Assert their Nationalism, 1880–1914* (London, 1988).

FITZROY, SIR A., *Memoirs* (2 vols., London, 1925).

FREUND, P., *The Supreme Court of the United States: Its Business, Purposes and Performance* (Cleveland, 1961).

FYSH, M., ed., *The Spycatcher Cases* (London, 1989).

GARDINER, G., and MARTIN, A., eds., *Law Reform NOW* (London, 1963).

GORDON, D. C., *The Dominion Partnership in Imperial Defence, 1870–1914* (Baltimore, 1965).

GRAVES, R., and HODGE, A., *The Long Week-end* (London, 1940).

GRIFFITH, J. A. G., *The Politics of the Judiciary* (1st edn. Manchester, 1977; 4th edn. London, 1991).

HARE, D., *Murmuring Judges* (London, 1991).

HARKNESS, D. W., *The Restless Dominion* (London, 1969).

HARRIS, K., *Attlee* (London, 1982).

HARTLEY, T. C., and GRIFFITH, J. A. G., *Government and the Law* (2nd edn. London, 1981).

HARVEY, C. P., *The Advocate's Devil* (London, 1958).

HEUSTON, R. F. V., *Lives of the Lord Chancellors, 1885–1940* (Oxford, 1964).

—— *Lives of the Lord Chancellors, 1940–1970* (Oxford, 1987).

HEWARD, E., *Lord Denning* (London, 1990).

HEWART, LORD, *Not Without Prejudice* (London, 1937).

—— *The New Despotism* (London, 1929).

Holmes-Laski Letters, ed. M. De W. Howe (2 vols., London, 1953).

HORNE, A., *Macmillan*, ii. *1957–1986* (London, 1989).

HUTBER, P., *Wanted, A Monopoly Policy* (London, 1960).

HYDE, H. MONTGOMERY, *Norman Birkett* (London, 1964).

JACKSON, R., *The Chief: The Biography of G. Hewart, Lord Chief Justice of England, 1922–40* (London, 1959).

Jackson, R. M., *Jackson's Machinery of Justice*, 8th edn., ed. J. R. Spencer (Cambridge, 1989).

JOWELL, J., and OLIVER, D., eds., *The Changing Constitution* (Oxford, 1985).

KEETON, G. W., *The Passing of Parliament* (London, 1952).

KOSS, S. E., *Lord Haldane: Scapegoat for Liberalism* (New York, 1969).

LEE, S., *Judging Judges* (London, 1988).

LEWIS, G. M. *Lord Atkin* (London, 1983).

LIDDELL, A. G. C., *Notes from the Life of an Ordinary Mortal* (London, 1911).

LOCKE, J., *The Works of John Locke* (9th edn. London, 1794).

MARSHALL, G., *Constitutional Theory* (Oxford, 1971).

MAUGHAM, LORD, *At the End of the Day* (London, 1954).

MAURICE, F., *Haldane* (2 vols., London, 1937–9).

MAY, E., *Parliamentary Practice*, 21st edn., ed. C. J. Boulton (London, 1989).

MORGAN, K. O., *The People's Peace: British History, 1945–1989* (Oxford, 1990).

MOUNT, F., *The British Constitution Now* (London, 1992).

MOWAT, C. L., *Britain between the Wars, 1918–1940* (London, 1962).

MOYLES, R. G., and OWRAM, D., *Imperial Dreams and Colonial Realities: British Views of Canada, 1880–1914* (Toronto, 1988).

PALLEY, C., *The Constitutional History and Law of Southern Rhodesia, 1885–1965* (Oxford, 1966).

PANNICK, D., *The Judges* (Oxford, 1987).

PATERSON, A. A., *The Law Lords* (London, 1982).

PAXMAN, J., *Friends in High Places: Who Runs Britain?* (London, 1990).

PIERSON, C. G., *Canada and the Privy Council* (London, 1960).

POLDEN, P., *Guide to the Records of the Lord Chancellor's Department* (London, 1988).

POLLOCK, G., *Mr Justice McCardie* (London, 1934).

ROSE, R., *Governing without Consensus: An Irish Perspective* (London, 1971).

ROUTH, G., *Occupation and Pay in Great Britain, 1906–1960* (Cambridge, 1965).

—— *Occupation and Pay in Great Britain, 1960–1979* (2nd edn. London, 1980).

SEARLE, G. R., *Corruption in British Politics, 1895–1930* (Oxford, 1987).

SELDON, A., *Churchill's Indian Summer: The Conservative Government, 1951–1955* (London, 1981).

SHETREET, S., *Judges on Trial: A Study in the Appointment and Accountability of the English Judiciary* (Amsterdam, 1976).

SLESSER, H. H., *Judgment Reserved* (London, 1941).

Smith and Bailey on the Modern English Legal System, ed. S. H. Bailey and M. J. Gunn (London, 1991).

SNELL, J. G., and VAUGHAN, F., *The Supreme Court of Canada: History of the Institution* (Toronto and London, 1985).

STEVENS, R. B., *Law and Politics: The House of Lords as a Judicial Body, 1800–1976* (Chapel Hill, NC, and London, 1983).

—— and YAMEY, B. S., *The Restrictive Practices Court: A Study of the Judicial Process and Economic Policy* (London, 1965).

SWINFEN, D. B., *Imperial Appeal: The Debate on the Appeal to the Privy Council, 1833–1986* (Manchester, 1987).

VILE, M. J. C., *Constitutionalism and the Separation of Powers* (Oxford, 1967).

WEILER, P., *In the Last Resort: A Critical Study of the Supreme Court of Canada* (Toronto, 1974).

WHISH, R., *Competition Law* (2nd edn. London, 1989).

WHITE, R. C. A., *A Guide to the Courts and Legal Services Act, 1990* (London, 1991).
WOOTTON, B., *The Social Foundations of Wage Policy* (2nd edn. London, 1962).
YALLOP, D., *To Encourage the Others* (London, 1971).
ZANDER, M., *A Matter of Justice: The Legal System in Ferment* (Oxford, 1989).

Index